The Bedside
Guardian 2018

The Bedside Guardian 2018

EDITED BY LISA ALLARDICE

guardianbooks

Published by Guardian Books 2018

2 4 6 8 10 9 7 5 3 1

Copyright © Guardian News and Media Ltd 2018

Lisa Allardice has asserted her right under the Copyright, Designs and
Patents Act 1988 to be identified as the editor of this work

First published in Great Britain in 2018 by
Guardian Books
Kings Place, 90 York Way
London N1 9GU

www.guardianbooks.co.uk

A CIP catalogue record for this book is available from the British Library

ISBN 978-1-5272-2979-2

Typeset by seagulls.net

Printed and bound in Great Britain by
CPI Group (UK) Ltd, Croydon CR0 4YY

Contents

WINTER

SPRING

SUMMER

Foreword

MARGARET ATWOOD

A large number of people have told me that the past 12 months have felt like being put through an automatic car wash, though without the car. They may not have put it quite that way, but I will. To summarise: battered by high-pressure jets, thwacked with sponges, drenched in toxic suds and steamed in clouds of hot air – and all of that just from reading the papers.

As we stagger across the room, drunk on information – some of it the quality of bootleg rotgut, and we know we will pay for this in the morning – we ask ourselves: What's going on? Why are people behaving like this? Where am I? Is this still planet Earth, and what does that mean any more now that the ice caps are melting? Are we about to re-enact the 1930s, either with a big financial crash or a clutch of preposterous but vicious authoritarian dictators, or both? Is there light at the end of the tunnel? Is this even a tunnel? Are women finally going forward, or is it one step up and two steps down? Did I just tread on someone's fingers? Will life as we know it soon be extinct? Is social media ruining sociability? And many equally troublesome questions to which no one stands poised to provide firm answers.

When in doubt about such matters I dedicate an egg to the altar of Hermes, concealer of secrets and opener of doors, and then consult the astrologers. They always have something to say. Here's the skinny:

Uranus – it sounds better if you put the emphasis on the first syllable – which is the planet of surprises, upsets and sudden events, had been transiting through Aries the Ram, sign of leadership, since March 2011. You wondered why Donald Trump got elected, why the Brexit vote turned out the way it did, and why #MeToo toppled Harvey Weinstein and ilk? Search no further! Unexpected leaders zizzed into power, established leaders hit the floor. There was a lot of revolutionary anger around – Aries and Uranus both facilitate anger – some of which propelled the successful yes campaign for reproductive rights in Ireland.

But Uranus moved into Taurus – a more stable position – in May, and the Argentinian vote for safe abortion was lost to a few old-style senators. Will things calm down on the world stage? Don't bet on that: Taurus is the sign of money and material possessions, so we could win the lottery or lose our shirts, or else you might get a new blow dryer. Innovative forms of currency may erupt – shells, large stones with holes in them – or the credit card may become obsolete. Taurus is an earth sign, so farmers may expect surprises: will there be bumper crops? Will vegans inherit the earth? And Uranus in Taurus can be good for tyrants: think 'radical' plus 'conservative'. The last time the explosive planet was in Taurus was the 1930s: the trains may run on time and there won't be riots in the streets, but that will be due to the crackdowns, the summary executions and the genocides.

On the other hand, Brexit may be shelved in favour of a return to the status quo. Or maybe it won't be: the astrologists can never be certain. So why not turn instead to the *Guardian*? Surely there's an equally good chance of truth and wisdom being found there! If we can't discover what's about to happen – though there are many scribbling pundits on call to cast the bones for us – at least we can get a handle on what just did happen. Or such is our desire.

I read the *Guardian* regularly, but I had missed a number of these pieces and welcomed the chance to regain lost time. Here, gathered together for all who, like me, enjoy reading the tea leaves backwards, is a treasure trove of informed opinions, interspersed with the occasional retrospectively embarrassing rant. No, I won't tell you which is which: you'll have to sort that out for yourself. But who could resist a compilation of 67 various and sprightly essays, conveniently arranged into seasons, like a Japanese calendar?

As one who counts such things, I determined – as well as I was able, given the indeterminacy of names – that almost half are by women – think of that! Almost half! Not too many are about health issues, riveting though we find these. And, showing remarkable restraint on the part of the curator, only a few are about Trump.

What kinds of things can happen in a year? People ate food (vegan, pre-processed), got it delivered in controversial ways (Deliveroo), drank alcohol (prosecco), remembered shooting drugs (heroin, John Crace), had art and photographic exhibitions, wrote books (Philip Pullman), worried about the loss of words from dictionaries, played music (Simon Rattle), went to fashion shows, and won literary prizes (Ishiguro). These the *Guardian* duly notes.

After doing these kinds of things for a while, people have a tendency to die. Various luminaries who'd been in our world for what seems like for ever vanished from the scene. Stephen Hawking; Philip Roth, keystone American novelist; Peter Preston, editor of the *Guardian* for 20 years; and Aretha Franklin, the Queen of Soul, are among those memorialised in these pages.

Others struggled with illness, and we learned more about those specific illnesses through them: George Monbiot writes about his prostate cancer in a surprisingly positive way, since it got dealt with; Hannah Jane Parkinson tells us how mental illness is simply not being dealt with; and Katharine White-horn of *Cooking in a Bedsitter* – so beloved by many generations of women, including mine – sadly cannot write any more since she has Alzheimer's, as Polly Toynbee tells us; though if she could, she'd be extolling the virtues of assisted dying.

It was a bumper year for news about women, and for changes in the way they are treated and perceived. The #McToo move-ment made huge waves, as Rebecca Solnit tells us; Ireland got new abortion laws in June of 2018 after a hard-fought campaign, explained here by Anne Enright; the gender pay gap closed some-what thanks to Harriet Harman's bill, and there was an all-female Shakespeare trilogy, thanks to the Donmar and Harriet Walter. (I saw *The Tempest*. It was astonishing.) Mary Beard met Hillary Clinton. But there was still trouble between certain kinds of femi-nists and some trans activists, as described by Gaby Hinsliff. As they say, stay tuned.

Amelia Gentleman wrote about earlier migrants of the Windrush generation, Hanif Kureishi about the difficulties of bringing diversity to publishing, Gary Younge tackled white America. The Syrian war raged on. Millions of people around the world continued to be forced from their homelands and suffer the miseries of displacement, and Ai Weiwei wrote about their plight and the dehumanisation to which they are subjected.

Beneath all this clamorous news of people there are stories that are more silent, but in the long run more momentous, because they are underpinning and affecting the human saga. Resource wars are being driven by climate change: more droughts, floods, hurricanes and fires mean less food. Zoe Williams writes light-heartedly about the 2018 summer heatwave, but it's not really a joke, as Jonathan Watts and Elle Hunt point out in 'Halfway to boiling: the city at 50C'. Plastic is a scourge that is choking land and water, but giving it up isn't as easy as you might think, say three people who tried it in February. Worse, the source of our nutrition – farming – may also be the architect of our doom, as it is killing the chain of life that sustains us, writes George Monbiot in 'Insectageddon'. Throw in the plight of the oceans, as Patrick Barkham does in his piece on the David Attenborough show, *Blue Planet*, and things look dire indeed. If the oceans die, we die – it's as simple, and as complex, as that.

Will we as a species go out with a whimper or a bang? Will we go out at all? How should we behave to avoid such a fate? Who will tell us what's really going on? What sources of information can we trust?

Ah, there's the rub, and it's a rub that's very much of our times. Which brings me to the final piece in this book: 'The *Guardian* view on the press and Trump: speaking truth to power'. This is scary stuff. 'Mr Trump's sweeping abuse of the press is grimly familiar now,' says the *Guardian*. It is even more grimly familiar to those of us old enough to remember the totalitarianisms of the 20th century: destruction of any voices other than their own was always one of their first goals. Let us hope that the independent press can survive the many pressures being brought to bear on it, for without it democracy is scarcely possible.

What will the coming year bring? Hang on tight, folks: it's been a wild ride lately, and it's not over yet.

Introduction

LISA ALLARDICE

'It is not the press's job to save the United States from Mr Trump. It is the press's job to report, delve, analyse and scrutinise as best it can and without fear.' On 16 August this year, the *Guardian* joined nearly 350 media organisations across America in publishing editorials in protest against Donald Trump's attacks on press freedom: his relentless undermining of facts as 'fake news' and branding journalists 'the enemies of the people'. 'Speaking truth to power' is the fitting final piece in this anthology.

The 'job' of the press is the subject of *Guardian* editor-in-chief Katharine Viner's inspiring lecture 'A mission for journalism in a time of crisis', given last November but (breaking with *Bedside Guardian* chronological convention) opening this anthology. 'What is the meaning and purpose of our work? What role do we play in society?' she asks. Pleasingly, this collection of some of the most acclaimed, noteworthy, amusing or simply elegantly written pieces published by the *Guardian* over the last year is thus bookended by reflections on the state of journalism itself: the changes and challenges it faces, as well as its potential for helping to create a better future. As befits a compendium, even more than a newspaper or website, I have tried – to borrow from Viner's essay – to choose 'work that speaks to the urgency of the moment, but lasts for more than a day'. I also looked for pieces that reflect her insistence on the importance of hope in our work: 'a faith in our capacity to act together to make change'.

This book presents a run of fearless, standout journalism that succeeded not only in uncovering stories and holding the powerful to account, but in so doing contributed to genuine cultural change: playing a part in toppling media moguls (the #MeToo movement), millionaires (the Paradise Papers) and ministers (Amelia Gentleman's powerful reporting on the Windrush scandal led to the resignation of home secretary Amber Rudd). We also took on the internet giants with Carole Cadwalladr's award-winning investigation into Cambridge Analytica, which resulted in a £500,000 fine, the maximum possible, for Mark Zuckerberg and Facebook over data breaches. Cadwalladr's pieces aren't included here because they first appeared in our sister paper, the *Observer*; but Jonathan Freedland's comment piece sagely sums up the implications of social media's fall from grace.

In January the newspaper itself underwent a radical transformation, relaunching as a tabloid, and it said goodbye to its former editor of 20 years, Peter Preston, who died that month (affectionately remembered here in a tribute from departing *Daily Mail* editor Paul Dacre). The *Guardian*'s ambitions remained as big as ever and it is now funded more by readers than advertisers.

In the world at large, while 2018 might not have been defined by the momentous shocks of its predecessors, no one could claim it has been a cheery year. Immersing oneself in 12 months of journalism is not unlike binge-watching a terrifying mash-up of the bleakest hit TV shows (*The Handmaid's Tale*, *The Wire*, *The Bridge* ...) without an off switch.

The overwhelming global crises posed by climate change, the plight of refugees, ongoing wars and oppression demand our attention with ever greater urgency. This was the year, perhaps, that we began to absorb the consequences of 2016's EU referendum and US election (I tried to keep an eye on those column-inch bullies Brexit and Trump – they have had two anthologies now); but also when dire warnings of previous decades began to make themselves felt: the weather was weird from Japan to Iceland; the rise of the far right continued across Europe, even reaching Sweden; knife crime on the streets of London increased to the highest rate in ten years. Poor mental health, obesity, poverty and air pollution are storing up greater problems for the future. The world is becoming more toxic. We are in mourning for old certainties, and, on my reading of a year's outpourings, if we were to assess our well-being on a scale of the seven stages of grief, we are stuck somewhere between 'anger and bargaining' and 'depression, reflection, loneliness'.

But I didn't want this book to be the stuff of nightmares; it is called *The Bedside Guardian* after all. And there have been great moments of shared joy, particularly in the UK. The patriotic fervour inspired by the royal wedding in May (even *Guardian* commentators found something to cheer in the arrival of Meghan Markle) rose with the temperature as England's young football team made it to the semi-finals of the World Cup in Moscow (waistcoats, thanks to Gareth Southgate, became summer's hottest fashion statement – literally, it was too sweltering to wear them) and the nation celebrated the seventieth anniversary of the NHS. A giant blimp floated across the London skyline in defiance of President Trump's UK visit. A Welshman won the Tour de France. And then there was *Love Island*, which drew in record numbers of fans – the final a true water cooler moment. We all needed cooling off.

Outside our own (endlessly debated) borders, in July the world's attention was focused on another football team, the young Wild Boars who had been trapped in caves in Thailand for more than 13 days. The successful rescue of all 12 boys and their coach, just minutes before the caves collapsed, was an all too rare happy ending. Here was hope.

We couldn't include everything – in particular stories that hadn't reached their conclusions: in the interval between sending the extracts to press and writing this introduction, the Salisbury poisoning suspects have been named, for example; the antisemitism row engulfing the Labour Party and Jeremy Corbyn remains unresolved; and, like Steve Bell's cartoon on which the collection ends, the fate of Theresa May (and her Chequers deal) is left painfully dangling. America is braced for terrible storms of one kind and another. And, as I write, one question unites the nation: who killed the Home Secretary? (In Jed Mercurio's *Body-guard*, the biggest TV drama of the decade.)

It is customary for the editor to use this space to apologise to colleagues whose work is not included. I am really sorry – there was too much great stuff. I packed, re-packed, stuffed and sat on this suitcase in an attempt to have all seasons covered – but you always find you've left something crucial behind. I'm sorry, too, if I missed out any of your favourites. I hope you enjoy reading it as much as I have enjoyed editing it. It has been a harrowing, humbling and, yes, hopeful experience.

I would like to thank Katharine Viner for asking me to do it; all of the section editors who spared the time to look back over their highlights (I know how hard it is to remember what you put in the paper last week, let alone last year); former *Bedside* editors Claire Armitstead and Gary Younge for their tips; and not least Lindsay Davies, for so cheerfully keeping me – vaguely – on track and with such a judicious eye on our luggage allowance. Most of all, thank you Margaret Atwood, for responding – yet again – to my demand for words, and as generously and brilliantly as always. Praise be. Of course, she saw it all coming decades ago – the *New Yorker* didn't dub her 'the prophet of dystopia' for nothing. But as she reminded me when I interviewed her at the beginning of this year: 'There is always hope. Otherwise why get up in the morning?'

A mission for journalism in a time of crisis

KATHARINE VINER

'No former period, in the history of our Country, has been marked by the agitation of questions of a more important character than those which are now claiming the attention of the public.' So began the announcement, nearly 200 years ago, of a brand-new newspaper to be published in Manchester, England, which proclaimed that 'the spirited discussion of political questions' and 'the accurate detail of facts' were 'particularly important at this juncture'.

The man who drafted this announcement, a 28-year-old English journalist named John Edward Taylor, had attended an enormous demonstration for parliamentary reform in St Peter's Field in Manchester on 16 August 1819, and witnessed how the city's magistrates, intimidated by the size of the 60,000-strong crowd and their demands, ordered armed cavalry to charge, killing at least 11 people. Taylor's relentless effort to report the full story of Peterloo strengthened his own reformist political views – and he became determined to agitate for fair representation in parliament. His newspaper, the *Manchester Guardian*, was launched with great confidence and optimism, by a man who believed that, 'in spite of Peterloo and police spies, reason was great and would prevail'. It was founded in a mood of great hope, and faith in ordinary people.

Now we are living through another extraordinary period in history: one defined by dazzling political shocks and the disruptive impact of new technologies in every part of our lives. The public sphere has changed more radically in the past two decades than in the previous two centuries – and news organisations, including this one, have worked hard to adjust.

But the turbulence of our time may demand that we do more than adapt. The circumstances in which we report, produce, distribute and obtain the news have changed so dramatically that this moment requires nothing less than a serious consideration of what we do and why we do it.

The Scott Trust, which owns the *Guardian*, stated a very clear purpose when it was established in 1936: 'to secure the financial and editorial independence of the *Guardian* in perpetuity and to safeguard the journalistic freedom and liberal values of the *Guardian* free from commercial or political interference'. As an editor, it's hard to imagine a finer mission for a proprietor: our sole shareholder is committed only to our journalistic freedom and long-term survival.

But if the mission of the Scott Trust is to ensure that *Guardian* journalism will exist for ever, it is still left to us to define what the mission of that journalism will be. What is the meaning and purpose of our work? What role do we play in society?

After working at the *Guardian* for two decades, I feel I know instinctively why it exists. Most of our journalists and our readers do, too – it's something to do with holding power to account, and upholding liberal values. We know what defines a *Guardian* story, what feels like a *Guardian* perspective, what makes something 'very *Guardian*' (for better and for worse).

In my own work as editor of the *Guardian* in Australia, and then as the editor of the *Guardian* in the US, I tried to conceptualise the *Guardian* with a different accent – to identify the essential qualities of *Guardian* journalism and bring them to new audiences. Now, as the editor-in-chief of the *Guardian* and the *Observer*,

I believe our time requires something deeper. It is more urgent than ever to ask: who are we, fundamentally?

Many of our core values – honesty, cleanness (integrity), courage, fairness, a sense of duty to the reader and a sense of duty to the community – were laid out by editor CP Scott on the 100th birthday of the *Guardian*, with his justly celebrated centenary essay of 1921. It was here that Scott introduced the famous phrase 'comment is free, but facts are sacred', and decreed that 'the voice of opponents no less than that of friends has a right to be heard'.

Our moral conviction rests on a faith that people long to understand the world they're in, and to create a better one. We believe in the value of the public sphere; that there is such a thing as the public interest, and the common good; that we are all of equal worth; that the world should be free and fair.

These inspiring ideas have always been at the heart of the *Guardian* at its best – whether the paper is called the *Manchester Guardian* or the *Guardian*, the name it adopted in 1959 – and they are enshrined in our independent ownership structure, in which the *Guardian* is owned solely by the Scott Trust. Any money made must be spent on journalism.

This is the mission that has motivated so many of the great moments in *Guardian* history, from our independent reporting of the Spanish civil war to the dramatic Edward Snowden revelations; from taking an anti-colonial position in the Suez crisis to standing up to Rupert Murdoch, the police and politicians in the phone-hacking scandal; from sending Jonathan Aitken to jail to the Panama and Paradise Papers.

These values, beliefs and ideas are well-established and enduring. But the past three decades – since the invention of the world wide web in 1989 – have transformed our idea of the public in ways that could not have been imagined. As its creator, Tim Berners-Lee, put it, 'this is for everyone'. At first, it felt like the beginning of a thrilling new era of hyper-connectivity, with all the world's knowledge at our fingertips and every person empowered to participate – as if the internet was one big town square where all our problems could be solved and everyone helped each other.

While many news organisations saw the internet as a threat to the old hierarchies of authority, forward-looking editors like Alan Rusbridger, who led the *Guardian* from 1995 until 2015, embraced this hopeful new future for journalism, by investing in digital expansion and by understanding that journalists, in this new world, must be open to challenge and debate from their audience. From making the *Guardian* the first British news organisation to employ a readers' editor to launching an opinion site that inverted the traditional model of top-down newspaper commentary, he put the *Guardian* at the forefront of digital innovation and the changed relationships of this new era.

But it has become clear that the utopian mood of the early 2000s did not anticipate all that technology would enable. Our digital town squares have become mobbed with bullies, misogynists and racists, who have brought a new kind of hysteria to public debate. Our movements and feelings are constantly monitored, because surveillance is the business model of the digital age. Facebook has become the richest and most powerful publisher in history by replacing editors with algorithms – shattering the public square into millions of personalised news feeds, shifting entire societies away from the open terrain of genuine debate and argument, while they make billions from our valued attention.

This shift presents big challenges for liberal democracy. But it presents particular problems for journalism.

The transition from print to digital did not initially change the basic business model for many news organisations – that is, selling advertisements to fund the journalism delivered to readers. For a time, it seemed that the potentially vast scale of an online audience might compensate for the decline in print readers and advertisers. But this business model is currently collapsing, as Facebook and Google swallow digital advertising; as a result, the digital journalism produced by many news organisations has become less and less meaningful.

Publishers that are funded by algorithmic ads are locked in a race to the bottom in pursuit of any audience they can find – desperately binge-publishing without checking facts, pushing out the most shrill and most extreme stories to boost clicks. But even this huge scale can no longer secure enough revenue.

Trust in all kinds of established institutions – including the media – is at an historic low. This is not a blip, and it should not be a surprise, when so many institutions have failed the people who trusted them and responded to criticism with contempt. As a result, people feel outraged but powerless – nothing they do seems to stop these things happening, and nobody seems to be listening to their stories.

This has created a crisis for public life, and particularly for the press, which risks becoming wholly part of the same establishment that the public no longer trusts. At a moment when people are losing faith in their ability to participate in politics and make themselves heard, the media can play a critical role in reversing that sense of alienation.

To do this well, journalists must work to earn the trust of those they aim to serve. And we must make ourselves more representative of the societies we aim to represent. Members of the media are increasingly drawn from the same, privileged sector of society: this problem has actually worsened in recent decades. According to the government's 2012 report on social mobility in the UK, while most professions are still 'dominated by a social elite', journalism lags behind medicine, politics and even law in opening its doors to people from less well-off backgrounds.

'Indeed,' the report concludes, 'journalism has had a greater shift towards social exclusivity than any other profession.'

After 71* people died in the devastating Grenfell Tower fire in west London – of which residents had forewarned for years – the Channel 4 News presenter Jon Snow said that the failure to attend to these warnings showed that the media was 'comfortably with the elite, with little awareness, contact or connection with those not of the elite'. As Gary Younge, the *Guardian* editor-at-large, has put it: 'They're not "us" – "their" views are not often heard in newsrooms, and they know it.'

If journalists become distant from other people's lives, they miss the story, and people don't trust them. The *Guardian* is not at all exempt from these challenges, and our staff is not diverse enough. We are committed to addressing these issues – but there is still a long way to go.

Meanwhile, those in power have exploited distrust of the media to actively undermine the role of journalism in the public interest in a democracy – from Donald Trump calling the 'fake news' media 'the enemy of the American people' to a British cabinet member suggesting that broadcasters should be 'patriotic' in their Brexit reporting. All over the world – in Turkey, Russia, Poland, Egypt, China, Hungary, Malta and many other countries – powerful interests are on the march against free speech. Journalists are undermined, attacked, even murdered.

In these disorientating times, championing the public interest – which has always been at the heart of the *Guardian*'s mission – has become an urgent necessity. People are understandably anxious in the face of crises that are global, national, local and personal. At the global level, these crises are overwhelming: climate change, the refugee crisis, the rise of a powerful super-rich who bestride

---

* In January 2018, the final death toll rose to 72.

the global economy. It is easy to feel that humanity is facing a great shift, about which we were not consulted. Overwhelming technological, environmental, political and social change has precipitated what the philosopher Timothy Morton memorably describes as 'a traumatic loss of coordinates' for all of us.

These global upheavals have plainly destabilised national politics, producing the shocks and surprises of the past two years: the unexpected result of the Brexit referendum, which leaves Britain facing a deeply uncertain future; the stunning election of Donald Trump; the collapse of support for traditional parties across Europe, and the rise of Emmanuel Macron in France. These events confounded the experts and the insiders who confidently declared them impossible. In the UK, Jeremy Corbyn appeared to have torn up the rulebook that had governed electoral politics for two decades – finding a surge of support in the June snap election, particularly among young people, by promoting socialist ideas that had long been dismissed. Bernie Sanders tapped into a similar mood in the US Democratic primary.

Skyrocketing inequality between the rich and poor has bred resentment at the political and economic establishment. In October it was revealed that the world's super-rich now hold the greatest concentration of wealth for 120 years – many of them taking elaborate steps to avoid tax in the process, as the Paradise Papers showed.

What is becoming clear is that the way things have been run is unsustainable. We are at a turning point in which, in writer Naomi Klein's words, 'the spell of neoliberalism has been broken, crushed under the weight of lived experience and a mountain of evidence'. (Klein defines neoliberalism as 'shorthand for an economic project that vilifies the public sphere'.) Perhaps the markets don't have all the answers after all. The *Financial Times* columnist Martin Wolf, who says that many had not understood how 'radical the implications' of worsening inequality would be, suggests that the political backlash to globalisation could possibly produce a 'fundamental transformation of the world – at least as significant as the one that brought about the first world war and the Russian Revolution'.

In many local areas, in our neighbourhoods and our communities, we see the collapse of civic life, from public space sold off cheaply to developers to the closing of libraries to the underfunding of schools and hospitals. It is not hard to imagine what has produced the growing tide of resentment that has shaken our politics. It is painful to see the rich getting away with it in the big cities while you're struggling in your small town. Older people lament the loss of community life; younger people are unlikely to be able to find a good job or afford somewhere decent to live.

All of these dislocations have led to another set of crises at a personal level. This year, the World Health Organization announced that cases of depression had ballooned in the past decade, making it the leading cause of disability worldwide. Loneliness is now being recognised as an epidemic throughout the west.

Our lives are increasingly atomised, but you can see the pleasure that comes from communal or civic participation. People long to help each other, to be together, to share experiences, to be part of a community, to influence the powers that control their lives. But in everyday life, such togetherness is hard to achieve: workplaces in the era of the gig economy no longer offer a solid place to gather; religion has declined; technology means that we often communicate via screens rather than face to face.

This is a dangerous moment: these are fertile grounds for authoritarianism and fascistic movements, and it's no surprise that people feel anxious and confused. The desire to belong can just as easily find a home in dark places; new ways of participating can just as easily be used to foster hate.

One response to this crisis is despair and escapism: to bury our heads in our phones, or watch some dystopian TV. Another is to declare that the whole system is broken, and everything must be torn down – a view whose popularity may partly explain our recent political tremors.

But despair is just another form of denial. People long to feel hopeful again – and young people, especially, yearn to feel the hope that previous generations once had.

Hope does not mean naively denying reality, as Rebecca Solnit explains in her inspiring book *Hope in the Dark*. 'Hope is an embrace of the unknown and the unknowable, an alternative to the certainty of both optimists and pessimists,' Solnit writes. It's a belief that actions have meaning and that what we do matters. 'Authentic hope,' she says, 'requires clarity and imagination.'

Hope, above all, is a faith in our capacity to act together to make change. To do this, we need to be bold. 'Not everything that is faced can be changed,' James Baldwin wrote in 1962. 'But nothing can be changed until it is faced.' We need to accept the limits of the old kind of power, and work out what the new kinds will be. We need to be engaged with the world, uncynical, unsnobbish, on people's side.

If people long to understand the world, then news organisations must provide them with clarity: facts they can trust, information that they need, reported and written and edited with care and precision.

If people long to create a better world, then we must use our platform to nurture imagination – hopeful ideas, fresh alternatives, belief that the way things are isn't the way things need to be. We cannot merely criticise the status quo; we must also explore the new ideas that might displace it. We must build hope.

We must embrace the new ways that people are engaging in the world, not long for a lost past when the ballot box and a handful of powerful media was the end of the story. As Ethan Zuckerman says, 'if news organisations can help make citizens feel powerful, like they can make effective civic change, they'll develop a strength and loyalty they've not felt in years'.

The *Guardian* is now funded more by our readers than by our advertisers. This is not only a new business model. It is an opportunity to focus on what readers value in *Guardian* journalism: serious reporting that takes time and effort, carefully uncovers the facts, holds the powerful to account, and interrogates ideas and arguments – work that speaks to the urgency of the moment, but lasts for more than a day. Being funded by our readers means we must focus on the stories that are most meaningful. It also means that we must spend money carefully, trying to produce – as one writer described CP Scott's ambition for the *Guardian* a century ago – 'a great paper without any of the airs of a great paper'.

Of course, in a serious age, the appetite for thoughtful, clever features beyond the news is possibly greater than ever. Our readers want to be nourished – by meaningful journalism about technology, economics, science, the arts – not fattened up with junk. They want useful, enjoyable reporting on how we live now, spotting trends, catching the mood, understanding what people are talking about – life-affirming, inspiring, challenging. We can be fun, and we must be funny, but it must always have a point, laughing with our audience, never at them. Their attention is not a commodity to be exploited and sold.

We will give people the facts, because they want and need information they can trust, and we will stick to the facts. We will find things out, reveal new information and challenge the powerful. This is the foundation of what we do. As trust in the media declines in a combustible political moment, people around the world come to the *Guardian* in greater numbers than ever before, because they know us to be rigorous and fair. If we once emphasised the revolutionary idea that 'comment is free', today our priority is to ensure that 'facts are sacred'. Our ownership structure means we are entirely independent and free from political and commercial influence. Only our values will determine the stories we choose to cover – relentlessly and courageously.

To steal Rainer Maria Rilke's phrase, we must 'live the questions now': constantly examining our assumptions, our biases, how the world is changing, what it means. To do this, we will follow five principles: we will develop ideas that help improve the world, not just critique it; we will collaborate with readers, and others, to have greater impact; we will diversify, to have richer reporting from a representative newsroom; we will be meaningful in all of our work; and, underpinning it all, we will report fairly on people as well as power and find things out.

Since I became editor-in-chief, we have experienced a huge number of political and social shocks, a dramatic undermining of the business model for serious journalism, and what many believe is an unprecedented level of disruption to our planet, our nation states, our communities, ourselves. It is a searching time to be an editor, a journalist and a citizen – but also a privilege to be grappling with these questions, with a possibility of helping to turn this era into something better, to turn this moment to 'beneficial account', as our founding manifesto proclaimed. And to do what has been the mission of the *Guardian* since 1821: to use clarity and imagination to build hope.

Autumn

On Kazuo Ishiguro's Nobel win

SEBASTIAN BARRY

Kazuo Ishiguro has won the Nobel prize. His fellow writers, his readers, his friends, his colleagues and translators all over the world, will have sat up straighter suddenly with an exclamation of simple joy at the news. With the death of Seamus Heaney you had the gnawing sense that the heart had gone out of the writing world. Seamus was a radiant and extraordinary soul, and you can apply exactly the same words to the great Ishiguro.

How clever and astute are the Nobel prize committee. Having given the prize last year to Bob Dylan, they have given this year's prize to Dylan's biggest fan. Joseph Conrad busied himself with writing seven or eight masterpieces in a row; Ishiguro has done exactly the same. Are we allowed to say that he, like Seamus, is one of the most truly gentlemanly writers in the history of the literary world, the most agreeable, the most storied, the most kind? Perhaps none of that should matter – but it does, somehow. Between genius and gentleness he has taken his measure of the world, and is himself a measure of the best that humankind can be. How delightful that the Nobel has alighted in his garden.

6 OCTOBER

The fall of Raqqa: hunting the last jihadists in Isis's capital of cruelty

MARTIN CHULOV

Abu Awad, a stalwart fighter for Islamic State, was unsettled. His battered men, sheltering in the rubble of bombed-out buildings, were running low on supplies and they were losing patience – and discipline.

'Abu Osama,' he said on a radio frequency that his pursuers were monitoring two streets away, from the other side of the frontline of the battle for Raqqa. 'We don't have water for ablutions, and we don't have enough medicine to treat our injured.'

'Cleanse yourself with dirt and I will get some to you in the morning,' a man replied in a tired voice.

A young Kurdish rebel was listening on a handheld radio and recognised the voice. 'He's Syrian,' he said, as others from his unit crouched around in the courtyard of a commandeered home. 'That's their leader, Abu Osama. One time [Isis] told us [on the same frequency]: "We will burn you, then bury you." There was no point replying.'

Around 300 Isis fighters are all that are thought to be left in the city, clinging to a corner of the capital of their so-called caliphate, which five months of relentless battle has reduced to three annihilated neighbourhoods. The Old City mud wall that had stood for more than a millennium flanks one side of the battleground, and a wasteland that was once an industrial area is on the other. Smoke from burning buildings mixed with raised grey dust from airstrikes shrouds both under an already dull autumn sky.

The extremists who have stayed have nowhere to go. Their fate is almost certain to be sealed in the apocalyptic ruins of the city where it all began for Isis in Syria more than four years ago.

What remains of the fight for Raqqa is now concentrated on a maze of ruined streets and homes that lead towards Clock Tower Square, where severed heads were placed on stakes after executions by Isis that residents were summoned to witness. Since 2013 the simple ringed roundabout has been scorched into the global psyche as an emblem of Isis's menace. In the eyes of many, its looming loss will seal the terror group's demise.

Bricks and twisted metal cover two empty boulevards leading to the square. Isis snipers line either side. Capturing it will symbolically destroy the group's hold on territory it conquered and has been steadily losing for the past year. Through a hole in a wall used by a Kurdish sniper team, the square and its towering clock can be seen just under 500 metres away.

While Isis used the Great Mosque of al-Nuri in Mosul to lay claim to be a group inspired by faith, Clock Tower Square showcased its naked savagery and intimidation. 'There were around 13 executions a month,' said a local pharmacist, Ismael, who fled the city six months ago and joined a US-backed coalition known as the Syrian Democratic Forces (SDF). 'They used to line the roundabout wearing masks, and go around the streets with a loudspeaker ordering people to watch.

'If you were a spy they cut your throat from the front. The same if you were a blasphemer or murderer. Magicians were beheaded from the back. Women were always shot.'

Fighters all along the frontline, men and boys – many of them also Raqqa locals – spoke matter-of-factly about events that would have been unfathomable before the Isis reign. 'They came to get my brother from our home,' said Moussa, 21, pointing at the ruins of a home down the road. 'They cut his head and hung his body on a crucifix near Aleppo. We weren't even allowed to ask why.' Rami, another Arab fighter from Raqqa, also lost a brother to Isis members who came to his home. 'They were Syrian, from among us, or else they wouldn't have worn masks,' he said. 'They also killed my mother at a checkpoint.'

The men had based themselves in a grey three-storey building less than two miles south of the clock tower. The rooms festered with rotting food and flies. A toppled semi-trailer blocked one entrance to the base, and sand berms closed off another. On the second floor, Hazam, 28, a Kurd from Kobani, incessantly barked instructions into a radio that he held in his only hand. His left hand was lost to a mortar in the fight for his home town two years ago, and when he pointed the stub of his wrist to direct his men, it seemed to have extra effect.

Just past a graveyard, in which Isis had shattered every tombstone, six young fighters had been sent the night before to flank the jihadists, but their position had been exposed. Two had been hit by an RPG, and the rest of the unit had been sent to rescue them. Hazam paced across a balcony as airstrikes thumped into Isis positions ahead. The blast wave shot past the brown mud walls of the Old City and into the headquarters. Shortly afterwards, his radio sparked to life. 'Send the Hummer. We have two martyrs,' a man shouted. 'And injuries. Four of them.'

An hour later, the US-supplied armoured Jeep – the only one the unit had – roared up the street, the legs of the dead dangling out the back, the wounded crammed up front. A utility truck backed towards the Hummer and the two bodies were lifted on blankets and gently transferred to the open canopy. The wounded climbed in beside them. Dazed and deafened, one wounded boy rested his head on a corpse as the truck set off for a medical clinic, past an overturned lorry and jagged, abandoned homes.

Not a single civilian was left in east Raqqa. In their absence, graffiti sprayed on ruins spoke for them, as well as for the vanquished occupiers – and international groups who had come to fight. 'The difference between men and apostates is prayer,' said one message scrawled by an Isis member. 'Raqqa will be purified from the filth of the terrorists,' said another. Greek anarchists fighting alongside the Kurds and Arabs had also left their mark: 'Rouvikonas, Raqqa 2017', they had written, on a wall near the battle zone.

On both sides of the front, men and women from around the world have lined up to fight. Members of global leftist groups – Americans, Turks, Germans and Spanish, among others – flesh out the ranks of Kurdish and Arab fighters. And within the SDF, minorities from around the region have taken prominent positions.

At a medical centre, two Yazidi girls from Iraq – in their late teens, but looking much older – hosed and swept a courtyard where the two dead fighters had been brought a few hours earlier. Their four wounded colleagues squatted nearby. 'I swear we didn't even see them,' said one wide-eyed boy from Raqqa with a bandaged head. His colleague clasped his hands over his damaged ears.

The clinic's doctor, Akif, a Kurd from the Turkish mountains, sat down and quickly dismissed the boys' injuries. 'They are just clumsy lads who need vitamins,' he said. 'They can go back and fight.'

Akif held rank at the clinic, as did Turkish Kurds in two other frontline areas – where Hazam was based, and further away from the front in the suburb of Raqqa Samra, where Hevda, a woman in her late 30s, led a small but sensitive base. She swept the floors, cooked meals, kept guard, and held court whenever she wanted.

'When you want something and you know it is right, it will come to you with courage and conviction,' she said. Kurds and Arabs in the base deferred to her, as they did to Dalil, from the Turkish city of Batman, who sat alongside Hazam in the forward base.

'The problem with Turkey is that it's an intersection of capitalism and totalitarianism,' he said. 'They have played an unfortunate role in the region.' Using a pejorative for the Turkish leader, Recep Tayyip Erdoğan, he added: 'The sultan's time is ticking.'

Arab volunteers, many of them locals, are prominent on the frontlines and, though neither group will acknowledge it publicly, recruiting local men has fired the battle with a sense of personal vengeance.

Near the frontline, with an Isis radio in one hand and another device to talk with his own men in the other, Elyas, 25, from Hasaka, said the role of the Raqqa ranks had been instrumental in the gains so far, as had precision airstrikes by a US-led coalition. '[Isis] know we don't torture them if we catch them. I don't even hate them,' he said. 'They are ignorant people. They have been brainwashed. If we treat them like they treat us, we become like them.'

Elyas led his men through a hole blown in a wall near the front, then more holes smashed into adjoining homes, through which both the extremists and their pursuers moved. A bicycle stood incongruously amid the wreckage of war in one room. Strewn clothes and Islamic books covered the floor in another, alongside more rotting food. On the rooftop, Arab fighters crouched behind a wall as a rocket from a fighter jet crunched into an Isis position. Smoke from the blast drifted over nearby grain silos and silhouetted the graveyard. 'I love the feeling of battle,' Elyas said as the sky darkened. 'It's delicious.'

As Isis withdrew, it burrowed underground to avoid the jets above. Tunnels are found most days, and nearly all have been booby-trapped. 'The amount of energy they have put into laying mines is incredible,' said Elyas in a building up ahead. 'We lost a comrade in the courtyard here.'

The stench of death lingered where both a tunnel and an improvised bomb had been found. An Isis man had been discovered there the day before. His body was buried nearby.

As the terror group's fighters tire, the men hunting them say the fall of Raqqa has galvanised them. Commanders believe the city will fall within four to six weeks, and there is increasingly nowhere left to hide for the diehard extremists in the rubble and tunnels of what was once the centre of their rule in Syria.

The overwhelming destruction of Raqqa speaks of a place that has been through more than just war. The shattered psyche of the city hangs heavily over the battlefield. 'Everything is broken,' said Ahmed Issa, a 25-year-old student. 'My parents will never come back here. And I won't let my sisters come. We are haunted by bad spirits here. Something needs to cleanse us.'

Additional reporting by Mohammed Rasool.

11 OCTOBER

'I had to defend myself': the night Harvey Weinstein jumped on me

LÉA SEYDOUX

I meet men like Harvey Weinstein all the time. I have starred in many films over the last 10 years and have been lucky enough to win awards at festivals like Cannes. Cinema is my life. And I know all of the ways in which the film industry treats women with contempt.

When I first met Harvey Weinstein, it didn't take me long to figure him out. We were at a fashion show. He was charming, funny, smart – but very domineering. He wanted to meet me for drinks and insisted we had to make an appointment that very night. This was never going to be about work. He had other intentions – I could see that very clearly.

We met in the lobby of his hotel. His assistant, a young woman, was there. All throughout the evening, he flirted and stared at me as if I was a piece of meat. He acted as if he were considering me for a role. But I knew that was bullshit. I knew it, because I could see it in his eyes. He had a lecherous look. He was using his power to get sex.

He invited me to come to his hotel room for a drink. We went up together. It was hard to say no because he's so powerful. All the girls are scared of him. Soon, his assistant left and it was just the two of us. That's the moment where he started losing control.

We were talking on the sofa when he suddenly jumped on me and tried to kiss me. I had to defend myself. He's big and fat, so I had to be forceful to resist him. I left his room, thoroughly disgusted. I wasn't afraid of him, though. Because I knew what kind of man he was all along.

Since that night in his hotel room, I've seen him on many other occasions. We are in the same industry, so it's impossible to avoid him. I've seen how he operates: the way he looks for an opening. The way he tests women to see what he can get away with.

He also doesn't take no for an answer. I once went with him to a restaurant and when he couldn't get a table he got angry and said: 'Do you know who I am? I am Harvey Weinstein.' That's the kind of man he is.

I've been at dinners with him where he's bragged openly about Hollywood actresses he has had sex with. He's also said misogynistic things to me over the years. 'You'd be better if you lost weight,' he said. That comment shocked me.

One night, I saw him in London for the Baftas. He was hitting on a young woman. Another time, at the MetLife ball, I saw him trying to convince a young woman to sleep with him. Everyone could see what he was doing.

That's the most disgusting thing. Everyone knew what Harvey was up to and no one did anything. It's unbelievable that he's been able to act like this for decades and still keep his career. That's only possible because he has a huge amount of power.

In this industry, there are directors who abuse their position. They are very influential, that's how they can do that. With Harvey, it was physical. With others, it's just words. Sometimes, it feels like you have to be very strong to be a woman in the film industry. It's very common to encounter these kinds of men.

The first time a director made an inappropriate comment to me, I was in my mid-20s. He was a director I really liked and respected. We were alone and he said to me: 'I wish I could have sex with you, I wish I could fuck you.'

He said it in a way that was half-joking and half-serious. I was very angry. I was trying to do my job and he made me very uncomfortable. He has slept with all of the actresses he filmed.

Another director I worked with would film very long sex scenes that lasted days. He kept watching us, replaying the scenes over and over again in a kind of stupor. It was gross.

Yet another director tried to kiss me. Like Weinstein, I had to physically push him away, too. He acted like a crazy man, deranged by the fact that I didn't want to have sex with him.

If you're a woman working in the film industry, you have to fight because it is a very misogynistic world. Why else are salaries so unequal? Why do men earn more than women? There is no reason for it to be that way.

Hollywood is incredibly demanding on women. Think about the beauty diktats. All of the actresses have Botox at 30. They have to be perfect. This is an image of women that is bizarre – and one that ends up controlling women.

This industry is based on desirable actresses. You have to be desirable and loved. But not all desires have to be fulfilled, even though men in the industry have an expectation that theirs should be. I think – and hope – that we might finally see a change. Only truth and justice can bring us forward.

Léa Seydoux is a French actor. She was awarded the Palme d'Or at the Cannes film festival for her film Blue Is the Warmest Colour.

12 OCTOBER

The fall of Harvey Weinstein should be a moment to challenge extreme masculinity

REBECCA SOLNIT

This past week was not a good week for women. In the United States, it was reported that a man who allegedly raped a 12-year-old girl was granted joint custody of the resultant eight-year-old boy being raised by his young mother.

Earlier in the week, the severed head and legs of Swedish journalist Kim Wall, who disappeared after entering inventor Peter

Madsen's submarine, were discovered near Copenhagen. A hard drive belonging to Madsen, Danish police said, was loaded with videos showing women being decapitated alive.

A Swedish model received rape threats for posing in an Adidas advertisement with unshaven legs. The University of Southern California's dean of medicine was dumped after reports resurfaced that he had sexually harassed a young medical researcher in 2003. A number of men at liberal publications were revealed to have contacted Milo Yiannopoulos, urging him to attack women – 'Please mock this fat feminist,' wrote a senior male staff writer at Vice's women's channel, since fired. And, of course, movie mogul Harvey Weinstein was described by the *New York Times* as a serial sexual harasser; his alleged offences, according to a TV journalist, include trapping her in a hallway, where he masturbated until he ejaculated into a potted plant.

This week, the *New Yorker* ran a follow-up story by Ronan Farrow (the biological son of Woody Allen, who has repudiated his father for his treatment of his sisters), expanding the charges women have made against Weinstein to include sexual assault. He quotes one young woman who said 'he forced me to perform oral sex on him' after she showed up for a meeting. She added, 'I have nightmares about him to this day.' Weinstein denies any non-consensual sex.

Saturday 7 October was the first anniversary of the release of the tape in which the United States president boasted about sexually assaulting women; 11 women then came forward to accuse Donald Trump. And last week began with the biggest mass shooting in modern US history, carried out by a man reported to have routinely verbally abused his girlfriend: domestic violence is common in the past of mass shooters.

Underlying all these attacks is a lack of empathy, a will to dominate, and an entitlement to control, harm and even take the lives of others. Though there is a good argument that mental illness is not a sufficient explanation – and most mentally ill people are non-violent – mass shooters and rapists seem to have a lack of empathy so extreme it constitutes a psychological disorder. At this point in history, it seems to be not just a defect from birth, but a characteristic many men are instilled with by the culture around them. It seems to be the precondition for causing horrific suffering and taking pleasure in it as a sign of one's own power and superiority, in regarding others as worthless, as yours to harm or eliminate.

Or perhaps it's an extreme version of masculinity that has always been with us in a culture that gives men more power and privilege than women; perhaps these acts are the result of taking that to its logical conclusion. There must be terrible loneliness in that failure to perceive or value the humanity of others, the failure of empathy and imagination, to consider oneself the only person who matters. Caring about others, empathising, loving them, liberates each of us; these bereft figures seem to be prisoners of their selfishness before they are punishers of others.

Much has also been written to explain why the mass shootings are not terrorism (except when the shooter is, as he is rarely, Muslim), but perhaps terrorism can be imagined as a cultural as well as political phenomenon, a desire to instil fear, assert dominance, devalue the rights and freedoms of others, assert the power of the violent and of violence. There is an ideology behind it, even if not an overtly political ideology, of self-aggrandisement, cruelty, the embrace of violence, and hate.

This is also a week in which white supremacists marched in Charlottesville again, where activist Heather Heyer was mowed down in August, and where black, Jewish and Asian friends of mine have been menaced by violence and hate. This ideology of dominance and idealisation of violence has its racial dimensions too. And it has its president now, in the racist misogynist in the White House.

It's the authoritarianism of violence that seems too often overlooked, the acts that are the opposite of the democratic ideal that all people are created equal, with certain inalienable rights. There is no greater authoritarianism than that of someone who violates the will, the body, the wellbeing, or takes the life of another. The crimes in question, from sexual assault to mass killings, seem designed specifically as assertions that the perpetrator has the power of a god, the victims are powerless.

That powerlessness of others seems to be desired and relished in these cases. It's time to talk about the fact that many men seem erotically excited by their ability to punish, humiliate, inflict pain on women – the subject of a lot of porn. When you jerk off while cornering an unwilling woman, you're presumably excited by her powerlessness and misery or repulsion. Another of Weinstein's victims told the *New Yorker*, 'The fear turns him on.' Fox News founder and CEO Roger Ailes took pleasure, according to his victims, in degrading the employees he sexually exploited and harassed. Journalist Gabriel Sherman reported in 2016, 'The culture of fear at Fox was such that no one would dare come forward' until Gretchen Carlson broke the silence with a lawsuit. This year several black employees sued the network for racial discrimination.

We've also recently had a host of obituaries for Hugh Hefner. Some included the arguments that Hefner and his magazine were harmless or liberating. But they insisted that women were for men to use if they met a narrow definition of attractiveness, and to mock or ignore if they were not. While often portrayed as part of the sexual revolution, the magazine and Hefner were instead part of the counter-revolution, figuring out how to perpetuate women's subordination and men's power in a changing era.

The young women who lived in – and sometimes described feeling trapped in – the Playboy mansion were there to please the old goat at the centre of it and his friends, and not the other way around. Some of the playmates ended up dead – Dorothy Stratten's face blown off by an estranged ex-husband at 20, Paula Sladewski's body found 'burned beyond recognition' in a Miami dumpster, and so forth. News anchor – and Roger Ailes victim – Andrea Tantaros said of the Fox network, 'behind the scenes, it operates like a sex-fuelled, Playboy mansion-like cult, steeped in intimidation, indecency and misogyny,' which is not an endorsement of the Playboy mansion.

There is a solution, but I don't know how we reach it, except in a plethora of small acts that accrete into a different worldview and different values. It's in how we raise boys, in what we define as erotic, in how men can discourage each other from the idea that dominating and harming women enhances their status. Perhaps it's in young men in power learning from the fall of Roger Ailes, Bill Cosby, Bill O'Reilly, and now Harvey Weinstein – and myriad Silicon Valley executives and more than a handful of academics – that women have voices and, sometimes, people who listen believe them, and the era of impunity might be fading from view. Though the change that really matters will consist of eliminating the desire to do these things, not merely the fear of getting caught.

In Darren Aronofsky's film *Mother!*, Jennifer Lawrence plays a young earth goddess of a woman restoring her poet husband's house to the best of her ability, alone, while he ignores her requests to have some say in what does and doesn't happen, who does and does not enter their home. You can interpret the story, as Aronofsky intended, as an environmental allegory in which the house is the Earth, the destruction is environmental destruction, the recklessness that accompanies selfishness. Or you can just see it as a film about things going increasingly wrong in an unequal marriage between an egomaniac without empathy and a woman who is all too giving and not respected, by her husband or by the increasingly destructive guests. It works either way.

It's a film for our time and one I can only hope captures a moment that will pass, because I want the ideals of democracy to be at last fulfilled, because it's past time to talk seriously about the poisonous lack of empathy and imagination that lies behind the corpses and the nightmares and the everyday fears.

20 OCTOBER

Thrive: the new showing-off online is showing off that you're not online

PASS NOTES

Name: Thrive.

Appearance: Dark, sleek, slightly sinister.

Age: Minus two months.

What is it? It's an app that turns your phone off, developed by Samsung and Arianna Huffington. It will be released in December, exclusively for Samsung phones.

It sounds a little like the 'off' button that my phone already has. Yes, but Thrive works automatically. It monitors how much time you spend using different apps, and stops you receiving notifications for set periods. That way you can concentrate on other things.

I've got an app quite like that in my brain. I call it 'Decide'. I'm happy for you, but not everybody feels the same. Huffington quotes research that the average American smartphone user touches their device 2,617 times a day.

Does she quote any proof that this is bad for you? Goodness, no, but many people feel a bit addicted to their phones. The British charity YoungMinds urges young people to have at least 15 phone-free minutes every day. Their survey found that 60 per cent of 18- to 25-year-olds thought they would benefit from a break.

Yet they don't take one? Not always, no. The Huff's plan is 'to help people take control of their lives and their technology – instead of being controlled by it'.

So people who don't trust themselves to make good decisions about their phone should authorise the phone to make the decisions for them? Exactly.

And Huffington thinks that stops people being controlled by technology? That's what she says. And maybe it will help. 'If you're a parent,' Huffington says, 'the Thrive app will allow you to spend time with your child and be fully present.'

Because if your child's happiness can't motivate you, Huffington's app will? That's right. People trying to message you during special family time will get a reply saying that you're 'in Thrive mode'.

Aha! So the new showing-off online is showing off that you're not online? Exactly. Huffington wants this app to spread socially, to be 'more than just a product' and 'create new cultural norms about what we value'.

But only among people with Samsung phones. Um, yes. That's right.

Do say: 'I'm sorry I can't come to the phone right now. I'm too busy living an authentic life.'

Don't say: 'I'm sorry I can't come to the phone right now. It won't let me.'

Insectageddon: farming is more catastrophic than climate breakdown

GEORGE MONBIOT

Which of these would you name as the world's most pressing environmental issue? Climate breakdown, air pollution, water loss, plastic waste or urban expansion? My answer is none of the above. Almost incredibly, I believe that climate breakdown takes third place, behind two issues that receive only a fraction of the attention.

This is not to downgrade the danger presented by global heating – on the contrary, it presents an existential threat. It is simply that I have come to realise that two other issues have such huge and immediate impacts that they push even this great predicament into third place.

One is industrial fishing, which, all over the blue planet, is now causing systemic ecological collapse. The other is the erasure of non-human life from the land by farming.

And perhaps not only non-human life. According to the UN Food and Agriculture Organization, at current rates of soil loss, driven largely by poor farming practice, we have just 60 years of harvests left. And this is before the 'Global Land Outlook' report, published in September, found that productivity is already declining on 20 per cent of the world's cropland.

The impact on wildlife of changes in farming practice (and the expansion of the farmed area) is so rapid and severe that it is hard to get your head round the scale of what is happening. A study published this week in the journal *PLOS One* reveals that flying insects surveyed on nature reserves in Germany have declined by 76 per cent in 27 years. The most likely cause of this Insecta-geddon is that the land surrounding those reserves has become hostile to them: the volume of pesticides and the destruction of habitat have turned farmland into a wildlife desert.

It is remarkable that we need to rely on a study in Germany to see what is likely to have been happening worldwide: long-term surveys of this kind simply do not exist elsewhere. This failure reflects distorted priorities in the funding of science. There is no end of grants for research on how to kill insects, but hardly any money for discovering what the impact of this killing might be. Instead, the work has been left – as in the German case – to recordings by amateur naturalists.

But anyone of my generation (ie in the second bloom of youth) can see and feel the change. We remember the 'moth snowstorm' that filled the headlight beams of our parents' cars on summer nights (memorialised in Michael McCarthy's lovely book of that name). Every year I collected dozens of species of caterpillars and watched them grow and pupate and hatch. This year I tried to find some caterpillars for my children to raise. I spent the whole summer looking and, aside from the cabbage whites on our broccoli plants, found nothing in the wild but one garden tiger larva. Yes, one caterpillar in one year. I could scarcely believe what I was seeing – or rather, not seeing.

Insects, of course, are critical to the survival of the rest of the living world. Knowing what we now know, there is nothing surprising about the calamitous decline of insect-eating birds. Those flying insects – not just bees and hoverflies but species of many different families – are the pollinators without which a vast tract of the plant kingdom, both wild and cultivated, cannot survive. The wonders of the living planet are vanishing before our eyes.

Well, I hear you say, we have to feed the world. Yes, but not this way. As a UN report published in March explained, the notion that pesticide use is essential for feeding a growing population is a myth. A recent study in *Nature Plants* reveals that most farms would increase production if they cut their use of pesticides. A study in the journal *Arthropod-Plant Interactions* shows that the more neonicotinoid pesticides were used to treat rapeseed crops, the more their yield declines. Why? Because the pesticides harm or kill the pollinators on which the crop depends.

Farmers and governments have been comprehensively conned by the global pesticide industry. It has ensured its products should not be properly regulated or even, in real-world conditions, properly assessed. A massive media onslaught by this industry has bamboozled us all about its utility and its impacts on the health of both human beings and the natural world.

The profits of these companies depend on ecocide. Do we allow them to hold the world to ransom, or do we acknowledge that the survival of the living world is more important than returns to their shareholders? At the moment, shareholder value comes first. And it will count for nothing when we have lost the living systems on which our survival depends.

To save ourselves and the rest of the living world, here's what we need to do:

1 We need a global treaty to regulate pesticides, and put the manufacturers back in their box.
2 We need environmental impact assessments for the farming and fishing industries. It is amazing that, while these sectors present the greatest threats to the living world, they are, uniquely in many nations, not subject to such oversight.

3 We need firm rules based on the outcomes of these assessments, obliging those who use the land to protect and restore the ecosystems on which we all depend.

4 We need to reduce the amount of land used by farming, while sustaining the production of food. The most obvious way is greatly to reduce our use of livestock: many of the crops we grow and all of the grazing land we use are deployed to feed them. One study in Britain suggests that, if we stopped using animal products, everyone in Britain could be fed on just 3 million of our 18.5 million hectares of current farmland (or on 7 million hectares if all our farming were organic). This would allow us to create huge wildlife and soil refuges: an investment against a terrifying future.

5 We should stop using land that should be growing food for people to grow maize for biogas and fuel for cars.

Then, at least, nature and people would have some respite from the global onslaught. And, I hope, a chance of getting through the century.

23 OCTOBER

Owning a car will soon be a thing of the past

JOHN HARRIS

If ours is an age in which no end of institutions and conventions are being disrupted, it shouldn't come as a surprise that one of the most basic features of everyday life seems under serious threat. If you are fortunate enough to live in a house with a drive, look outside and you will probably see it: that four-wheeled metal box, which may well be equipped with every technological innovation imaginable, but now shows distinct signs of obsolescence.

To put it another way: after a century in which the car has sat at the heart of industrial civilisation, the age of the automobile – of mass vehicle ownership, and the idea (in the western world at least) that life is not complete without your own set of wheels – looks to be drawing to a close. *Top Gear* is a dead duck. No one writes pop songs about Ferraris any more. The stereotypical boy racer appears a hopeless throwback. And in our cities, the use of cars is being overtaken by altogether greener, more liberating possibilities.

The sale of diesel and petrol cars is to be outlawed in the UK from 2040. But only 10 days ago Oxford announced that it is set to be the first British city to ban all petrol and diesel cars and vans – from a handful of central streets by 2020, extending to the entire urban centre 10 years later. Paris will ban all non-electric cars by 2030, and is now in the habit of announcing car-free days on which drivers have to stay out of its historic heart. In the French city of Lyon, car numbers have fallen by 20 per cent since 2005, and the authorities have their sights set on another drop of the same magnitude. London, meanwhile, has shredded the idea that rising prosperity always triggers rising car use, and seen a 25 per cent fall in the share of journeys made by car since 1990.

Last week, highlighting the increasingly likely arrival of driverless vehicles, General Motors announced that it will soon begin testing autonomous cars in the challenging conditions of New York City, apparently the latest step in the company's rapid and handsomely funded move towards building a new fleet of self-driving taxis. Earlier this year, forecasters at Bank of America tentatively claimed that the US may have reached 'peak car', acknowledging that 'transportation is costly and inefficient, making the sector ripe for disruption'. Their focus was on ride-sharing services, car-pool apps and the collective use of bikes: what they were predicting had the sense of a reality that is already plain to see.

There are caveats to all this, of course. Although cities in the world's rising economies are just as fond of car-sharing and bike use as anywhere in the west, car ownership in India and China is rising vertiginously. And as one of the 25,000 residents of a West Country town that is expanding fast and now prone to gridlock, I can confirm that in swaths of this country, the idea that we will soon surrender our vehicles can easily look rather far-fetched. The recent farcical launch by Great Western Railway of its new inter-city trains (plagued by technical problems, and now taken out of service) highlights how our public transport remains woeful. Even if it brings regular twinges of guilt, there is currently little alternative to owning a car, and using it every day.

But deep social trends do point in another direction. In 1994, 48 per cent of 17- to 20-year-olds and 75 per cent of 21- to 29-year-olds had driving licences. According to the National Travel Survey, by 2016 these figures had dropped respectively to 31 per cent and 66 per cent. Some of this, of course, is down to the deep financial insecurities experienced by millennials, and the stupid costs of car insurance. But in the context of technological change, it looks like it might have just as much to do with the likely shape of the future. If you buy most of your stuff online, the need to drive to a supermarket or shopping centre dwindles to nothing; if you are in daily touch with distant friends and family online, might a time-consuming visit to see them feel that bit less urgent? Meanwhile, at the other end of the demographic spectrum, an ageing population will soon have equally profound consequences – for levels of car ownership, and the demand for alternatives.

Many huge social changes creep up on us, and the fact that politicians tend to avert their eyes from incipient revolutions often serves to keep them out of public discourse. But this one is surely huge. I am from a generation for whom the promise of your own car represented a kind of personal utopia. Go-faster stripes were signifiers for aspiration; Margaret Thatcher's reputed claim that 'a man who, beyond the age of 26, finds himself on a bus can count himself as a failure' chimed with the newly discovered joys of conspicuous consumption. Now, even if some of this lingers on, it does not feel nearly as culturally powerful. The rising global emergency focused on fatal levels of air pollution confirms the motor industry's dire environmental impacts; and concerns about the sub-prime loans that now define a huge swath of the car market suggest that the supposed joys of driving might be unsustainable in plenty of other ways.

The birth pangs of something better are inevitably messy, as evidenced by the stink currently surrounding Uber – an archetypal example of those modern disruptors who point to the future, while obscuring their visions in a great cloud of arrogance. But whatever Uber's failings (and it has to be said: in a city as diverse as London, the idea of traditional black cabs, mostly driven by white British men, representing a comparatively progressive option seems flimsy, to say the least), its innovations are hardly going to be put back in their box. In the US, the average cost per mile of the UberX service is put at around $1.50; in New York City, car ownership works out at around $3 a mile. As and when Uber and Lyft – and whatever ride-hailing services either join or displace them – go driverless in cities and suburbs across the planet, the financial maths will become unanswerable.

At a time of all-pervading gloom, make no mistake: this is good news. At the heart of it all are amazingly emancipatory prospects: mobility no longer dependent on a huge cash outlay and on the organised extortion of motor insurance; everybody, regardless of age or disability, able to access much the same transport. With the requisite political will, dwindling numbers of cars will bring opportunities to radically redesign urban areas. The environmental benefits will be self-evident. And as cities become more and more car-free, towns will cry out for their own changes. Neglected railway branch lines may well come back to life; the hacking-down of bus services that came with austerity will have to be reversed. With any luck, the mundane term 'public transport' will take on a new vitality.

Is this utopian? No more, surely, than the dreams of the people whose visions of a car outside every house and busy highways eventually came true, with no end of grim consequences. 'The remains of the old must be decently laid away; the path of the new prepared,' said Henry Ford. How ironic that the same wisdom now applies to the four-wheeled dreams he created, and their final journey to the scrapyard.

28 OCTOBER

How Deliveroo's 'dark kitchens' are catering from car parks

SARAH BUTLER

A tatty car park under a railway line is squeezed between a busy road, an industrial site and a semi-derelict pub covered in graffiti. It's one of the grittiest parts of east London and probably the last place you would imagine some of the trendiest eateries in the country to be preparing meals.

But the grimy spot is just a short moped ride from the gleaming office towers of Canary Wharf and upmarket docklands apartments, and is therefore the perfect location for the latest idea from Deliveroo, the food courier service. It is setting up dozens of 'dark kitchens' in prefabricated structures for restaurants that want to expand their businesses without opening expensive high-street premises.

Ten metal boxes of a similar size to a shipping container are on this site in Blackwall. They are fitted with industrial kitchen equipment, and two or three chefs and kitchen porters are at work in each, preparing food for restaurants including the Thai chain Busaba Eathai, the US-style MEATliquor diners, the Franco Manca pizza parlours and Motu, an Indian food specialist set up by the family behind Mayfair's Michelin-starred Gymkhana.

The boxes have no windows and many of the chefs work with the doors open, through which they can be seen stirring huge pans or flipping burgers. Outside there are piles of spare equipment, mops in buckets, gas cylinders for the stoves and large cans of cooking oil.

This is one of the biggest of 11 sites currently operated by Deliveroo that are home to 66 dark kitchens. Five sites use the metal structures, known as Rooboxes or Deliveroo Editions, while others are in adapted buildings. The majority are in London, but there are others in Leeds, Reading and Hove, tucked away in car parks or on industrial estates. All are close to residential and office areas filled with customers hungry for upmarket takeaways.

The locations may be unglamorous, but one dark kitchen in Southwark, south London, is turning out rotisserie chicken for the pricey Notting Hill-based specialist Cocotte. There are also outposts for Gourmet Burger Kitchen, the trendy pizza joint Crust Bros and the Soho sushi bar Yoobi.

Deliveroo has big ambitions for its Rooboxes, with plans to open more in London's Swiss Cottage, Nottingham and Cambridge soon, and Manchester and Birmingham lined up for more boxes next year. Deliveroo finds and equips the locations, then rents them out to the restaurants, which employ and train the kitchen staff.

Two chefs tell the *Guardian* that working in the metal boxes is either hot or cold, depending on the weather and whether they are cooking or prepping. In one kitchen, there is only a small fan heater for cold days. Another houses a pizza oven that takes up more than a third of the space and makes it extremely hot.

Javed Akhtar, the operations director of Franco Manca, says the company is testing out a Roobox at the Blackwall site so diners and chefs at its busy nearby restaurant can avoid being troubled by takeaway delivery drivers. Franco Manca chefs get extra money for working in the box, he says, because 'there is no interaction with front-of-house staff'. It also encourages chefs who may not be keen to work in a metal box in a car park.

But more chefs are likely to soon be swapping central locations for less salubrious surroundings.

Deliveroo's sales soared sevenfold to £128.6 million last year as it expanded its operations in the UK and overseas, to 25,000 restaurants in more than 140 cities and 12 countries. The food delivery market, which includes the Deliveroo rivals Just Eat and Uber Eats as well as traditional takeaways, is expected to increase by 10 per cent a year to £53 billion by 2020, according to the market analyst NPD.

But it is not all straightforward for Deliveroo. The company had planned to have more than 200 dark kitchens on 30 sites across the UK by the end of 2017, and even more overseas. That target has been missed and there have been complaints from residents and councils, who accuse the company of bypassing planning rules.

The Roobox site in Camberwell, south London, may be forced to close after Southwark council said the noise of delivery vans and mopeds was a nuisance to neighbours and the operations had been set up without planning permission.

Dan Warne, Deliveroo's UK and Ireland managing director, admits the company did not move quickly enough to speak to the council and residents in Southwark, but says Roobox kitchens are clean, hygienic and checked by the Food Standards Agency.

He says Deliveroo is considering the use of more pushbikes to deliver food, rather than mopeds, in order to reduce noise where that is a problem. The company has a team of staff specially to deal with queries and complaints from councillors and residents. 'We are keen to adapt our operations to meet the concerns that people raise,' Warne says. 'We do understand this is a new thing coming into an area and some people will have questions about it.'

Some residents living in and around Rooboxes say they welcome the opportunity for jobs for young people. But in Dulwich, south London, Pasquale Mereu, a chef at the nearby Italian restaurant Il Mirto, says Deliveroo has been a 'very bad thing' for the business. He says the restaurant's delivery orders have more than halved in the past year and they have had to lay off one of two couriers.

30 OCTOBER

Paddington, go home: should our fantasy stories be more truthful?

STEVE ROSE

Back in 2014, an immigration lawyer pointed out that, under current UK law, Paddington would most likely be deported back to Peru or held in a detention centre. Since he was not fleeing persecution, the little bear would be refused asylum, nor would the Home Office believe he was a minor, owing to his lack of paperwork. The bear's citizenship claim is unlikely to improve with the forthcoming *Paddington 2*, in which he takes up window cleaning, presumably without a work permit. He also dreams of bringing his Aunt Lucy to London, possibly followed by other family members, who would claim benefits and flood the NHS with their marmalade-related health problems.

Paddington is a fine ambassador for Britain's once-proud history as a haven for the persecuted, but did he make a difference? If Theresa May ever read or saw him growing up, her heart and policies remained resolutely unsoftened. Every generation has had these children-orientated 'let's be nice to immigrants' fables. Postwar Americans had a rural Kansas couple who took in an orphan from another planet and named him Clark Kent (by good fortune, he had the same skin colour as them, otherwise who knows?). In recent issues of the comic, Superman saves migrants from white supremacists. In real-world Kansas, meanwhile, Donald Trump won the state with a fairly comfortable majority in 2016.

In the 1980s we had ET, an alien embraced by small-town America. As is so often with kid-meets-alien stories (*Lilo & Stitch*, *The Iron Giant*), *ET* contrasted the innocence of children with the heartlessness of adults. That these prejudice-free kids might grow into heartless adults is a possibility we don't like to contemplate.

Some current multiplex fixtures might also be of interest to the authorities. Does Wonder Woman have a valid visa from Themyscira? Admittedly, she'd ace any points-based immigration system. And what about the Minions: stateless economic migrants whose language no one can understand? Or *Thor: Ragnarok*, which ends (spoiler alert) with an entire spaceship-load of refugees in search of a new home. They can cross Earth off their list.

In the same way we lie about Santa Claus, maybe we tell children these feelgood stories not for their benefit but our own. We know the reality is crushingly grim, but we want to believe in something rosier, like we did when we were children. It might make for a better world one day, but let's not kid ourselves.

5 NOVEMBER

Why we are shining a light on the world of tax havens again

NICK HOPKINS

Most people do not understand the complexities of offshore tax. They have no need to – because they do not have enough money to consider the schemes and arrangements that are on offer in tax havens. The 'ordinary' world and the 'offshore' world have coexisted for decades, separated by the secrecy that remains one of the important attractions of the sector.

This secrecy – and inconsistent scrutiny – has served it well.

Over the past 40 years, offshore tax regimes have grown exponentially; back in the 1970s, they were a way for individuals to hide their money from corrupt and predatory governments in unstable countries, or for banks to move cash around to avoid fluctuations in currency rates.

Then, the lack of transparency and advantageous tax regimes made them the investment place of choice for the rich and famous who wanted legitimate but tax-efficient investments for their wealth.

That cottage industry has developed into a sprawling kingdom for the rich, and there has been little political appetite to thoroughly review what has been going on in this new realm.

That began to change in April last year with the Panama Papers exposé. Millions of people in the UK who had been enduring a 'we are all in it together' austerity since 2008, and countless others in countries around the world, saw in vivid detail that some people were hurting more than others.

The papers showed how some of the world's wealthiest individuals and businesses had been able to shelter their money in companies that did not bear their name, buy luxury goods and homes at cheaper prices, or invest in 'vehicles' that kept the tax they paid to a minimum.

Most of this was entirely lawful, but that was not the point. As the then US president Barack Obama noted: 'The problem is that a lot of this stuff is legal, not illegal.'

The Panama Papers posed a fundamental ethical question: is this fair?

The insights were provided by more than 11 million documents leaked from one law firm, Mossack Fonseca. This was a Panamanian company making the most of the offshore options available to its clients, while simultaneously showing a disregard for its obligations, as set out by regulators who are supposed to ensure money launderers and corrupt politicians are not using offshore schemes to squirrel away their cash.

As a direct result of the publication of stories by the *Guardian*, and a consortium led by the German newspaper *Süddeutsche Zeitung* and the International Consortium of Investigative Journalists, politicians, academics and financiers began to debate more seriously the morality of offshore tax havens, and how they have been policed.

In one notable intervention, more than 300 economists, including the Nobel prize winner Sir Angus Deaton, signed a letter to world leaders that argued: 'The existence of tax havens does not add to overall global wealth or wellbeing; they serve no useful economic purpose.'

There were demands for greater transparency from across the political spectrum, but this eventually led to compromises over the disclosure of information and assurances from prominent figures in the offshore sector. They argued that Mossack Fonseca was the exception rather than the rule.

For instance, the International Financial Centres Forum (IFC), a body representing offshore law firms, insisted British overseas territories and crown dependencies had 'the highest regulatory standards'.

It said more transparency would lead to more money laundering and would only be a boon for criminals, NGOs and investigative journalists. Changes to the sector would only do harm, the group insisted.

One prominent member of the IFC is Appleby.

Last year, a partner in the company told a journalist that criticism of the sector was unfair. 'It's a bit like saying that because Harold Shipman murdered his patients, that all doctors should be thrown in jail,' they said.

We know this because the remark appears on a document that forms part of a second substantial leak. This new cache of documents will allow politicians and the public to test whether the 'Dr Shipman' claim stands up to scrutiny.

Appleby certainly has a reputation as a respectable company.

One of the 'magic circle' of offshore law firms, with offices in 10 jurisdictions, it has a blue-chip clientele that includes some of the wealthiest companies and individuals in the world. The service Appleby provides them has won it the title of 'offshore firm of the year' on a number of occasions. This year, it was the official law firm to, and sponsor of, the America's Cup yacht competition.

Appleby regards itself as a Rolls-Royce operation. Thanks to the leaked files, journalists from some of the world's leading media organisations, including *Süddeutsche Zeitung*, the *New York Times*, the BBC and *Le Monde*, have had a chance to peek under its bonnet.

The insights the documents provide raise new questions about the offshore industry, those who regulate it and how much notice is taken of them.

The files also highlight myriad legitimate ways the company's super-rich customers can minimise the tax they pay – extraordinary methods, bewilderingly complex in some instances, that run counter to the original philosophy of the offshore sector, have been condemned by bodies such as the European commission and the OECD, and appear to have become increasingly unpalatable to ordinary people.

There is a political dimension too, which was not apparent in the Panama Papers. The files show the IFC speaking of its influential 'penetration' of the UK government with lobbying of ministers and civil servants. It boasted that this behind-the-scenes activity may have prevented world leaders from agreeing more wide-ranging transparency measures at a G8 summit in 2013.

Appleby certainly did not want more transparency. Internally, it argued any changes would mean 'eye-watering' costs for its business.

The lobbying effort is particularly significant because the files show that, in 2013, Appleby's Bermuda operation was under scrutiny from the Bermuda Monetary Authority.

The BMA did not like what it found. In a critical report, it red-flagged Appleby in nine areas, demanding 'high priority' changes in, among other things, the company's anti-money-laundering and anti-terrorist-financing risk assessments.

This was not the first time Appleby had been called out over its handling of such issues. The files show it being criticised for flawed compliance procedures in 12 confidential audits over a

10-year period in the Isle of Man, the Cayman Islands, Bermuda and the British Virgin Islands (BVI).

So, at the same time Appleby was pushing back against greater transparency in offshore tax havens, and arguing that such moves would be counterproductive and unnecessary, it was consistently failing to keep to standards that campaigners say are not tough enough anyway.

The company has insisted – in a preemptive public statement – that it has investigated all the allegations put to it by partners in this project and found it did nothing wrong.

But it declined to answer specific questions, for instance, about clients such as Glencore, and how it secured mining rights in the Democratic Republic of the Congo, one of the most corrupt and impoverished nations on Earth.

And what did Appleby really know about a network of companies it set up for associates of the president of Angola, who has been repeatedly accused of corruption and human rights abuses?

The documents reveal other worrying vignettes, including one involving a billionaire client designated as a PEP – politically exposed person. PEPs require extra scrutiny and due diligence.

This particular billionaire wanted to do some business through Appleby's Bermuda office, but the BMA resisted. It wanted more checks conducted on him, because the businessman had very obviously provided misleading information about his background on an important application form.

But Appleby did not want to do this extra due diligence work; instead, it suggested rerouting the application through the BVI, where it 'does not appear that the same issues arise'.

The documents show some partners in the firm were clearly unhappy. 'This is strange stuff,' one said. 'Perhaps leave me out of the group for now in case there's something I'm not supposed to know.'

There was deep unease, too, around another PEP who had been a client of the company since 1984. In 2013, Appleby realised he was not the man they thought he was.

The client, staff discovered, had connections to a scientist accused of being one of the architects of Saddam Hussein's nuclear weapons programme, and his company had, in the early 1990s, been accused of being a front for Saddam.

When Appleby was alerted to the link, managers flew into a panic. According to a document seen by the *Guardian*, a senior partner asked: 'Is there any evidence we detected this before? How can we not have known this earlier?'

None of them could explain how the company had been oblivious to this for 28 years, or who had introduced the client in the first place.

For all of this, it is the variety and nature of the tax avoidance schemes revealed in the papers that may cause the most concern outside the elites that use them. From ways to avoid paying VAT on superyachts and private planes, to brain-achingly complex structures designed to help multinational companies – they are all in the files.

In 2012, the then chancellor George Osborne described some aggressive schemes as 'morally repugnant'. The then prime minister David Cameron said they were 'not fair and not right'.

More recently, the iniquities of tax havens were an issue that united the US president, Donald Trump, and Bernie Sanders, who ran Hillary Clinton close for the Democratic presidential nomination last year.

Sanders struck a chord when he said it was time for the largest corporations in the US to 'pay their fair share of taxes so that our country has the revenue we need to rebuild America'. Trump appeared to agree. He said he wanted to bring back 'trillions of dollars from American businesses that is now parked overseas'.

Awkwardly for him, though, some of his own lieutenants and donors seem to be among those with money in offshore schemes. And the Paradise Papers show corporate America is in no hurry to bring its money back onshore. The opposite seems to be the case.

In the UK, the Conservative election manifesto boasted of 'vigorous action against tax avoidance and evasion'. It has not happened yet.

Labour has demanded a public inquiry into the questions raised about offshore tax regimes. On Wednesday, the party's leader, Jeremy Corbyn, goaded Theresa May, saying: 'When it comes to paying taxes, does the prime minister think it is acceptable that there is one rule for the super-rich and another for the rest of us?'

Thanks to the Paradise Papers leak, the world will get a chance to scrutinise and pass judgment on the tapestry of schemes and networks politicians say they find so unpalatable – and many ordinary people find offensive and unfair.

6 NOVEMBER

My travels in white America – a land of anxiety, division and pockets of pain

GARY YOUNGE

Jeff Baxter's enduring memory, from childhood, is the glow. Coming down over the hill overlooking the coke plant in Johnstown, Pennsylvania, the molten iron would make itself known – both as a vision and an aspiration. 'It's like the sun landed there,' says Baxter, a burly, bearded retiree, who achieved his boyhood dream of becoming a steelworker.

Today, the plant, like the one Baxter worked in for 30 years, stands derelict – a shell that represents a hollowing out not just of the local economy but of culture and hope – as though someone extinguished Baxter's sun and left the place in darkness. Buildings in the centre of town that were once testament to the industrial wealth produced here stand abandoned. More than 40 per cent of the population now live below the poverty line; 9.1 per cent are unemployed.

Cambria County, where Johnstown sits, was once a swing county. Al Gore won it in 2000; George W Bush took it in 2004; it went to Barack Obama in 2008 and Mitt Romney in 2012 – each time by fairly narrow margins. Last year, Donald Trump won it in a landslide.

Baxter, who once backed Obama, voted for Trump, the first time he had ever voted Republican. 'I liked [Obama's] message of hope, but he didn't bring any jobs in ... Trump said he was going to make America great. And I figured: "That's what we need. We need somebody like that to change it."'

Over at the century-old Coney Island Lunch, this once-bustling institution famous for its chilli dogs and sundowners is virtually empty. 'A lot of people have left town,' explains Peggy, who has been serving at the diner for nine years. 'There are no jobs. If you're going to have a life or a steady income, you know, you need to get out of here, because there's nothing here. I expect a lot of towns go this way. You know, when the steel mills died and the coal died. It's sad, it's very sad.'

Across from the counter, Ted sits in a T-shirt emblazoned with a Native American in full headdress. He thinks white America is getting a rough deal and will soon be extinct. 'There's not many white Americans left. They're a dying breed. It's going to be yellow-white Americans, African-American white Americans, you know what I'm saying? The cultures are coming together,' he says, with more than a hint of melancholy. 'Blending and blending, and pretty soon we'll just be one colour.'

Ted also voted for Trump. 'I liked him on TV. I voted for him, all right, but it was because he was supposedly going to make America great, and what's he done so far? He hasn't done anything.'

Two days after I spoke to Ted and Peggy, Coney Island Lunch closed down.

In the 12 years I reported from the US I saw no end of white journalists opine on black America. This summer, I took a trip through white America, driving from Maine (the whitest state) to Mississippi (the blackest), to flip the script. Talking only to white people, I attended a white supremacist conference, accompanied an emergency health worker who sought to revive people who had overdosed, and went to a comedy club in the French Quarter of New Orleans to see the 'Liberal Redneck' perform. I was told the Ku Klux Klan were liberals (they weren't), that Confederate general Robert E Lee didn't own slaves (he did) and that I could not be British because I'm black (I am).

It was a few weeks before the disturbances in Charlottesville, when a mob of white supremacists, including neo-Nazis and Klansmen, converged on a college town in Virginia, terrorising protesters and leaving one dead and many injured. Just seven months after the US had bid farewell to its first black president, his successor said there were 'some very fine people' marching with the neo-Nazis who chanted: 'Jews will not replace us.' A poll shortly afterwards showed that almost half of white Americans thought they were 'under attack' and one in three thought the country needs to do more to preserve its white European heritage.

Any reckoning with how the US got to this point, politically, demands some interrogation of how white America got to this place economically and culturally; that takes into account both their relative privilege and their huge pockets of pain.

White Americans make up a majority of the country. Compared with other races, they may enjoy an immense concentration of wealth and power. But these privileges are nonetheless underpinned by considerable anxiety. Their health is failing (white people's life expectancy has stalled or dipped in recent years), their wages are stagnating (adjusting for inflation, they are just 10 per cent higher now than they were 44 years ago) and class fluidity is drying up (the prospect of poor white Americans breaking through class barriers is worse now than it has been for a long time). Out-traded by China (in 2016 the trade deficit with the country was $347 billion); soon to be outnumbered at home (within a generation white people will be a minority); and outmanoeuvred on the battlefields of the Arab world and beyond (neither of the wars launched in response to 9/11 have ended in victory), these vulnerabilities are felt at home and abroad. Meanwhile, Black Lives Matter protesters are in the streets over police brutality, football players are taking a knee, and the movement to bring legal status to large numbers of undocumented people grows. White Americans feel more pessimistic about their future than any other group. Almost two-thirds of white working-class people think the country has changed for the worse since the 1950s.

I covered the last presidential election from Muncie, Indiana, once seen as the archetypal US town thanks to the Middletown project, a sociological study first published in the 1920s. Many of the white working-class areas on the south side of Muncie were similar to Johnstown. The head of Middletown Studies at the city's Ball State University, James Connolly, told me this was the area he had found most difficult when it came to finding contacts. Whereas African Americans in the north-east of the city had strong churches and campaigning organisations, he explained, the poorer white areas had few champions.

'Nobody speaks up for the poor,' said Jamie Walsh, a white working-class woman who grew up in Muncie, explaining Trump's appeal to those she grew up with on Muncie's Southside. 'There is systemic racism, but black people have advocates. Poor white people don't. They're afraid. They're afraid that they're stupid. They don't feel racist, they don't feel sexist, they don't want to offend people or say the wrong thing. But white privilege is like a blessing and a curse if you're poor. The whole idea pisses poor white people off because they've never experienced it on a level that they understand.

'You hear privilege, and you think "money and opportunity", and they don't have it. I understand how it works but I don't think most people do. So when Trump says stuff, they can understand what he's saying and he speaks to them in a way other people don't. And then you've got people calling them stupid and deplorable. Well, how long do you think you can call people stupid and deplorable before they get mad?'

Increasingly, for many white Americans, their racial privilege resides not in positive benefits of work and security but in the sole fact that it could be worse – they could be black or Latino. In other words, their whiteness is all they have left. In few areas is this clearer than the opioid epidemic, which is disproportionately affecting white America. Wander down Oxford Street, home to one of the main shelters in Portland, Maine, and you can see people, distraught, disoriented and desperate, openly struggling with their addiction long into the night.

'In the past, we might go months and not have an overdose call,' said paramedic Andrea Calvo, as we drove around Portland. 'And we had a day, not too long ago, when I think we did 14 overdoses ... the majority of people, certainly in this area in this state, probably in the country, are somehow affected by addiction issues.' A member of her family struggles with addiction. She constantly worried that one day she would be called to assist her.

Thanks to contamination through needle sharing, the opioid epidemic is also turning into an HIV crisis, which is particularly acute in rural white areas. Of the most vulnerable 5 per cent of counties at risk of an HIV outbreak, almost all voted for Trump.

In late October, Trump called it a 'public health emergency', while offering little in the way of new funding. When your privilege amounts to this amount of pain, no wonder you can't see it. But just because you can't see it, it doesn't mean it's not there.

If there's one thing that 200 years of slavery and 100 years of segregation did for African Americans, it was to temper their investment in the myth that the US is a meritocracy. The notion that if you worked hard and kept your nose clean, you would get on was always stymied by the grim realities of racial barriers. 'America was never America to me,' wrote the Harlem renaissance poet Langston Hughes in 1935's 'Let America Be America Again'. 'There's never been equality for me / Nor freedom in this "homeland of the free".'

But, for many white Americans, the expectation that each year would be better than the next and each generation healthier and wealthier provided the core for optimism. However, with those assumptions being eroded, the mood is now more reminiscent of a post-colonial country. People are looking back for a sense of hope. Ask Trump voters when they would like to go back to if they wanted to make America great again and they will give you a date. Jeff Baxter wants to go back to the glow of the 1960s, Ted to the 1980s, others to the 1950s and beyond.

There are, of course, many white Americans looking forward, fighting for their place in a more equal and just, multiracial future. Heather Heyer, a 32-year-old paralegal, was killed while protesting against the neo-Nazi march in Charlottesville when a car, allegedly driven by a neo-Nazi sympathiser, ploughed into the crowd. 'She wanted equality,' her father, Mark Heyer, said. 'And in this issue of the day of her passing, she wanted to put down hate.'

Her mother, Susan Bro, refused to take the president's condolence call. 'I've heard it said that the murder of my daughter was part of making America great,' Bro added. 'The blood on the streets ... is that what made America great? Attacking innocent people with a vehicle ... is that what made America great?'

When American Renaissance, a white supremacist group straining to put a veneer of intellectualism and respectability on its bigotry, came to Montgomery Bell state park near Nashville in the summer, they were met by a crowd of mostly white protesters, chanting: 'No Klan, no hate, no racists in our state.'

One told me that Trump's election had shaken some white people out of their complacency. 'We were asleep at the wheel,' she said. 'We can no longer find comfort in silence. We have to dig up all the courage we have, to take a stand for what's morally right.' On the journey back to Nashville I stopped at a second-hand shop on the roadside, selling Confederate paraphernalia, owned by Nikki who had a complicated relationship to the stars and bars. 'I'm a proud southerner,' she said. 'But you and I both know the [American] civil war's basically about slavery,' she told me. 'Thank God we lost, thank God ... but it doesn't mean that we still don't wanna honour our dead.'

Trump did not create this anxiety or this division. References to the civil war and the Klan illustrate for just how long white America has been riven by its sense of moral purpose and material privilege. What is new is that Trump has emboldened the bigots and channelled their thinking in a fashion not seen in modern times. A president who draws a moral equivalent between neo-Nazis and anti-fascist protesters, who baits black athletes and black journalists, brands Mexicans rapists and Muslims terrorists.

One of those to whom he has given confidence is Richard Spencer, the intellectually unimpressive, historically illiterate huckster who rallied the far right in Charlottesville. Spencer, who wants to create an 'ethno-state' for white people, claims to have coined the term 'alt-right' – a sanitised word for the extreme right. In July last year, Trump's former chief strategist, Steve Bannon, boasted that his website Breitbart News was a 'platform for the alt-right'.

When I encountered Spencer at Montgomery Bell park, he emerged carrying a glass of what smelled like bourbon, and an entourage of adoring bigots soon surrounded me in the car park. More odious troll than eloquent polemicist, he claimed, among other things, that Africans had benefited from white supremacy and that, despite having been banned from 26 European countries, Europe would always be more his home than mine. 'If Africans had never existed, world history would be almost exactly the same as it is today,' he claimed. 'Because we are the genius that drives it.' Like a vulture preying on the anxiety, and with few alternatives on offer – as much as people cited Trump as the problem, few offered Democrats as the solution – he felt confident.

'People are now aware of the term "alt-right" ... I don't think Trump shares the ideal of the ethno-state ... But he wouldn't have run the campaign that he ran if he didn't feel some sense of loss, that America has lost something,' he said.

He felt he was gaining influence. This was one of the few accurate things he actually said. And by far the most chilling.

18 November

Life in the shadow of Grenfell: the tower next door

SIMON HATTENSTONE

Joe Walsh looks out the window of his flat on the 14th floor of Whitstable House in west London. The skyline is magnificent. On a clear day, you can see many of the capital's landmarks, the view stretching from the giant wheel of the London Eye to the arch of Wembley Stadium. But overshadowing everything, a few hundred metres away, is the blackened shell of Grenfell Tower.

Our first meeting comes six weeks after the fire that killed 71 people in the early hours of 14 June. The crowds of reporters and TV crews are long gone, and this unassuming corner of the city feels quiet and ghostly. Everywhere you look there are tributes: messages of love, teddy bears, candles, hand-drawn hearts, roses that have rusted and died.

Walsh, 58, is a small, tough man. From his Dr Martens to his shaved head, he looks like someone not to be messed with. He says as much himself. But Joe the scrapper is only part of the story; Walsh is better known locally for helping people out. It was he who opened the Maxilla at 2am when Grenfell was on fire, to provide a haven for those who had escaped and for neighbours who wanted comfort. 'We did teas and coffees for 26 hours, right through until the next day,' he says. 'From then on, we did 18 hours a day, because we became a donation centre.'

The victims of the fire were part of a close community composed of two neighbouring council estates. Whitstable House, where Walsh lives, forms part of the Silchester Estate; Grenfell stands on the Lancaster West Estate. Today, an aerial photograph would show you the wreckage of Grenfell Tower surrounded by the four smaller towers of Silchester. 'I knew quite a few families in there – some who got out, some who didn't,' Walsh says. 'I would meet one fella, Steven, with his dogs. He had three Staffies, and I had to keep my dog away from his. His daughter escaped, but he wouldn't leave his dogs.'

Walsh's wife, Siobhan, left London soon after the fire: 'She went to Ireland for a few weeks to get away. She got a bit emotional. Strained.' Walsh insists he's coping. 'I'm all right. It's part of life. You have to go on.' But he doesn't look all right; he looks broken.

Soon after the fire, a narrative emerged: that this was a deeply polarised part of London where the very wealthy and the very poor lived side by side but never met. It is true that this area, the Royal Borough of Kensington and Chelsea, houses some of London's richest people: walk a couple of hundred yards and you will find yourself on streets where modest-sized houses cost £3–4 million. Go a little farther and you reach the celebrities' even pricier homes.

But what residents of these two estates have found harder to accept is the way their lives have been depicted: as bleak, impoverished, dangerously overcrowded. Some suspect that Grenfell was deliberately portrayed this way, to create a sense that residents had made their own environment unsafe. After the fire, the government announced there would be a one-year amnesty for undocumented migrants who had been living in Grenfell; so far, there have been no reports of any. The media portrait of council residents as chaotic, and Grenfell as a kind of favela, created considerable ill feeling. 'There are teachers, bus drivers, nurses and social workers in this block,' Walsh says of his own tower. 'The way it was put – that it was subsidised housing, mainly unemployed – was just a way of putting us all down. It ain't that sort of area.'

The remains of Grenfell are expected to be razed to the ground by the end of 2018 – but Walsh worries that Whitstable, a 20-storey tower of 80 mainly council-owned flats, may also be torn down in the near future. Two years ago, its residents were told by the council that their estate was going to be regenerated. About time, they thought: their homes were overdue a lick of paint; the lifts were unreliable; the drainage wasn't what it should be. But Walsh was shocked when he discovered what regeneration might really mean. The council presented residents with a range of options: do nothing; modernise the existing buildings; partial redevelopment; or knock down the whole estate and start again. 'They made it clear which one they preferred,' he says. 'The knockdown was the only one they talked about.'

Walsh was informed that, if the 'complete' regeneration plan went ahead, the council would impose a compulsory purchase order on his flat, for £475,000. It appeared a generous offer – 10 per cent above market value – but then he was given another figure: 'They said if I wanted the same-sized flat on the new property, it's going to cost me £800,000. Where am I going to find another £325,000? It's social cleansing.'

Musician Peaky Saku briefly became a public figure in the aftermath of the fire. In a series of memorable television interviews, he was one of the first locals to suggest that Grenfell's new cladding – added to the tower in 2016 – had been done on the cheap and largely for cosmetic reasons. 'There needs to be more care for human life rather than money,' he told reporters.

His encounter with fame has left him feeling raw. Saku always wanted to be recognised for his music, but now he's not sure he wants to be recognised for anything. After his interviews went viral, people discovered he'd been to private school (something he had never made a secret of) and the online response was vitriolic. On Twitter, there were suggestions he was an impostor, or a government stooge. 'They said I was some sort of devil worshipper,' a still bewildered Saku says.

If there is one person on the estate who exemplifies the complexity of social identity in 21st-century London, it is this 23-year-old. A working-class man who talks the language of the streets, at the age of 13 Saku took up an academic bursary to Charterhouse school, where boarding fees are £36,774 a year.

Today, he has asked if we can meet on the Whitstable House landing where he shot the video for his Grenfell tribute song, 'I Don't Wanna Go Back'; his mother is at home and her nerves have been too affected by the fire for us to talk there.

Saku has spent many long hours on this landing with friends, smoking and shooting the breeze. 'They make out we're all bums and criminals, just smoking weed and plotting crime. That's not true. Sure, we'd stand there busting jokes, but if someone walks down with shopping, we'll open doors for them. Before all of this madness, I would say Whitstable was definitely a good place to live.'

Since the fire, however, his feelings have changed. 'Even my mum doesn't feel secure now, living this high.' He asks me to try opening the fire door to the landing: 'See how hard it is? You've got these because people used to slam the old doors. Now they're too heavy. My mum can't open them.'

Saku tells me the Grenfell fire is not the first tragedy to have struck here. On 31 May 2008, 10-year-old Christian Castano was waving to friends on the ground while leaning against his kitchen window in this tower. Residents had previously complained to the council that the windows were dangerous because they opened at the bottom and locks were faulty. Christian fell 18 floors to his death. Five days later, the *London Evening Standard* reported: 'Residents claim the council had failed to repair the window, which should only have opened a few inches, despite requests.' The inquest later reached a verdict of accidental death, the coroner concluding that a restrictor was in place and nobody was to blame.

We are talking in September, nearly three months after the fire, and Saku says life has yet to return to normal. After he appeared on television, locals would stop him in the street. He found it difficult: they seemed to be looking for guidance, but he wasn't coping himself. Did he know anybody who died in the fire? 'There was one older lady who used to look after me. She gave me a card when I was about five, and I've still got it. I didn't take the chance to reconnect with her. You think, there'll be another day; I've got more important things to do. And then something mad happens and it's like, "Oh, that's that."'

Nahid Ashby stops to say hello to a neighbour. Then another, and another. She apologises: 'It's only a tiny walk, but because we're a community, from here to there, I might say hello to five or six people.'

When we finally reach the estate's communal garden, Ashby, who is chair of the residents' association, exhales extravagantly and smiles. 'Ah, my beautiful trees. It's like an oasis of calm. The air changes, the smell changes – everything. And, if you're lucky, you hear the birds.'

Walking from tree to tree, cupping a hand to her ear, she gives me a potted history of the area. 'Charles Dickens wrote about it. When they dug up the ground to get clay to make bricks, it was full of pig waste and human waste and rainwater. People lived here in hovels, and the authorities only did anything about it when cholera broke out.'

The Silchester Estate was built in the late 1960s in Notting Dale, an area renowned for its piggeries in the 19th century, its slums in the 1930s and its race riots in the 1950s. The estate's four towers were part of a utopian vision, creating new communities in the sky, surrounded by open land. Ashby is more proud of the open land than anything else: while the nearby Westway is clogged with traffic pumping out pollution, this garden, which is open to the general public, allows the area to breathe.

'People used to be scared of coming down to Latimer Road station, because they thought there was antisocial behaviour. But then the culture changed: everybody was happier. Some of them don't even know it's because of the trees that they are having a better time.' We stand underneath her favourite tree, a willow. 'You don't get this diversity anywhere else in this area. I've counted 38 different trees in this garden.'

Since Grenfell, does she think there has been much support from the council? 'No. We have been pretty much ignored. We are less than 200 metres away, and we all saw the fire. We heard it, we felt it, we smelled it. Everybody has been affected.'

Ashby lives in one of the other towers on the Silchester Estate. Her living room window is huge, and the burnt-out tower looms large, like a giant flatscreen television that shows only one channel. She says she is trying to learn how to look beyond Grenfell. 'It's a survival instinct, because if I keep looking at it, I keep remembering – and it makes me want to cry.'

As well as the estate's communal garden, Whitstable House has an allotment carefully nurtured by Rama, a retired carpenter from Germany. Actually, he says, 'allotment' is too grand: 'It's just a tiny, tiny space. But we've got a raised bed for vegetables, and the potatoes taste good.'

Rama, who moved in 20 years ago and looks part-wizard, part-veteran rocker, is digging them up as we speak, but he won't be eating any of this season's crop. 'There was black ash and burnt plastic all over the place. I've got bin bags full of them,' he says. 'We had the windows closed in the house for three weeks –

my missus was totally freaked – and we still have a blind over the kitchen window, so we don't have to look at Grenfell.'

Rama was asleep when the fire started. 'I was woken by my neighbour, who is a Muslim and was breaking her fast. It was just before 2am. I still don't want to know what I saw that night.'

He says it's extraordinary how everyone got together to help – and how invisible the authorities were, both on the night and afterwards. 'There was nobody from the council. But the Maxilla opened and people came from all over. My daughter was sorting through baby stuff for three days.'

Rama shows me around Whitstable, pointing out its faults. 'There is no sprinkler system. The doors are a fire risk because of their PVC frame. There are open-ended pipes and they run upwards, meaning the water will only run away to a certain point. This tower was built to a decent standard, but they've let it go.'

Does that mean he supports the plan to demolish the tower to make way for new, fit-for-purpose homes? Rama looks amazed: 'No, of course not.' The tower's problems are not cosmetic, he says, but they are easy enough to fix. 'This place has been run down on purpose. They use the complaints to say, "People don't want to live here, we have to regenerate." Then what we get is expensive housing. We've seen it all over London.'

As far as Rama is aware, there has been no health and safety inspection or fire drill since the Grenfell fire. But Whitstable is basically safe, he says – unlike Grenfell: 'When you put gas pipes through the staircase in a tower block, as they did there ...' He is so upset, he can't complete the sentence. 'You should be shot for that,' he says eventually.

You're getting worked up, I say. 'I can't help it,' he replies. 'I'm so angry about this whole thing.'

After the fire, it was reported that Kensington and Chelsea had reserves of £274 million, making it one of the richest councils in the country. It was also revealed that the fire-resistant zinc cladding approved by Grenfell residents had been replaced in the refurbishment contract with combustible aluminium panels, to save £293,368 on the tower's £10 million regeneration bill.

Rama looks up at the charred remains of Grenfell from his vegetable patch, and says he hopes it doesn't get knocked down. 'I would put a big flame on top of that building, so everybody can see it for miles. It can stand as a great monument to incompetence and greed: a symbol of shame.'

It is November, and Grenfell Tower is being covered in a white protective wrap – a long, laborious process. Outside Whitstable House, the veg patch has gone to seed, and Rama will have to wait until next year for a new crop. Nahid Ashby is spending her time in meetings, fighting for the estate's residents. They have just been told that the front door to every flat will be replaced or upgraded after an investigation by LBC radio confirmed they were flammable. The Kensington and Chelsea Tenant Management Organisation has just sent out letters admitting that 'further works are required to fit upgraded fire-rated features'.

I pop into the Maxilla to say goodbye to the Walsh family. I ask Walsh how he is feeling. 'Emotional and drained,' he says. 'Utterly drained.'

It is already getting dark on this cold, crisp November afternoon. As I leave, I look back at Whitstable House. The tower, illuminated by a glorious sunset, looks magnificent.

'The people are free': Zimbabweans react to the fall of Robert Mugabe

JASON BURKE

The news came at 5.30pm, as Zimbabwe's MPs and senators debated a motion to impeach their president in the conference hall of a five-star hotel in Harare.

Helton Bonongwe, the minister for parliamentary affairs, approached the stage holding a sheet of paper in his hand. There was a moment of silence, and then the hall erupted. After 37 years in power, Robert Mugabe had resigned.

The cheers spread in concentric waves, through the 400 MPs and senators, out into the Rainbow Towers hotel's reception and bars, through the drivers waiting in the MPs' luxury SUVs, and on to the streets of Harare, where people sang and whistled and danced in a massive shout of relief and joy.

Some shouted political slogans, calling for the appointment of Emmerson Mnangagwa, the vice-president whose sacking two weeks ago triggered the crisis that led to the end of Mugabe's rule. But most simply voiced their excitement and, above all, their hope.

'I never thought it would happen so soon,' said Nancy Thembi, a 21-year-old student on secondment to the hotel who danced as she heard the news. 'Everyone is calling it a new era. It is history in the making. The people are free.' Thembi, like so many in this youthful nation, had never known any other leader than Mugabe.

'Change is good,' said 25-year-old Phionah Kusere, a receptionist who conscientiously continued to check guests in despite the chaos around her because, she explained: 'I am a Zimbabwean so I work hard.'

In the halls of the Rainbow Towers – a kitsch hotel, casino and conference centre with marbled floors and a brass spiral staircase – opposition politicians embraced government loyalists who have long been bitter enemies.

'It is an example to the rest of Africa. To follow our route, of engagement, unity and the rule of law,' said David Chapfika, a veteran MP from the ruling Zanu-PF party.

Mike Carter, a senator from the Movement of Democratic Change (MDC), the brutally suppressed main opposition party, said the moment was 'wonderful'.

'This is what we have been struggling for for 25 years,' he said.

Much of the anger of the past week has been directed not at 93-year-old Mugabe, who maintains his reputation as a liberation hero across much of the continent as well as at home, but at his wife, Grace.

'He was my leader and will always be my leader. He was my father and my friend. But that woman was his problem,' said Matanga Takamurumbira, a 75-year-old veteran of the brutal bush wars of the 1960s and 1970s that won Zimbabwe its independence and ended rule by a white supremacist regime.

Soldiers, long feared and reviled, were surrounded by cheering crowds. A couple sat with their toddler on an armoured vehicle, posing for photographs.

'The joy I feel is for my son. This is a new sunrise in Zimbabwe. He has a new future,' said Avril Chimesa, 31.

White Zimbabweans joined the throngs too. 'Now we can move forward,' said Lloyd Herschel.

Trevor Ryamuzihwa, an IT consultant, had just bought a round of drinks at a central Harare bar. He was born in 1980, the year Mugabe took power. 'It is bittersweet. We still respect what he did. But he should have retired 15 years ago. It would be wrong to go after him, to prosecute or something. He's 93 years old. Let him rest.'

As for the first lady, Ryamuzihwa said: 'That's a different story. She should pay back the money. She should go to jail.'

The barman apologised to another client that the beer was not cold. The response was quick: 'Just give me the bottles. We have been drinking warm beer for 37 years. No one is going to sleep tonight.'

In Epworth, one of the poorest neighbourhoods of Harare, the news brought people out on to the streets for impromptu barbecues. Cheap Scuds beer fuelled the celebrations. Here there was less respect for the former president.

'We don't care what happens next,' said Blessing Nyathi, 37, whose husband, a veteran of the liberation war, died 10 years ago, leaving her six children to bring up on her own.

'Anything has got to be better than before. [Mugabe] gave us nothing but promises and words. The children were suffering. No one tended the grave of my husband. I get a worthless pension. We are hungry. They say respect him but I say curse him.'

Zimbabwe's economy is close to collapse. Its currency is worthless. Millions live in the deepest poverty. Its once-admired infrastructure lies largely in ruins. There are deep social and political divides.

For now, the ruling Zanu-PF remains in power and may even have been emboldened by the events of the last week. Mnangagwa, who may be sworn in as an interim president on Wednesday, was Mugabe's ruthless right-hand man. There are concerns that coming elections won't be held, or will be rigged.

But for the most part the crowds that thronged the streets of Harare, Bulawayo, Masvingo and elsewhere were not worrying about the future.

'He has gone and I am so happy. We have been waiting for this for 37 years. I feel a great excitement,' said Bacillia Makhaya, an MDC representative of Mashonaland Central, as she watched the scenes of jubilation with her friend, fellow MDC MP Josephine Chitembwe, 65. 'We know there are challenges ahead and difficulties to come. But now we will celebrate.'

27 NOVEMBER

Mark Foster: 'I tiptoed around in the shadows for so long, but now is the time to come out'

DONALD McRAE

Sunlight streams through the huge windows that make Mark Foster's front room such a light and airy space as he reaches the moment he has avoided for 30 years. It is a cold and beautiful morning in Hertfordshire and, from the converted barn where he lives, Foster can look down at the little river below where two swans lead their cygnets in a stately paddle.

The mood appears as serene in Foster's home but a deeper truth is about to surface. 'It's not like I've been pushed to come out,' the former world champion swimmer says as he prepares to tell the world he is gay. 'I've just swerved and swerved. Telling half-truths and not being my true self is only hurting me. I'm

47, a middle-aged man, and I'm no longer competing. And I'm not the first gay sportsman to come out. Gareth Thomas and Tom Daley led the way.'

I felt no real surprise when hearing that Foster wanted to talk publicly for the first time about his sexuality in this interview. Foster had not been tortured about being gay, or ashamed, and over the past 26 years he has lived with, and loved, two different men in long relationships. His family and friends are accepting and supportive.

Foster set eight world records as a freestyle and butterfly sprinter and won six world titles, 11 European championship gold medals, two Commonwealth golds and competed in five Olympic Games – even carrying the GB flag at the opening ceremony in Beijing in 2008. But he could not unlock a partially concealed secret about himself.

'I tiptoed around the issue for so long,' he says. 'I got really good at the dance of telling half-truths. I've supported the Terrence Higgins Trust, Stonewall, Ben Cohen's Stand Up to Bullying campaign. But I've always done it under the radar. At the Sochi Olympics [in 2014] I did a piece for *Huffington Post*. I was shocked by the treatment of gay people in Russia and needed to say something – without revealing anything about myself. So I half-said something. It's always been half-truths in public.'

Foster has done lots of television work, from *Strictly Come Dancing* to being a BBC pundit. Even during fevered gossip about a possible relationship with a fellow swimmer, the four-time Olympic medallist and BBC analyst Rebecca Adlington, during the 2016 Olympics, when she was filmed squeezing his leg under the table, an assumption that he might be gay did not seem to matter to anyone but Foster and those closest to him.

Yet it does matter, particularly in sport, where it can still feel terribly hard for people to come out. Foster is intelligent and articulate, a man who also works as a model and a motivational speaker, but he has struggled since the age of 17 to voice out loud the simple fact he is gay. The longer we talk, the clearer the reminder that being a gay sportsman still verges on the taboo.

When we turn to football, where the glass ceiling seems frosted and unbreakable to gay and bisexual men who play the game professionally while harbouring a secret, the importance of similar sportsmen talking openly is obvious. Foster, a Spurs supporter, understands why gay footballers might fear abuse from the terraces or uncertainty from teammates if they came out. Other stories need to be heard first.

'I was a bit nervous today,' Foster admits, 'but I kept busy. I was tidying the house for you [he laughs]. I was a little apprehensive but years ago I would have been fearful of how I would be judged. Maybe that's me being older and having a long time to get used to the idea. I went to the Attitude awards last month and gave Greg Louganis [the gay American diver and double Olympic champion] an award. I spent time with him and his partner and was backstage with Prince Harry and Kylie Minogue. I have a weird and wonderful life meeting all these people. They know about me – well, Prince Harry doesn't – and I felt such warmth and togetherness. I thought: "I've been tiptoeing in the shadows, but now's the time to come out." I wish I'd done it when I was 21 and met my first partner. But I wasn't ready. Sharing stuff was always the problem. I've got used to avoiding the truth and I never spent much time looking in the mirror. It's a fear of being vulnerable because if you open yourself up you could be hurt.

'But a lot happened over the last year. I had problems with my other half and we had a break from January to April for me to look at myself. Usually, I can't even read a book. I need to be busy. I don't like thinking. I'm a doer. Most athletes are doers. They don't use their minds anywhere near as much as their bodies. But I needed to look inside.

'I started seeing a therapist at the beginning of the year. It was really hard but I soon found I could tell him the truth because I didn't really know him. He also won't judge me and what I say stays with him. I then lost my dad in June. He knew I was gay but we never talked much. I kick myself because there were so many things I wanted to know because Mum and Dad split when I was 11. We had so many things we never shared. I now want to share my feelings.'

Foster had considered coming out publicly before – especially when the *News of the World* approached his first partner years ago, the *Daily Mail* alluded to his sexuality when he was on *Strictly* in 2008 and the *Sun* stalked Foster last December with creepy sensationalism. 'But I didn't want to be forced,' Foster says. 'There was that stuff about Becky [Adlington] but she knows I'm gay and knows my other half. We're good mates and when she doesn't want to answer anything on live television she'll squeeze my leg and I take over. But it became a huge story. I should have said: "Don't be daft. I'm gay."'

He can now talk about his private life on his own terms. 'When I was younger, I thought my feelings were just a phase. I had girlfriends. I never had a boyfriend. But I had sexual experiences with boys. At swimming competitions I would go with women to divert attention from the real me. It's not like I didn't enjoy the act – I just preferred boys. But I accepted I was gay when I fell in love with my first partner, Vincent.

'I was closest to my youngest sister and I told her. A year later I told Mum. She cried at first because her immediate reaction was thinking no grandkids and what had she done wrong? But after five minutes she showed unconditional love. She cuddled me and said: "I love you to bits."

'I wasn't like Gareth Thomas [the rugby player who came out as gay when married]. I was never in that dark place. I've lived an openly gay life to my friends and family. But I always hid it as a swimmer.'

Foster was also reluctant to come out while competing because of his focus on winning. But did all the shadowy half-truths have an impact on his swimming which, for all his success, was never capped by an Olympic medal? 'A mate of mine, who swam for Australia, said: "The reason you never won Olympic gold is that you were afraid of the spotlight. You never wanted to show the real you." I don't know if that's true but when you've spent your whole life shying away from scrutiny it must have some impact. I've lost races and broken world records by 100ths of seconds. I'm not saying I would've won the Olympics but, if I wasn't subconsciously processing all this stuff, I would have achieved more.'

In retirement, Foster says, 'there was a darker side', adding: 'I was worried about how coming out might affect my work. My swim schools cater for children and there's this insidious perception that gay equals paedophile/child molester. I never want to be perceived as being a threat to children.

'So I understand what's stopping gay footballers coming out. I've been to many football matches and seen that aggressive mob mentality. Because of dressing-room "banter" they don't want to show their real selves. Football is a weird testosterone-driven world and it's the last bastion. But if a gay footballer came out it would change so many attitudes.'

Outside the bubble of elite sport surely people are more tolerant? 'I play many charity and corporate golf days. I always get asked: "Are you married? How many kids?" They just presume because most people's perception of gay men is what they see on TV – camp chat-show hosts. They can't put me in that box. I'm conditioned not to share so I'll usually say: "I've got no kids but I've got a partner." If they ask, "What does she do?", I will either correct them or just say: "They're a civil servant" or "They're an antiques dealer". I'm very clever at dancing around stuff. But it's tiring and sometimes I have been honest and said: "No, I don't have kids. I'm gay." And a guy will surprise me and say: "Oh, but you could adopt kids." That's refreshing.'

I am pretty sure that reaction to Foster coming out publicly will be just as refreshing. 'I hope so. As you can tell from my bad moustache, it's Movember. I'll be clean-shaven in December but it's important to think about mental health and remember that the biggest killer of young men is suicide. I'd like to say to them it's important not to live your life in fear. I'm not scared of many things but, until now, I feared looking inside at the real me. None of us like being vulnerable but sharing with other people has helped me come out and say: "This is the real me."'

We talk for another half-hour, mostly about football, and Foster shows me jokey clips of Arsenal and Spurs. His sexuality is forgotten and it is only when he walks down to the water for a photo session that I remember his tiptoeing through the shadows is no longer needed. As I drive away he waves cheerfully. Mark Foster, a former world champion who just happens to be a gay man, looks happy and free in the winter sunshine.

28 November

'I can't eat or sleep': the woman threatened with deportation after 50 years in Britain

AMELIA GENTLEMAN

Paulette Wilson had been in Britain for 50 years when she received a letter informing her that she was an illegal immigrant and was going to be removed and sent back to Jamaica, the country she left when she was 10 and has never visited since.

Last month, she spent a week at Yarl's Wood detention centre before being sent to the immigration removal centre at Heathrow, where detainees are taken just before they are flown out of the country. It was only a last-minute intervention from her MP and a local charity that prevented a forced removal. She has since been allowed to return home, but will have to report again to the Home Office in early December and is still worried about the possibility of renewed attempts to remove her.

The experience of being detained and threatened with deportation to a country she has no links with has been profoundly upsetting for Paulette, a grandmother and former cook, who has paid national insurance contributions for 34 years and can prove a long history of working and paying taxes in this country.

Paulette, 61, arrived in the UK in 1968, went to primary and secondary school in Britain, raised her daughter, Natalie, here and has helped to bring up her granddaughter. For a while, she worked in the House of Commons restaurant overlooking the Thames, serving meals to MPs and parliamentary security staff.

More recently, she has volunteered at her local church, making weekly meals for homeless people.

She has been left furious and distraught by this sudden Home Office decision to categorise her as an illegal immigrant. The week of detention in Yarl's Wood was the worst experience of her life.

'I felt like I didn't exist. I wondered what was going to happen to me. All I did was cry, thinking of my daughter and granddaughter; thinking that I wasn't going to see them again,' she says while sitting in Natalie's flat in Wolverhampton. She was taken from the Home Office reporting centre in Solihull, Birmingham, in a secure van and told she was going to be sent out of the country. 'I couldn't eat or sleep; still now I can't eat and sleep properly.'

When staff told her after she had spent a week in Yarl's Wood that they were going to take her to the removal centre, she was allowed to call Natalie; she screamed in terror down the phone. 'I was panicking because that evening they took away a lady. I watched her crying and being taken away. It was very scary,' she says.

Paulette's solicitor, Jim Wilson, is working to persuade Home Office staff that Paulette has a legal right to stay in the UK because she moved here before the 1973 Immigration Act gave people who had already settled in Britain indefinite leave to remain. Although the decision to detain and remove her is extremely unusual, there is evidence that a large number of people who came legally to the UK in the 1960s have found themselves wrongly caught up in the 'hostile environment' Theresa May said she wanted to create for illegal immigrants in 2012.

Migrant rights charities around the country are increasingly coming across people who have been living here for 50 or more years – often people from the Commonwealth – who came to the UK when there was no need to apply formally for leave to remain. They have only recently encountered problems because they have no documents to prove their right to be here. (Newer arrivals, who came after immigration laws became tougher and less welcoming, are less likely to find themselves in Paulette's situation.)

In a separate case earlier this month, an urgent appeal was made to trace former pupils of a school in Maidenhead, to see if they could help save a homeless woman who also faces deportation. Eleanor Rogers, 71, arrived in Britain from Sierra Leone in 1966 and has lived and worked here since. She has lost her documentation and she, too, faces removal back to a country she hasn't lived in for 51 years unless she can find people who can help prove she has been here for five decades. In a report, 'Chasing Status: If Not British, Then What Am I?', immigration advisers warn of a 'virtually invisible and rarely acknowledged group who can't easily prove their legal status', who are surprised to find their right to live in the country where they have lived all their adult life being challenged.

When she was 10, Paulette's mother put her on a plane to the UK, to live with her grandfather, a factory worker, and her grandmother, a care worker. Her mother, who she never saw again, sent her here for a better life and, on the whole, Paulette has been happy here. She never travelled back to Jamaica and never applied for a passport. She never gave a thought to her immigration status.

In 2015, she was shocked to receive a letter informing her she was an illegal immigrant and that she had six months to leave the country. For a few days, she told no one. 'I was panicking. I was too scared to tell my daughter,' she says.

Her housing benefit and sickness benefits were stopped immediately, leaving her homeless. For two years, Natalie has been supporting her financially and a friend has let her stay in his flat. She was told to report monthly to the Home Office.

Natalie and her case worker, Daniel Ashwell, at the Refugee and Migrant Centre in Wolverhampton have gathered documents proving that she has been in the country for 50 years. Paulette's grandparents struggled to look after her for a while when she was in her teens and they sent her to a children's home. The family now has letters from Shropshire council, acknowledging that she was there in the 1970s. Her case worker believes there has been some bureaucratic confusion on the part of the Home Office, and a lack of understanding among junior staff about the law making it clear that Paulette has the right to remain.

'They have deprived her of everything,' Natalie says, detailing how her mother has been near destitution for the past two years. 'I am surprised we didn't lose her from the stress. She is normally so bubbly and sociable. Since she came out of Yarl's Wood she has withdrawn.' A few times in the last month, Paulette, who lives nearby, has come to her flat in the middle of the night, waking her to tell her she is scared that Home Office workers are going to come to take her away. She can't sleep until she gets into Natalie's bed. 'I feel very angry. They have put me through the worst heart-ache anyone could go through,' she says. Paulette's MP, Labour's Emma Reynolds, says: 'It is really shocking that the Home Office is detaining a woman in her 60s who has been here for 50 years. It seems to me that Paulette Wilson was detained wrongly and I am seeking clarification from the Home Office. My understanding is that she is here legally.'

Paulette is despairing at the pressure she is under to prove that she is British. The application to process leave to remain documents costs more than £240, money she does not have. Legal aid is no longer available for cases such as hers. She is terrified that she could be separated from her family. 'I don't know anyone in Jamaica. I had no passport so I couldn't go,' she says. Paulette does not like to be asked if she feels British. 'I don't feel British. I am British. I've been raised here, all I know is Britain. What the hell can I call myself except British? I'm still angry that I have to prove it. I feel angry that I have to go through this.'

Winter

Hillary Clinton meets Mary Beard: 'I would love to have told Trump: "Back off, you creep"'

DECCA AITKENHEAD

Hillary Clinton is sequestered in a hotel room, giving a big television interview, when Mary Beard arrives at Claridge's. While she waits outside on the sofa, though, it quickly becomes clear that the star of this conversation is the classicist. One by one, members of Clinton's staff approach in reverent tones to declare her their heroine. Even a passing cameraman stops to pay court and say: 'I love you!' Does this happen to Beard all the time? 'Yes,' she laughs, 'funnily enough, it does.'

Her latest book, *Women & Power: A Manifesto*, brings an illuminating historical perspective to the contemporary abuse of powerful women. Clinton is in London to talk about *What Happened*, her rivetingly candid if shellshocked account of her defeat to Donald Trump in last year's US presidential election. As soon as she appears, it becomes very hard to believe she lost because voters found her cold. She greets Beard with a whoop of delight, exclaims, 'This is fun!', does a very, very funny impersonation of Trump's voice and, over the course of an hour, laughs a lot.

The pair met briefly four years ago when both received honorary degrees at the University of St Andrews in Scotland. Beard had been advocating a more combative strategy towards trolls than Michelle Obama's famous injunction to 'go high ... when they go low'. The latter having failed to work for Clinton, she and Beard fall at once to discussing how women in public life can deal with misogyny ...

Mary Beard What I remember us talking about when we met was the sense that it was extremely important to say: 'Hang on a minute, mate, you are not right.' Or: 'Please take this tweet down.'

Hillary Clinton Learning about the ongoing grief you took over standing up for women's rights and accurate history was quite enlightening to me.

MB It's gone on, too, actually.

HC Well, as you rightly point out, it has only continued, and in some ways gotten worse. The ability of people in public life or in the media to say the most outrageous falsehoods and not be held accountable has really altered the balance in our public discourse, in a way that I think is endangering democracy.

MB To me, what's really interesting is that, although they look as if they're going for what we said, what they're really going for is the fact that we dared to say anything, almost. It's not about having an argument about, say, migration. It's about telling you to shut up.

HC That's right. I know that very well, and so do you, and we have perhaps thicker skin than a lot of other people. But it is still distressing to be told, either explicitly or implicitly: 'Go away. You have nothing to say.'

MB The friendly advice when it happens to you is always: 'Don't pay attention. Don't give them the oxygen of publicity. Block them and just move on, dear.' And you think, sorry, that is what women have been told to do for centuries. If somebody accuses you of having a smelly vagina that stinks of cabbage, you're supposed to say: 'Just block him.' Actually, no. Somehow, even among the people who are trying to support you, it's basically saying: 'Shut up.'

HC It's interesting you say that, because, in my book, I try to talk about the dilemma that a woman faces between 'be calm and carry on' ...

MB You're quite good at that!

HC Yes, I've had a lot of practice. You know, when Trump was stalking me [in the 2016 televised presidential debates] and leering and, oh, just generally trying to dominate me on this little stage, my mind was like: OK, I practised being calm and composed, you know, because that's what a president should be. But, boy, would I love to turn around and say: 'Back off, you creep.' But I didn't, because I thought then his side will say: 'See, she can't take it. If she can't take Donald standing there like the alpha male that he is, then how's she going to stand up to Putin?' A ridiculous argument, but nevertheless one that might get traction. And, as you say, even your friends are like: 'Oh, come on, don't take the bait. Don't take the bait.'

MB Being an academic gives you a bit of freedom to play around with things, because in the end what people think about me doesn't matter all that much. But I remember when I first did telly, a clever, nasty but well-respected TV critic here said, basically: 'You look like the back end of a bus. How dare you come into our living room with those teeth? If you're going to inflict yourself on us, please will you smarten up.' After the first shock, I thought, look, sunshine, if you line up a load of women between 55 and 65, they'll mostly look like me. So, I wrote a piece pointing out that he was not abusing me only; he was abusing every woman who looked a bit like me.

HC I think you touched a chord when you said: 'OK, this is what a woman looks like.' When you run for office, however, what a president looks like is not any kind of woman. So therefore how you feel about this particular woman is influenced by how you feel about women in really powerful positions. It's that

THE BEDSIDE GUARDIAN 2018

tightrope, that balance that we keep trying to figure out how to strike.

MB When I looked back to the ancient world about this, Romans in particular were always saying that women, in some way, are fake. The problem about a woman is that she's always made up, she's never what she seems. Reading your book, what was so interesting was that women in public life – and I'm happily removed from that – you've got to look the part *and* you've got to be authentic. And that's impossible.

HC Well, that is the core dilemma. Like, today, I have makeup on. You don't. But that is just part of the uniform that one wears in public life and politics, at least in my experience.

MB If I started to wear makeup now, I would get so abused on Twitter. I'm actually as trapped as you are, Hillary! [Laughter.]

HC Men can get a haircut; it doesn't change their authenticity. They can grow a beard; they are still who they are. Whereas we are constantly held to that good old double standard, which is so complex and deep and charged with historical and mythological and cultural totems.

But I wanted to ask you about that memorable debate you had with Boris Johnson over Greece versus Rome. He is a reality TV kind of character from my observation, don't you think?

MB Yes!

HC And he knows it and he knows how to play it. It's very deliberate. The same with Trump. I mean, it's a persona that they have assumed, which really works for them, even the same kind of hair. The hair is part of the whole deal.

MB And it is so contrived, and it is contrived to look so spontaneous, it makes you sick.

HC It's interesting, because men's roles in public life are somewhat evolving. It used to be: you go for the sober character on the right or the left, who you think represents your views and whose platform you support. They could come in different sizes and shapes, but there was an assumption they were serious people, even if they had a good sense of humour, right?

Now, because of what I think is the pressure of performance, which is more important than substance by a long shot, it is the performance that matters most. We're going to see more of this type. And I think then it's particularly hard to pin down and make the argument about position and facts versus performance and rhetoric.

MB When I debated with Boris about Greece versus Rome, it was a fun charity gig, but it revealed precisely that. Boris is very funny. He can work an audience. I admire it. I knew the only way I was going to have a chance of winning was by being fantastically prepared.

HC That sounds very familiar. [Laughter.]

MB I sat and I looked at any video I could find of Boris. I noted the mistakes and I thought, he's so busy, he's going to use the same examples – and I know they're wrong. I must have put about a week of studying Boris videos and reading everything Boris had written wrongly about the ancient world. That is fine for a one-off gig, but you can't write a long-term debate like that.

HC Or a campaign, in my experience. That's right. So, I was made fun of for preparing and, at one point in one of the debates, Trump actually said: 'Oh, well, she's prepared.' I said: 'Yes, you know what else I prepared for? To be president.' Then he gets elected and he goes: 'It's so much harder than I thought.'

MB It's back to the old version that was prevalent at university when I was an undergraduate – you know, that it was the women who were in on the Saturday nights doing the work, and they were very diligent, but they didn't really have that ...

HC They didn't have the creative ...

MB The flair. So, they were awfully reliable – and by awfully reliable, you mean very boring. Whereas, somehow, what both Boris and Trump have done is they've branded themselves around gaffes, so that it no longer makes a difference. One extra gaffe doesn't matter, because that's the brand.

HC Women are going to have to learn how to pull off that trick. I think it's difficult, but it has to be possible, because there's no alternative.

MB It's relatively easy for me. It's great fun being an academic, because you have a certain licence to be a bit of a joker. But I couldn't do this style in any form of politics. What do you think Chelsea's going to do when she comes one day and says: 'I think I'm going to run for Congress'?

HC Well, it hasn't happened yet. But part of what I'm trying to do now is not let my loss discourage young women from taking public positions, even running for office themselves. So I'm supporting organisations that are out recruiting women, training women, helping women run. And part of the lessons are how you grow a thick skin without losing your sense of humour, without becoming too grim and too serious.

MB I think, when I was 25, nobody in the world knew who I was. But if I'd got the sort of tweets then that I get now ...

HC You would have been crushed. You would have gone to bed.

MB I would have gone to bed. I wouldn't have even gone out.

HC That's the problem, but you have set a good example of how you overcome it. I am really envious of the kind of freedom that you have. But you've taken that freedom and your expertise, and used it to enhance the public debate. Mary, what do you think the moment was when you won the debate with Johnson?

MB It was when I said: 'Boris has been claiming that Roman literature really wasn't worth reading. But a leading politician said of Book IV of Virgil's *Aeneid*, on the death of his lover Dido, that it was: "The best book of the best poem of the best poet." Who do you think that was?' And Boris had to say: 'I think that might have been me.' [Laughter.]

HC Preparation!
MB It paid off.

10 December

'Pretend your food is disgusting': a Christmas survival guide for vegans

ROMESH RANGANATHAN

Veganism is a point of contention all year round. So much so that many vegans cut themselves off from the rest of society, huddling together for warmth and smugness, and using online forums to vent their disgust at the morally corrupt dairy- and meat-eating savages who make up most of the populace. But at Christmas, vegans are forced temporarily to reintegrate into mainstream society, which can be incredibly stressful for both them and the omnivores who host them. Here, then, are some basic guidelines for a happy vegan Christmas.

Avoid invitations, if possible

This is always my first strategy. This might imply I'm suggesting you invite people to your house. I am not. It's much easier for the vegan to remain at home and do their own Christmas dinner. That way, you can enjoy your food without someone making some hilarious comment about your stuffed pepper. I realise this won't work for ever, however, in which case please see my subsequent tips.

Accept you will be asked a lot of questions

Veganism is an unusual thing. Regardless of how many celebrities take it up, or how large the Free From section gets at Tesco, the fact is, you have chosen an extreme standpoint. Morally superior, without doubt, but unusual nonetheless. For that reason, you'd do well just to accept that you're going to be asked questions such as, 'Why are you vegan? Don't you miss scotch eggs? What if you were on a desert island and you had to eat animals to survive? If we were meant to be vegan, why is bacon so delicious? Are all your pizzas shit?'

Many vegans will throw up their arms and complain about being asked the same questions over and over again, but that only reinforces the stereotype that we are sanctimonious twats. What's much more effective is to wait for the first question to arrive, then answer it in such painstaking and mind-numbing detail that nobody else will even want to talk to you, let alone ask inane questions.

Accept that you are a difficult guest

People don't want to invite you round, because having a vegan round is a pain in the arse. They have to check all the ingredients and find vegan alternatives to all the traditional Christmas desserts, and they're terrified of giving you something that ends up not being vegan.

One year, I went to Christmas drinks at the house of one of my wife's mates, who went to great trouble to point out the vegan snack selection to me. When I commented on how delicious the vegan sausage rolls were, the colour drained from her face as she explained she had actually been pointing to the hummus selection behind the pork sausage rolls. I then had to pretend I didn't feel sick and she had to pretend she cared.

For this reason, it is nice to be a bit considerate of the challenge you present. If you are invited to someone's house, offer to take vegan food with you, or offer suggestions of good vegan stuff they could serve. There are loads of accidentally vegan things that people don't even think of getting, such as Waitrose Christmas pudding or Oreos: it's in your interests to be forthcoming. Basically, don't be a prick about it. Alternatively, be a massive prick to ensure you don't get asked back.

Don't let anyone touch your food

In terms of quantity of food available, you are always at a disadvantage. There will be less food made for you, plus there's the fact that everybody can eat your food, but you can't eat everyone else's. That's why it is essential to make it clear what food is vegan, and therefore yours and off-limits to your moral inferiors. I will never forget being told how much trouble a friend's mother had gone to making me vegan gravy from scratch, before watching her dad slather it all over his turkey, leaving me with a choice of chicken gravy or dry nut roast.

Sometimes, though, you don't get to decide what's yours. One year, we were having Christmas dinner at my dad's pub, and my mum made me an incredible spread of Sri Lankan curries. My parents invited a Muslim family round, and Dad ordered a halal turkey to be roasted by the pub chef. The chef delivered the turkey, covered in foil, and my father made a big show of bringing it to the table and peeling back the silver wrapper. He revealed a turkey covered in more bacon than I had ever seen in my life. So my parents and brother ate a turkey for six, while I shared my Christmas food with the Khans.

Pretend your food is disgusting

I hate sharing. This is not a dilemma I have to face often, thanks to vegan food's terrible reputation. Unless, of course, you make the mistake of displaying New Vegan Enthusiasm (NVE). The error that many vegans make is forgetting that our food has novelty value. Non-vegans think our food is awful, but are fascinated by the prospect of something vegan being delicious. They want to disprove it. The NVE error occurs when a vegan is given food that they have not tried before and announce how delicious it is to the rest of the party. Every other person then asks to try it, thereby finishing all of it, before stating, 'It's quite bland and would be better if it had chicken on it.'

It's far better to eat your food silently, and declare it disgusting to anyone who looks in your direction. For good measure, maybe tell somebody how messed up the dairy industry is, to ruin his or her meal.

Avoid vegan cheese

Supermarkets and specialist suppliers will have you believe there are great substitutes for cheese. There are not. No vegan cheese tastes anything like decent cheese, and melting cheese might as well be alchemy as far as the vegan cheese industry is concerned. People will tell you different. In the past year, I've spent more than £1,000 to find a great vegan cheese. I even bought a vegan 'world cheeseboard' for Christmas: it was like an international tour of disappointment. There are nut cheeses that taste passable, and even some that taste very good. But the fact is they Do. Not. Taste. Like. Cheese.

Take your own dessert

There are many vegan dessert options, particularly at Christmas: there are vegan mince pies, Christmas puddings, ice-creams, cakes. Identify your favourite and take it to the party, even if the host says there is a dessert for you. Because if you believe them and turn up empty-handed, you'll watch people tucking into pavlovas and gateaux while you nurse a fruit salad. And not a good fruit salad, either: it'll be mainly diced apple.

Be prepared to discuss isinglass

Most people know Baileys isn't vegan, so, unless you have secured a bottle of vegan equivalent, which is rarer than a Trump-supporting member of Mensa, you will have to endure the sound of creamy slurps and declarations of how 'Christmas isn't Christmas without a Baileys'. What many people don't know, however, is that many other drinks, such as red wine and some beer, use isinglass in their production, which is made from the swim bladders of fish, so rendering them 'non-veegs'. It's a pretty simple explanation, but you will be expected to clarify this repeatedly before someone says something along the lines of, 'Next you'll be telling me that Quorn isn't vegan!' Which, of course, it isn't (it contains milk and egg products).

Be ready for some terrible jokes

You have to accept that someone will say something like, 'Are you having carrots with your carrots?' and everybody will fall about in hysterics. And you'll know you can't have the carrots because they have butter on.

Do not preach

If you've made the decision to become vegan, you're doing so because you feel morally compelled or you're a huge Beyoncé fan. Whatever your reasons, it is pretty good practice not to bang on about them at Christmas. Most people are generally aware of the arguments regarding veganism and vegetarianism, and many people continue to eat meat and dairy despite being conflicted about the morality of their choices. What these people don't need is a vegan in their ear, explaining how milk is made up of mainly pus and cruelty, and how, if you eat turkey, you deserve to have stuffing inserted into your anal cavity to gain some perspective. The truth is, people don't like being lectured at the best of times, and they certainly don't want to be told about the horrors of animal slaughter when they're still dealing with the aftermath of their behaviour at the office party.

And if you're hosting a vegan ...

It's hard having a vegan round for Christmas, and your efforts are thoroughly appreciated, but it's in both of your interests for your guest to have ample supplies. In all likelihood, they are going to be far better informed than you as to what sort of things you should provide, so feel free to ask what they'd like. They will probably be grateful. If not, at least you know you've tried and you can give them a jacket potato without feeling guilty.

And if you want to encourage a vegan to leave? Ask how they manage to get enough protein. They will never speak to you again.

12 December

What David Attenborough should have said at the end of *Blue Planet*

PATRICK BARKHAM

We find the sea a great source of solace and peace. The author Ronald Blythe has written of the sea's 'most wonderful monotony', which 'can drug the watcher into forgetting past, present and future'. Watching *Blue Planet II* has been almost as hypnotic, with its sublime rendering of our turquoise oceans, a watery world almost without humans.

This lulling effect is at odds with the message the programme conveyed with new urgency in its final episode: that our oceans, upon which we depend, are under threat like never before.

The BBC Natural History Unit, which makes these incomparable, world-leading works of art and science has come under increasing criticism for not telling the most urgent story of our times: humanity's destruction of our planet. *Blue Planet II* is a riposte. Coral bleaching or plastic pollution, say, was not bundled into one final episode but scattered throughout the series.

Its finale combined breathtaking footage of the most charismatic sea creatures with the most noble broadcaster deploying every fibre of his authority to hit us with overfishing, noise pollution, plastics and other toxins, ocean acidification and sea-level rise.

So as not to swamp us, Sir David Attenborough's message was that hope, action and individuals can make a difference. This stirring stuff will help us do the easy bits – switch to reusable water bottles and coffee cups, or paper straws – and nudge policymakers towards tougher rules, such as outlawing single-use plastic and creating marine nature reserves (the campaign to protect 30 per cent of the global ocean is admirably ambitious).

Blame the ocean, perhaps, but I was still soothed as much as stirred. Sir David is a saintly man who has done more to save our planet than any living person. But I hoped to be a little more jolted by *Blue Planet II*'s concluding piece to camera. We needed to hear the following: sustainable growth is a lie; we must renounce economic growth as a societal goal; we must consume much, much less.

I use coloured pencils to show which key I'm writing in – D minor, at the moment

PHILIP PULLMAN

I get to my desk (in a very small room at the top of the house) at about 10, and fiddle about with the height of the desk and the chair until I'm comfortable. I have a desk that I can raise or lower according to the state of my aching back. Sometimes I stand at it, and sometimes I have it high up to write at, and sometimes a bit lower to type.

The desk is covered by an ancient kilim, because it looks nice, but that's not a good surface to write on, so I have one of those green safety cutting mats to support the paper I use, which is A4 narrow lined, with two holes. I love the shape of the A paper sizes. It's the only one of Andrea Palladio's recommended architectural shapes (the ratios of room length to width, and so on) that contains an irrational number, in this case the ratio of one to the square root of two. Very handy for illustrating Pythagoras's famous theorem, in fact.

Nearby is a basket full of coloured pencils, including some of the best of all, the Berol Karisma range, now unfortunately discontinued. For each book I write, the paper is authorised for writing on by means of a coloured stripe along the top edge. I fan the sheets out and colour a stack at a time. The current book is a warm blend of Karisma Pumpkin Orange and Faber Castell Venetian Red. I sometimes think I should make it clear which key

I'm writing a particular passage in – D minor, at the moment – but that would be silly, unlike colouring the pages, which makes perfect sense.

In front of me there's a little aneroid barometer, a present from my son Tom, which also tells me the temperature and the humidity. Near that is a piece of equipment given to me by the scientists at the Rutherford Appleton Laboratory, which came out of an instrument that detects dark matter, or tries to. It's a cylinder of glass in a copper casing, about the size of a small snowball but much heavier. I use it as a paperweight for my current manuscript, so it can go on detecting dark matter, or Dust, when I'm not around. I also keep some binoculars handy so I can watch any interesting birds through the window. The village heron lumbers past occasionally, and right now there's a red kite circling over the church tower.

One handy piece of equipment, which I recommend to any writer of fiction, is a set of Myriorama cards. I consult them frequently. I think the idea comes from the early 19th century. There are 24 of them, each one showing a slice of a landscape, sometimes with figures, sometimes without. You can put any of them next to any other, and the pictures join up perfectly, so you can make a vast number of different scenes. 'When in doubt, have a man come through the door with a gun,' said Raymond Chandler. Or pick a Myriorama card, or several, and see what comes to mind.

The newest occupant of my desktop is a beautiful 15th-century bronze Buddha from Myanmar, which my wife gave me for my birthday. The eyes have the characteristic asymmetry described by William Empson in *The Face of the Buddha*, written 70 years ago but only recently published.

In two or three untidy piles an arm's length away are the books I'm most reliant on at the moment: books about Central Asia, principally, and maps. Maps! They cover the walls, they stand in ranks behind my laptop, they absorb my attention for hours. Kazakhstan and Uzbekistan and Tajikistan and Kyrgyzstan! Mountains and deserts and movable lakes! But also books of poetry: Rainer Maria Rilke, Wallace Stevens, Paul Valéry. And dictionaries, of course.

Coming a little closer to the centre of things is my stack of newly coloured paper, and my pen. I write in pen because it works. A fountain pen is no good for writing in the way I do, because I'd have to decide, each time I stopped, how long I was likely to stop for, in order to know whether or not to put the cap on. But I never know. So instead I use a ballpoint, a Montblanc to be precise, the most comfortably balanced pen I've ever found. I am available for sponsorship.

I see I haven't said anything yet about the central activity itself. Instead I've been taking up time talking about all the bits and pieces I have around me, and I haven't even mentioned the magnifying glass or the Post-it notes or the worry beads. Wasting time, perhaps. Fiddling about and getting nowhere. But what else did you think writers do all day? Write?

3 JANUARY

I don't like Brexit – I just don't see how it can be stopped

OWEN JONES

If only Brexit would go away. It sucks the political oxygen away from the issues we should all be discussing: such as low wages, insecure jobs and the housing crisis. It is a rallying cry

for a noxious alliance of anti-immigrant demagogues and regu-
lation-stripping free marketeers. The bigotry, xenophobia and
racism stirred up by the official leave campaigns injected an ugli-
ness into British politics which never dissipated, and left hate
crimes surging. And, frankly, Brexit is just mind-numbingly, painfully, excruciatingly dull. So yes, if there was a big red button to
make it all just go away, I'd enthusiastically push it.

Yes, as a socialist, I had profound reservations about the current
incarnation of the EU, and even considered the case for leave. I
dismissed the argument because of persuasive pleas from European leftists to stand together to reform and change the EU, and
because it was clear that a hellish anti-immigration crusade beck-
oned. And so, alongside the Another Europe Is Possible alliance, I
passionately campaigned against the Brexit juggernaut. Then the
vote happened, and we lost. There seemed to be two conclusions
that fateful night. One, challenge the bigotry, authoritarianism
and intolerance of the Tory Brexiters. And two, try to reconcile a
bad result with the country's future.

Which brings me to the 'stop Brexit' campaign. Many decent and
honest people are committed to reversing the referendum result.
They fear a completely unnecessary national tragedy is befalling
Britain, driven by myths and lies, and believe economic turmoil
and national isolation await. It is perfectly legitimate to seek to
democratically challenge a referendum result. But it is difficult to
see how the current strategy, communication and leadership of
this cause achieve anything other than doom it to failure.

First off, I'm not convinced by the campaign's aim, and here's
why. Some stop Brexiters recite, almost as a mantra, that the
referendum was only advisory (despite the government sending
a pamphlet to every household in Britain promising them that
the government 'will implement what you decide'). If the referendum result was simply cancelled, it would be regarded as a

coup against democracy not just by leave voters, but by many remainers. Faith in democracy may never be rebuilt – 'more people voted for Brexit than for anything else in British history and the establishment thwarted it', the refrain would go. It would surely be the greatest shot in the arm for the radical right in British history – not least because the result was in part due to a sense of resentment against a contemptuous political elite.

Alternatively, a second referendum could easily be framed as the establishment holding votes until it got the right result. It would mean an even more bitter campaign than the last, leaving deeper national divisions than ever. Either the last result would be reconfirmed, with rightwing Brexiters more triumphalist and intolerant than ever; or – if remain scraped a narrow victory – furious Brexiter demands for yet another referendum would be impossible to resist. Would it be best of three? Furthermore, a focus on overturning the referendum surely risks abandoning the debate over what sort of Brexit deal Britain negotiates to the Tory extremists.

Then there's simple political maths. If Labour committed to overturning Brexit, the party would haemorrhage many of the 3 million or so of its voters who backed leave, losing seats as a consequence. Perhaps it would win a sliver of the 7 per cent of Britons currently supporting the main stop Brexit party, the Liberal Democrats: though even that paltry gain would be in urban remain seats already held by Labour. Indeed, if preventing Brexit is such an inherently appealing prospect, why the derisory level of support for Vince Cable's party? The consequence would surely be a decisive Conservative electoral victory, enabling the party to implement the most true blue of Tory Brexit deals, and continue everything from austerity to the failure to build affordable homes.

I'm genuinely open to having these arguments rebutted by stop Brexiters: actually, I'd like to be persuaded. But their campaign seems unable to learn from the failures of the official remain movement in the referendum, which was seen by many as an establishment push for the status quo in an era when millions feel angry and disillusioned.

Its prominent spokespeople – Tony Blair, Nick Clegg and unelected peers – simply cement the negative images of what was, after all, a failed campaign, however unfair that might seem to the most devout supporters. A successful movement would have to win over a significant chunk of leave voters as well as remainers resigned to the vote. But leavers are often dismissed en masse as racist and ignorant – which, again, does little but confirm their views. Even remainers who believe the vote has to be accepted – and polling suggests there are millions – are beyond the pale to the most committed stop Brexiters.

To have any chance of success, they need a completely different strategy. First, the messenger matters, not just the message. For many leave voters, a thwarted Brexit would be an establishment coup against the democratic will of the people. Having discredited and deeply unpopular politicians, or unelected peers, pushing for this surely reinforces these views. Second, if stop Brexit presents itself as a defence of the status quo – at a time of popular ferment – it will fail: it should combine its signature policy with radical demands.

Third, it should launch itself as a grassroots, populist insurgency: rather than hosting EU flag-waving marches in remain citadels, it should hold mass public meetings and leafleting campaigns in leave areas, focusing on a positive case directed at those who are not enamoured with the EU (which is most people, including many remain voters). Its aim should be to shift public opinion so dramatically that calls for a new referendum become unanswerable.

Instead, it seems that too many stop Brexiters are making the same mistakes some leftists have traditionally made: looking for traitors, not converts; defined by what they are against, not what they are for; purist; cult-like; treating the wider public as politically backward; angrily dogmatic; yelling at people on Twitter.

No, I'm not convinced by their case as things stand, and can't see clear answers to the questions I pose. A Labour-managed Brexit that doesn't shred our links with the EU and turn Britain into a low-regulation tax haven still seems preferable. But the case to stop Brexit does deserve to be made, and deserves to be made well.

12 JANUARY

Harriet Harman on exposing the pay gap: 'This is kind of ... revolutionary'

DECCA AITKENHEAD

Harriet Harman is being photographed when I arrive at her south London home. As I fall to admiring her fabulously billowy skirt, she laughs and says: 'Ah, well, you see, I've evolved beyond the sharp jacket. I don't need to bother about looking authoritative any more, now that I'm a "former". We're now in a new mode which is more, well, kind of more droopy. Which suits me perfectly.'

Except that eight years after leaving government, and 35 since entering parliament, from the twilight of her political afterlife Harman is about to witness what may well prove to be the most radical achievement of her career.

The country has been agog over Carrie Gracie's resignation and the BBC gender pay gap. But, come April, thanks almost entirely to the former deputy Labour leader, most women are likely to discover another industrial-scale case of #MeToo.

'There's going to be an avalanche in April. It's going to be unbelievable. Because everybody's going to go: "Bugger this", just like Carrie. This is a really huge, structural earthquake – and now it's all happening.' She pauses and allows herself a gleeful grin. 'Usually, policies all fall apart after a while, and you think,' she winces, '"Oh God." But this one is a cracker, there's no doubt about it.'

In April, a clause of the 2010 Equality Act will come into force, requiring every company of 250 or more employees to publish its gender pay gap. Were it not for Harman, the act would instead have mandated companies merely to commission internal equal pay audits. 'And I said no, no, if you have consultants doing an equal pay audit paid for by the management, they will just tell them that it's all fine. It would have been the worst of all worlds. Businesses would have had to spend money on it and it wouldn't have moved the needle on equal pay. So, I went absolutely bonkers and said no, let's have pay transparency instead. Because if people can see what's happening in their workplace, that is going to empower people to say we've got to change.'

She faced near-universal resistance from the equality sector – and even the TUC. 'There was this kind of orthodoxy around the mantra of equal pay audits. And I was like, that is just a process, it doesn't empower the individual woman. I just knew that it's the secrecy of it that stops anything changing.' She wanted every woman, like Gracie, to know what her male colleagues earned. 'Exactly. As Carrie says in her resignation letter: "I always suspected it, but it wasn't until the figures were published forcibly that I actually saw that." And I thought, that is precisely what I was aiming for in the Equality Act.'

Right now, the BBC's critics may be having a field day, observes Harman, but come April they may look a lot less holier than thou.

'I don't think the BBC is even unique among broadcasters, let alone among the wider economy.' Some companies have already published their gender pay gap, and the figures are arresting. For Phase Eight, a women's clothes shop, the average hourly pay for women is an eye-watering 65 per cent lower than it is for men.

'What this does is expose the hypocrisy in lip service, because basically everybody says: "Pay gap? Terrible! No, no, we wouldn't have one of those. Oh, we're totally against unequal pay, and we'd never have it here. That's other people." So what this does is it blows the lid off the fact that people are saying one thing and doing another.'

Politicians, too, may regret their haste to castigate the BBC. 'I asked the Labour party and the Tory party to publish their own pay gap [years ago]. I definitely thought that the Labour party should do it, because it was our policy, but they haven't published yet. So that is going to be a corker, when the political parties all reveal their pay gaps.'

It is nearly half a century since the Equal Pay Act was passed. The fact that so many employers have paid lip service to it for so long, Harman reflects, may be maddening, but now has turned out to be rather useful.

'The argument that it's unfair has blossomed on the basis that people didn't think they were going to have to do anything about it. People adopted the rhetoric because they felt they had impunity – because it was all undercover, if you like. Therefore, we've got the rhetoric very nicely developed. And now suddenly the facts are marching up to the rhetoric and tapping it on the shoulder. And it's going to be: bang! Now it's the day of reckoning.'

The obvious danger is that the figures will be published, women will be furious for a while and nothing will be done. Before I can even put this to Harman, however, she hands me copies of letters she has written to the heads of the Equalities and Human Rights Commission and the TUC. She urges the EHRC to publish annual gender pay gap league tables showing the discrepancies, both by sector and region, to set annual targets for companies to close the gap, and to support legal action brought by individual women against those that don't.

'Because the act is not supposed to be just revealing the discrimination and the shamefulness of it. It's about a spur to action – so you can say, if you work in Virgin Money: "Why has NatWest got less of a pay gap when it's the same sector as us?" So, the EHRC is absolutely key in this. And the TUC has to place closing the pay gap at the heart of national pay bargaining.'

Even if the EHRC and the TUC adopt all of Harman's proposals, and every organisation in the land dutifully resolved to close its gap, how would it be done? It would be wildly unrealistic, I suggest, to expect every employer to magic up funds for whopping pay rises overnight to all its female employees.

'It is hard to bring about change which is deeply entrenched,' Harman agrees. 'And I don't think it's easy. There isn't a get-out-of-jail-free card. There's not a magic wand you could wave on this. But there is no point getting ourselves to this point, looking over the edge of the precipice and thinking: "Well, we're not going to do anything about it." So, you've got a choice: you either perpetuate it or you change it. And the transition will be ragged.'

One approach she offers will be to effect change through staff turnover. For example, when a man earning £100,000 a year vacates the post, the man who replaces him could find the new salary is £80,000. 'The point is, these jobs change hands, so you don't have to cut men's pay.' That would mean a period when some very highly paid men find themselves working alongside men paid significantly less – even those in roles senior to them. That's going to cause havoc, isn't it?

'The fact that you've got somebody who is your junior earning twice as much as you, well, that's the way it's going to be. But, actually, if that is what's necessary, it's going to have to happen. I think that, basically, there's got to be a gritting of the teeth for a while and a recognition that our normal sense of a pay hierarchy is going to have to be suspended, because we're in a transitional period. We're transitioning from entrenched discrimination to equality.'

Another way to close the gap, of course, would be to fill the highest-paid roles with women. 'Some people say the oddest things,' Harman offers, rolling her eyes. 'Like, they say: "Well, we have got a pay gap, but that's because all the men are at the senior levels."' If one consequence of the act is that employers have a tangible incentive to promote women to positions of power within organisations, it will do much more than merely close the pay gap. 'Oh, totally,' Harman agrees. 'It is kind of,' and she drops her voice to a stage whisper, 'revolutionary.'

A lifelong feminist, born in 1950, Harman has been a leading figure in the women's movement for as long as almost anyone can remember. Parliament was 97 per cent male when she arrived in 1982, and her first Commons question to Margaret Thatcher concerned the lack of childcare provision during school holidays. Maternity leave and pay, all-women shortlists, Sure Start centres, even the abolition of the arcane provocation law 'which basically said it was a woman's fault if her husband killed her', were all down to her work for women's rights. Yet for decades she was mocked as Harridan Harperson, even on her own benches. The enduring mystery, if not miracle, is how she stuck at it. As she talks at her kitchen table now, she has the quiet satisfaction of sensing history on her side.

'This pay gap information comes at a time where women are not minded any more to accept phoney explanations and justi-fications. There is this sense now about what women are not prepared to put up with, which is very like that spirit of the 60s and 70s women's movement. The spirit of "We're not having this any more, this is wrong" is abroad again.' When Harman published her memoir, *A Woman's Work*, last year, which revealed that her university tutor had offered to upgrade her degree result if she slept with him, the *Daily Mail* and other critics savaged the claim. 'I was told: "Either you made it up or you should have said it at the time or you're being mean to somebody who's dead." That was just a few months before the Harvey Weinstein thing.'

Harman was still busy with book publicity when Theresa May called last year's snap election. Like most of her colleagues, Harman braced herself for the worst. She thought Labour would be wiped out. 'Oh, the atmosphere in the PLP was slightly less cheerful than a Dignitas waiting room. I mean, everybody thought they were on their way out. Literally half the PLP was saying goodbye to each other and hugging.'

And now? Were Jeremy Corbyn's office to call and offer her another front bench role, I ask, what she would say? 'No, definitely, I'm a former. There's lots of amazingly good people and they are the future.'

Many Harman fans still bitterly regret her decision not to stand for the Labour leadership in 2010. The same constituency is determined to see a woman succeed Corbyn, but when I ask if Harman is in favour of introducing a constitutional mechanism to guarantee it she spreads her hands.

'Well, I might be if somebody works out a good way of doing it. I'm totally not against it – but I couldn't work one out that didn't seem to have loads of downsides. But, actually, we need to recognise that we've got some fantastic men in the Labour party, new men coming forward who are rightly ambitious. And we ought to really be encouraging them, and admiring the great work that they're doing and saying: "You will go far, you will really go far. You could aspire to be deputy." What we've got to have is a generation of men who know that the height of their ambition is to support a woman leader.'

18 JANUARY

I wrote *The Art of the Deal* with Trump. He's still a scared child

TONY SCHWARTZ

'I alone can do it.' These five extraordinary words kept coming back to me as I reflected on Donald Trump's first year as president of the US. He made this claim during his speech accepting the Republican nomination in July 2016. At the time, it struck me simply as a delusional expression of his grandiosity. Looking back, I also hear the plaintive wail of a desperate child who believes he is alone in the world with no one to care for him. 'I alone can do it' is Trump's survival response to: 'I must do it all alone.'

There are two Trumps. The one he presents to the world is all bluster, bullying and certainty. The other, which I have long felt haunts his inner world, is the frightened child of a relentlessly critical and bullying father and a distant and disengaged mother who couldn't or wouldn't protect him.

'That's why I'm so screwed up, because I had a father who pushed me so hard,' Trump acknowledged in 2007, in a brief and rare moment of self-awareness.

Trump's temperament and his habits have hardened with age. He was always cartoonish, but compared with the man for whom I wrote *The Art of the Deal* 30 years ago, he is significantly angrier today: more reactive, deceitful, distracted, vindictive, impulsive and, above all, self-absorbed – assuming the last is possible.

This is the narrative I've been advancing for the past 18 months. With the recent publication of Michael Wolff's *Fire and Fury*, it turns out that even those closest to Trump recognise his utter lack of fitness to be president, even if they are too cowed and cowardly to do anything about it.

Fear is the hidden through-line in Trump's life – fear of weakness, of inadequacy, of failure, of criticism and of insignificance. He has spent his life trying to outrun these fears by 'winning' – as he puts it – and by redefining reality whenever the facts don't serve the narrative he seeks to create. It hasn't worked, but not for lack of effort.

In his first year in office, Trump has lambasted any facts he dislikes as 'fake news', while making nearly 2,000 false or misleading claims of his own – more than five a day. In a single half-hour interview with the *New York Times* in late December, he made 24 such claims. This is the very definition of gaslighting – lying until you get people to doubt their own reality – and it is both frightening and disturbing. Because the office Trump now occupies makes him the most powerful man on Earth, his fears, and the way he manages them, have necessarily become ours.

We fear Trump because he is impulsive, irrational and self-serving, but above all because he seems unconstrained by even the faintest hint of conscience. Trump feels no more shame over his most destructive behaviours than a male lion does killing the cubs of his predecessor when he takes over a pride.

Trump has made fear the dominant emotion of our times. This, I believe, is his primary impact on the body politic after a year in office. He began his campaign by describing immigrant Mexicans as rapists, Muslims as terrorists, and more recently all black and brown people, and entire countries, as inferior. Trump skilfully exploited the fears of supporters who felt powerless and disenfranchised by presenting himself as their angry champion, even though the policies he has since pursued are likely to make their lives worse.

About the only thing Trump truly has in common with his base is that he feels every bit as aggrieved as they do, despite his endless privilege. No amount of money, fame or power has been enough to win him the respect he so insatiably craves. His anger over this perceived injustice is visceral and authentic. Trump's unwinding of government programmes such as Barack Obama's Affordable Care Act will fuel yet more fear among the millions of people who will lose their healthcare in the year ahead. The tax plan Trump pushed through most benefits him, his family and his fellow billionaires and provides the least relief to those who need it most. In both cases, the victims of these policies will include millions of his supporters, who may find someone else to blame, but whose suffering will inexorably increase.

The fearful divide Trump has exacerbated is not simply between his supporters and his detractors, the rich and the poor, or Democrats and Republicans, but between the best and the worst in each of us.

In the face of fear, it is a physiological fact that our most primitive and selfish instincts emerge. Control of our behaviour shifts from the prefrontal cortex to the emotionally driven amygdala – sometimes referred to as 'fear central'. As we move into fight-or-flight mode, we become more self-centred, and our vision narrows to the perceived threat, which in the modern world is less to our survival than to our sense of value and worthiness. We lose the capacity for empathy, rationality, proportionality and attention to the longer-term consequences of our actions.

This is the reactive state Trump has tapped into with his followers and which he has prompted in his opponents. It serves none of us well. Think for a moment about the immense difference between how you feel and behave at your best and your worst. It is when we feel safest and most secure that we think most clearly and expansively. It's also when we are most inclined to look beyond our self-interest, and to act with compassion, generosity, consideration and forgiveness.

I have never observed any of these qualities in Trump. Over the past year I have frequently been asked whether he has any redeeming qualities. I've thought about this as objectively as I can, and the only one I've come up with is his relentless drive. But because Trump uses this quality solely in the service of his self-aggrandisement and domination, it scarcely qualifies as a virtue.

So what does resistance to Trump look like? This is a question that has preoccupied me and millions of other Americans this past year. If fear gets sufficiently intense, or persists for long enough, we eventually move into 'freeze' – meaning numbness and submission. This is my own greatest fear. As Trump violates one norm after another day after day, the risk is that we lose our sense of outrage and our motivation to speak out.

The challenge we face is to resist our own fear without sacrificing our outrage. That requires widening our perspective beyond Trump's, and beyond Trump himself. The future is ours to shape, not his. Dispiriting as I found it to write *The Art of the Deal* with a man I progressively came to view as a black hole, the experience prompted me to redirect my life in almost complete opposition to the values and worldview that he represents. My own path over the past two decades – prompted in reaction to my experience with him – has been to help business leaders become more wholly human, and to humanise workplaces.

Trump's actions over the past year have already prompted an extraordinary wave of new activism among people in their 20s and 30s, who are now the biggest segment of the US electorate, and represent the next generation of leaders. The 19 women who stepped forward to accuse Trump of sexual assault have helped to galvanise a rapidly growing, worldwide movement to empower women and to call out sexual abuse in the workplace. Thanks in large part to Trump, hundreds of new female candidates are now running for political office.

Trump himself has become the embodiment of the limits of traditional masculinity. 'We raise boys,' writes the author Terrence Real, 'to live in a world in which they are either winners or losers, grandiose or shame-filled ... perpetrators or victims. Society shows little mercy for men if they fail in the performance of their role. But the price of that performance is an inward sickness.'

Trump represents an extreme version of a sickness from which most men suffer, to some extent. The most powerful stand we can take in opposition to Trump's values and behaviour is to pursue a higher purpose every day, seek more common ground amid our differences, and find better ways to take care of others and add value wherever we can. As he looks backward, we must look forward.

The Trumpian worldview is narrow, dark and deficit-driven. Each of us shares some of those instincts: the fear of inadequacy is uniquely and universally human. But we are also capable of so much more. My hope and belief is that Trump will no longer be president by this year's end. My personal commitment is to pay much less attention to him, and more to making a difference to others affected by his policies. Whatever happens, may the worst of Trump inspire the best in us.

We, together, can do it.

Tony Schwartz wrote The Art of the Deal *with Donald Trump in 1987.*

20 JANUARY

I loved that boy to the point where I felt close to fainting

ELENA FERRANTE

Some time ago, I planned to describe my first times. I listed a certain number of them: the first time I saw the sea, the first time I flew in an aeroplane, the first time I got drunk, the first time I fell in love, the first time I made love. It was an exercise both arduous and pointless.

For that matter, how could it be otherwise? We always look at first times with excessive indulgence. Even if by their nature they're founded on inexperience, and so as a rule are not very successful, we recall them with sympathy, with regret. They're swallowed up by all the times that have followed, by their transformation into habit, and yet we attribute to them the power of the unrepeatable.

Precisely because of this innate contradiction, my project began to sink right away and shipwrecked conclusively when I tried to describe my first love truthfully. I made an effort to search my memory for details and I found few. He was very tall, very thin, and seemed handsome to me. He was 17, I 15. We saw each other every day at six in the afternoon. We went to a deserted alley behind the bus station. He spoke to me, but not much; kissed me, but not much; caressed me, but not much. What primarily interested him was that I should caress him. One evening – was it evening? – I kissed him as I would have liked him to kiss me. I did it with such an eager, shameless intensity that afterwards I decided not to see him again. But already I don't know if that really happened then, or in the course of other brief loves that followed. Certainly I loved that boy to the point where, seeing him, I lost every perception of the world, and felt close to fainting, not out of weakness but out of an excess of energy.

Consequently, I discovered, what I distinctly remember of my first love is my state of confusion. Or rather, the more I worked on it, the more I focused on deficiencies: vague memory, sentimental uncertainties, anxieties, dissatisfaction. Nothing, in fact, was sufficient; I expected and wanted more, and was surprised that he, on the other hand, after wanting me so much, found me superfluous and ran away because he had other things to do.

All right, I said to myself, you will write about how altogether wanting first love is. But, as soon as I tried, the writing rebelled; it tended to fill gaps, to give the experience the stereotypical melancholy of adolescence. It's why I said, that's enough of first times. What we were at the beginning is only a vague patch of colour contemplated from the edge of what we have become.

Translated by Ann Goldstein. This was Elena Ferrante's first column for Guardian Weekend.

31 JANUARY

In 2011 Preston hit rock bottom. Then it took back control

ADITYA CHAKRABORTTY

The city of Preston in Lancashire dates back to Roman times. It is listed in the Domesday Book as Prestune. It's where inventor

Richard Arkwright kickstarted the cotton trade. Yet ask local people to tell you its history and they jump straight to 2011. That was Preston's year zero, when the grand schemes for the city fell apart. For more than a decade the council had bet everything on a massive shopping mall. The Tithebarn would sprawl over the city centre, cost £700 million and be built by two of the biggest developers on the planet. It was going to have a Marks & Sparks, a multiplex and a huge John Lewis store. It was the lottery ticket, said the council leader. The lifeline, the turnaround, the magic bullet.

Then came the banking crash, and cranes across the country stopped dead. Businesses grew cooler on the Tithebarn until, in November 2011, John Lewis pulled out. The council found its sums no longer added up, and killed the entire scheme. Where once there was a masterplan, Preston now had a vacuum.

Such stories lie scattered all over post-industrial Britain. During the boom, lest we forget, ex-mining town Barnsley proposed to turn itself into a 'Tuscan hill town'. Yet 'the T-word' serves two purposes for Prestonians. The story reminds them of the precariousness of their perch. It also marks the point at which everything changed.

Small cities trailing big histories rank among the flotsam of 21st-century capitalism. With a big enough dowry (some subsidies, perhaps, or free roads and cheap labour), they might catch the eye of a passing multinational bearing some dubious inward investment. A distribution warehouse, say, with poverty-pay jobs, or a high-street killer of a retail park. That was Preston at the start of this decade – and it's several other places still.

But the city council no longer plays that game. Instead it has adopted a guerrilla localism. It keeps its money as close to home as possible so that, amid historically drastic cuts, the amount spent locally has gone up. Where other authorities privatise, Preston grows its own businesses. It even creates worker-owned co-operatives.

Now Labour leader Jeremy Corbyn praises Preston for its 'inspiring innovation'. Westminster thinktankers talk about 'making a pilgrimage' – and they are only half-joking. Even actor Michael Sheen has dropped by.

There is much talk of a 'Preston model', of this place being Corbynism on Earth. But what's most remarkable is how somewhere so beaten-up – with its streets a mix of empty shops and rough sleepers, and having the highest suicide rate in England – got itself off the floor. How a council that only a few years back hugged multinational Lendlease now espouses localism. How a place that has been on the wrong end of the past 40 years mustered the confidence to strike out on its own. The answer each time has something to do with Matthew Brown.

When the Tithebarn dream died, Brown was in the council cabinet, although not in the Labour mainstream. His days are spent in a clerical job with the Department for Work and Pensions; evenings are devoted to books on leftwing economics. Early in his teens he was watching the BBC's *Question Time* when Tony Benn came on – and it was as if postwar Britain's most eloquent socialist was talking directly to him. Thatcher was in charge and Preston was on the slide ('Some of the social housing was like a third world country'). His commitment to social justice and economic democracy made him marginal, even within Labour – until 2011 came along and the council began groping around for new ideas. In meetings, Brown quoted research showing 'big supermarkets cost jobs' and urged colleagues to expand the city's handful of co-operatives. 'People were like, "Can this stuff work?" The council officers were suspicious.' Yet in 2012 Preston declared itself the first living-wage employer in the north of England. To take on the loan shops, the council backed a credit union. But the transformative moment came as Brown worked with a Manchester-based consultancy, the Centre for Local Economic Strategies (CLES), on how to harness public services.

Public services are something Preston has a lot of. Come out of the train station and on the left are the grand county council offices. In the centre is the city council, right next to the municipally owned Harris Museum. A few minutes farther on and you are amid a forest of buildings belonging to the University of Central Lancashire. Then there is the police force, the sixth-form college, the housing association ... Like so many other towns and cities, while Preston's private sector has shrivelled, its public sector has grown and grown to fill the gap.

These public bodies account for thousands of jobs and hundreds of millions in spending. Yet calculations in 2013 showed that a mere fraction – one quid for each £20 spent – stayed in Preston. Much of the rest was going to building firms headquartered in London, say, or to global catering companies.

Years before PFI builder Carillion keeled over and the rest of the country realised the importance of which particular private firms take public money, Preston had already begun fretting about where its pounds were going. 'There was all this money in the community and it was leaking out,' says Brown. The Federation of Small Businesses has published research by CLES showing that for every pound spent with a small or medium-sized firm, 63p is re-spent locally. That drops to 40p for every pound given to a large or multinational company.

Brown's team persuaded six of the public bodies on their doorstep to commit to spending locally wherever possible. It sounded commonsensical; yet it defied procurement convention, which trades cost against quality and rarely thinks about the environment or society. 'You don't go in saying, "Have you thought about an alternative to neoliberalism?"' says CLES chief executive Neil McInroy. 'It's practical. You say to the housing association, "How would you like to do more for your residents so they'll be better off and pay their rent on time?"'

To hear how that conversation sounded from the other side of the table, I visited Community Gateway, which manages 6,500 homes around Preston. In a tower overlooking the docks, where ships once came in, head of finance Phil McCabe explained what the new regime meant to his team. Once they outsourced repairs and grass cutting; now they are in-house. There's been no drop-off in quality, only marginal rises in cost, at most. In 2015, Lancashire county council put a contract to provide school meals out to tender. That was impossibly large for local firms, so officers broke it into bite-size chunks. There was a tender to provide yoghurt, others for sandwich fillings, eggs, cheese, milk and so on. One contract was split into nine different lots. It meant officials actually shaping a market to fit their society – and it worked. Local suppliers using Lancashire farmers won every contract and provided an estimated £2 million boost to the county.

In 2013 the six local public bodies spent £38 million in Preston and £292 million in all of Lancashire. By 2017 those totals stood at £111 million in Preston and £486 million throughout the county. That is a huge turnaround, especially as their budgets shrank from £750 million to £616 million. The county's pension fund is now building student accommodation in the city and doing up a hotel. Over the next few months Brown will get two new worker co-ops off the ground – one in IT, the other in food. He talks about establishing a local bank for Lancashire. But right now his pride is the multimillion-pound revamp of the covered market, built by family firm Conlon using local contractors, which opens in February.

A few minutes from the market is a lovely Georgian square where, among the solicitors' and accountants' firms, stands a statue of Robert Peel. Residents built it in gratitude for the Conservative's repeal of the corn laws in 1846, the point at which Britain converted to free trade. It remains the establishment creed, but Preston's guerrilla protectionism suggests how it might break down.

For decades this city has been one of many losers in Britain's political economy. Its great achievement has been to recognise how badly it has lost out at the hands of finance and Westminster – to London, in short. The tantalising possibility is that other towns and cities might also come out as losers: that Britain could form a coalition of loser regions, stretching from outer London through south Wales to Strathclyde.

Preston's ideas could spread, Brown thinks, to Birmingham, Oldham, Bristol: 'Imagine if every Labour city were setting up its own banks, supporting worker-owned businesses and credit unions? Imagine it. That would be our way of taking back control.'

2 February

The refugee crisis isn't about refugees. It's about us

AI WEIWEI

I was born in 1957, the same year China purged more than 300,000 intellectuals, including writers, teachers, journalists and whoever dared to criticise the newly established communist government. As part of a series of campaigns led by what was known as the anti-rightist movement, these intellectuals were sent to labour camps for 're-education'.

Because my father, Ai Qing, was the most renowned poet in China then, the government made a symbolic example of him. In 1958, my family was forced from our home in Beijing and banished to the most remote area of the country – we had no idea that this was the beginning of a very dark, long journey that would last for two decades.

In the years that followed, my father was sentenced to hard labour cleaning latrines in a work camp in north-west China. He was also forced to criticise himself publicly.

From my youth, I experienced inhumane treatment from society. At the camp, we had to live in an underground dugout and were subjected to unexplainable hatred, discrimination, unprovoked insults and assaults, all of which aimed to crush the basic human spirit rooted in my father's beliefs. As a result, I remember experiencing what felt like endless injustice. In such circumstances, there is no place to hide and there is no way to escape. You feel like your life is up against a wall, or that life itself is a dimming light, on the verge of being completely extinguished. Coping with the humiliation and suffering became the only way to survive.

I share this personal background because it sheds light on my emotional connection to the current global refugee condition, which I documented in the film *Human Flow*. My experience clarifies why I identify so deeply with all these unfortunate people who are pushed into extreme conditions by outside forces they are powerless to resist.

In the months since the film's release, some of the areas we covered have deteriorated even further. The Rohingya refugee situation in Myanmar, for example, has erupted in a wave of more than half a million newly displaced people, adding to the already existing 65 million refugees worldwide.

Observing and researching recent and historical refugee events makes some conclusions abundantly clear. Not a single refugee we met had willingly left their home, even when home was impoverished and undeveloped. The promise of economic prosperity is not more important than place. People left their homes because they were forced to by violence which caused the deaths of family members, relatives and fellow citizens. Often it is not just a single house that is destroyed, but entire villages vanish under indiscriminate bombing. There is simply no way for them to stay. Fleeing is the only choice they have to preserve their own lives and the lives of those they love.

A common argument is that many of the people who try to reach the west are economic migrants who wish to take unfair advantage of its prosperity. However, this view ignores the contradiction between today's physical borders and the real political and economic boundaries of our globalised world. Also implicit is a refusal to acknowledge that through globalisation, certain states, institutions and individuals have greatly profited at the direct expense of those in many parts of the world who are vulnerable and increasingly exploited.

At this moment, the west – which has disproportionately benefited from globalisation – simply refuses to bear its responsibilities, even though the condition of many refugees is a direct result of the greed inherent in a global capitalist system. If we map the 70-plus border walls and fences built between nations in the past three decades – increasing from roughly a dozen after the fall of the Berlin Wall – we can see the extent of global economic and political disparities. The people most negatively affected by these walls are the poorest and most desperate of society.

In nature there are two approaches to dealing with flooding. One is to build a dam to stop the flow. The other is to find the right path to allow the flow to continue. Building a dam does not address the source of the flow – it would need to be built higher and higher, eventually holding back a massive volume. If a powerful flood were to occur, it could wipe out everything in its path. The nature of water is to flow. Human nature too seeks freedom and that human desire is stronger than any natural force.

Can physical borders stop refugees? Instead of building walls, we should look at what is causing people to become refugees and work to solve those conditions to stem the flow at its source. To do so will require the most powerful nations in the world to adjust how they are actively shaping the world, how they are using political and economic ideology – enforced by over-whelming military power – to disrupt entire societies. How do we think the poor, displaced or occupied can exist when their societies are destroyed? Should they simply disappear? Can we recognise that their continued existence is an essential part of our shared humanity? If we fail to recognise this, how can we speak of 'civilised' development?

The refugee crisis is not about refugees; rather, it is about us. Our prioritisation of financial gain over people's struggle for the necessities of life is the primary cause of much of this crisis. The west has all but abandoned its belief in humanity and support for the precious ideals contained in declarations on universal human rights. It has sacrificed these ideals for short-sighted cowardice and greed.

Establishing the understanding that we all belong to one humanity is the most essential step for how we might continue to coexist on this sphere we call Earth. I know what it feels like to be a refugee and to experience the dehumanisation that comes with displacement from home and country. There are many borders to dismantle, but the most important are the ones within our own hearts and minds – these are the borders that are dividing humanity from itself.

Ai Weiwei is a contemporary artist, activist and advocate of political reform in China.

13 FEBRUARY

Recipe for pasta cacio e pepe

RACHEL RODDY

Of all the classic Roman pasta dishes, cacio e pepe was the one I tasted first – and still the one I like best. It has just three ingredients: pasta, cacio (aka pecorino romano) and freshly cracked black pepper. In cooking, though, the pasta creates another ingredient: the cloudy cooking water slightly thickened with starch that has seeped from the pasta as it boils. This cooking water is a sort of culinary negotiator, melting and then emulsifying the cheese into a rich, creamy sauce on the strands of pasta.

Unsurprisingly, there are as many ways and opinions about how best to make a cacio e pepe as there are cooks. Some like to add a little olive oil; others have ways with double boilers and grated ice, which, as far as I can see, require the almost gloopy starchy water of a trattoria pasta cooker and the wrists of a chef. But one thing people seem to agree on is that the enemy of cacio e pepe is chilly china – that is, cold plates – which can make the cheese clump into almost Plasticine-like blobs from which there is no coming back. Happily, it is an enemy easily overcome by warming the vessel in question. Most agree, too, that the smaller the quantity, the better the result. With this in mind, here are two ways to prepare two main-course portions of cacio e pepe.

For both methods, 300g of fresh tonnarelli or 220g of dried spaghetti or bucatini are cooked and mixed with a generous 120g of grated pecorino and black pepper to taste (my taste being 12 grinds). Both begin by bringing a pan of well-salted water to the boil and adding the pasta, grating the cheese – ideally to a grainy texture on the unlovable but effective star-shaped holes of your box grater – and warming a bowl, which I do first by running it under the hot tap, then sitting it near the warm hob.

First way: pasta first. Once the pasta is al dente (tender but with bite), lift it from the pan directly into the warm bowl, ideally using tongs or a sieve, so there's still some residual water clinging to it. Keep the pasta cooking water.

Next, tip almost all the cheese on to the pasta, grind in the pepper and toss using a fork and spoon, lifting the wetter pasta from the bottom of the bowl up and over, then swirling together. You'll see the cream forming as the cheese mixes with the watery pasta. If it doesn't look slippery enough, add more cooking water and toss again.

Second way: cheese first. While the pasta is boiling, put most of the grated cheese and plenty of pepper into the warm bowl, then, little by little, add enough water from the boiling pasta pan and mix until you have a paste the consistency of soft cream cheese. When the pasta is ready, lift it from the pan, with residual water clinging, and toss and swish. Add more cooking water if you think it needs it – you will quickly learn the feel as the sauce forms.

When it works, cacio e pepe is a culinary eureka. The sharp and salty cheese, flecked with enough pepper to make the back of your throat feel warm, transforms into a soft coat. It is also a recipe that sums up the everyday genius of Roman cooking: a few ingredients put together cleverly to make a downright delicious dish that's both bowl- and heart-warming.

Inside the *OED*: can the world's biggest dictionary survive the internet?

ANDREW DICKSON

In February 2009, a Twitter user called @popelizbet issued an apparently historic challenge to someone called Colin: she asked if he could 'mansplain' a concept to her. History has not recorded if he did, indeed, proceed to mansplain. But the lexicographer Bernadette Paton, who excavated this exchange last summer, believed it was the first time anyone had used the word in recorded form. 'It's been deleted since, but we caught it,' Paton told me, with quiet satisfaction.

In her office at Oxford University Press, Paton was drafting a brand-new entry for the *Oxford English Dictionary*. Also in her in-tray when I visited were the millennial-tinged usage of 'snow-flake', which she had hunted down to a Christian text from 1983 ('You are a snowflake. There are no two of you alike'), and new shadings of the compound 'self-made woman'. Around 30,000 such items are on the *OED* master list; another 7,000 more pile up annually. 'Everyone thinks we're very slow, but it's actually rather fast,' Paton said. 'Though admittedly a colleague did spend a year revising "go".'

Spending 12 months tracing the history of a two-letter word seems dangerously close to folly. But the purpose of a historical dictionary such as the *OED* is to give such questions the solemnity they deserve. An Oxford lexicographer might need to snoop on Twitter spats from a decade ago; or they might have to piece together a painstaking biography of one of the oldest verbs in the language (the revised entry for 'go' traces 537 separate senses over 1,000 years). 'Well, we have to get things right,' the dictionary's current chief editor, Michael Proffitt, told me.

Ninety years after the first edition appeared, the *OED* – a distant, far bulkier descendant of Samuel Johnson's *Dictionary* – is currently embarked on a third edition, a goliath project that involves overhauling every entry (many of which have not been touched since the late-Victorian era) and adding at least some of those 30,000 missing words, as well as making the dictionary into a fully digital resource. This was originally meant to be completed in 2000, then 2005, then 2010. Since then, OUP has quietly dropped mentions of a date. How far had they got, I asked Proffitt. 'About 48 per cent,' he replied.

The dictionary retains a quiet pride in the lexical lengths to which it will – indeed, must – go. Sometime in the late 1980s, Proffitt's predecessor as chief editor, John Simpson, asked the poet Benjamin Zephaniah about the origins of the noun 'skanking'. Zephaniah decided that the only way to explain was to come to *OED* headquarters and do a private, one-on-one performance. Skanking duly went in, defined as 'a style of West Indian dancing to reggae music, in which the body bends forward at the waist, and the knees are raised and the hands claw the air in time to the beat'.

When the *OED*'s second edition was published in March 1989 – 20 volumes, containing 291,500 entries and 2.4 million quotations – there were complaints that this wasn't really a new edition at all, just a nicely typeset amalgam of the old ones. The entry for 'computer' defined it as 'a calculating-machine; esp an automatic electronic device for performing mathematical or logical operations'. It was illustrated by a quotation from an 1897 journal.

By astonishing coincidence, another earthquake, far bigger, struck the very same month that *OED2* appeared in print: a proposal by an English computer scientist named Tim Berners-Lee for 'a large hypertext database with typed links'. The world wide web, as it came to be called (*OED* dates the phrase to 1990), offered a shining path to the lexicographical future. Databases could be shared, and connected to one another; whole libraries of books could be scanned and their contents made searchable. The sum of human text was starting to become available to anyone with a computer and a modem.

The fact that so much text is now available online has been the most cataclysmic change. Words that would previously have been spoken are now typed on social media. Lexicographers of slang have long dreamed of being able to track variant forms 'down to the level, say, of an individual London tower block', says the slang expert and *OED* consultant Jonathon Green; now, via Facebook or Instagram, this might actually be possible. Lexicographers can be present almost at the moment of word-birth: where previously a coinage such as 'mansplain' would have had to find its way into a durable printed record, which a researcher could use as evidence of its existence, it is now available near-instantly to anyone.

Most people, of course, now never go near a dictionary, but simply type phrases into Wikipedia (used more often as a dictionary than an encyclopedia, research suggests) or rely on Google, which – through a deal with Oxford Dictionaries – offers thumbnail definitions, audio recordings of pronunciations, etymology, a graph of usage over time and translation facilities. If you want to know what a word means, you can just yell something at Siri or Alexa.

Dictionaries have been far too slow to adjust, argues Jane Solomon of Dictionary.com. 'Information-retrieval is changing so fast,' she said. 'Why don't dictionaries respond intelligently to the semantic or user context, like figuring out that you're searching for food words, and give you related vocabulary or recipes?' And not just words: 'I'd love to include emojis; people are so creative with them. They've become a whole separate language. People sometimes need explanation; if you send your daughter the eggplant emoji, she might think that's weird.'

Some have dared to dream even bigger than polysemous aubergines. One is a computer professor at the Sapienza University of Rome called Roberto Navigli, who in 2013 soft-launched a site called Babelnet, which aims to be the dictionary to beat all dictionaries – in part by not really being a dictionary at all. Described as a 'semantic network' that pulls together 15 existing resources including Wikipedia, Wiktionary and Microsoft Terminology, it aims to create a comprehensive, hierarchical root map of not just English but of 271 languages simultaneously, making it the largest lexicon/encyclopedia/thesaurus/reference work on the web. Navigli told me that his real aim was to use 'semantic technology' to enable the holy grail for software engineers everywhere: autonomous machine-reading of text. 'This is the dream, right?' he said. 'The machine that can read text and understand everything we say.'

For lexicographers, speech is the most precious resource of all, and the most elusive. If you could capture large samples of it – people speaking in every context imaginable, from playgrounds to office canteens to supermarkets – you could monitor even more accurately how we use language, day to day. 'If we cracked the technology for transcribing normal conversations,' the lexicographer Michael Rundell said, 'it really would be a game-changer.'

For *OED*'s editors, this world is both exhilarating and, one senses, mildly overwhelming. The digital era has enabled Oxford lexicographers to run dragnets deeper and deeper through the language, but it has also threatened to capsize the operation. When you're making a historical dictionary and are required

Military personnel investigate the poisoning of Russian double agent Sergei Skripal and his daughter in Salisbury in March – the first offensive use of nerve agent in Europe since the second world war. CHRIS J. RATCLIFFE/GETTY IMAGES

Paulette Wilson of Wolverhampton, threatened with deportation after 50 years in the UK. The *Guardian*'s exposure of the Windrush scandal led to the resignation of Amber Rudd as home secretary in April. FABIO DE PAOLA/GUARDIAN

Kicking off an extraordinary year for women, stars including Amy Poehler, Meryl Streep and Natalie Portman wear black to support the Time's Up campaign at the Golden Globes in January. AXELLE/BAUER-GRIFFIN/FILMMAGIC

Pro-choice supporters wear handmaiden robes at a rally in Londonderry, Northern Ireland. The Republic of Ireland voted overwhelmingly to overturn its ban on abortion in the referendum on 25 May. CHARLES MCQUILLAN/GETTY IMAGES

A Saudi woman practises reversing in Riyadh, ahead of the lifting of a ban on women driving – the only one of its kind in the world – in Saudi Arabia in the summer. YOUSEF DOUBISI/AFP/GETTY IMAGES

Meghan Markle walks down the aisle of St George's Chapel in Windsor Castle to marry Prince Harry on 19 May. The new Duchess of Sussex has vowed to use her role to champion feminist causes. DANNY LAWSON/AFP/GETTY IMAGES

In world news, Kim Jong-un and Donald Trump met in Singapore on 12 June. Trump declared the summit an unequivocal success, despite the vague wording of the peace deal. SAUL LOEB/AFP/GETTY IMAGES

An asylum seeker and her child are detained near the Mexican border. Public pressure forced the suspension of Trump's 'zero tolerance' policy towards undocumented migrants in June. JOHN MOORE/GETTY IMAGES

In July, the world became gripped by the plight of the 12 Thai boys and their football coach, trapped in a flooded cave. They spent 13 days underground before they were rescued. THAM LUANG RESCUE OPERATION CENTRE/AP

England manager – and unlikely fashion hero – Gareth Southgate consoles captain Harry Kane at the end of their World Cup run on 14 July. The young squad achieved England's second best-ever result. TOM JENKINS/GUARDIAN

Political pressure: Theresa May and Angela Merkel at the G7 summit in Canada, 8 June. May spent much of the year fending off leadership speculation and attacks from Brexit hardliners within her own party.

IAN LANGSTON/AFP/GETTY IMAGES

The 'Trump Baby' blimp flies over Parliament Square on 13 July as thousands gather to protest against the President's visit to Britain. Trump nonetheless described the UK/US relationship as 'the highest level of special'. ANDY RAIN/EPA

After a turbulent year in which he was rarely out of the news, Boris Johnson
– here with Jacob Rees-Mogg and Iain Duncan Smith – tries to stay awake as
he launches an alternative to the Chequers Brexit plan on 11 September.
DAN KITWOOD/GETTY IMAGES

Labour leader Jeremy Corbyn faced his own problems as an antisemitism
row engulfed the Labour party. The controversy, which had been rumbling
for three years, came to a head in early September. JACK TAYLOR/GETTY IMAGES

Wildfire sweeps across moorland in Stalybridge, Greater Manchester, in June. A series of fires across the UK – blamed on the unusually hot weather – smouldered for three weeks. ANTHONY DEVLIN/GETTY IMAGES

The heatwave continued throughout the whole of July, making it Britain's hottest summer for 42 years. SARAH LEE/GUARDIAN

to check each and every resource, then recheck those resources when, say, a corpus of handwritten 17th-century letters comes on stream, the problem of keeping the dictionary up to date expands to even more nightmarish proportions. Adding to that dictionary to accommodate new words – themselves visible in greater numbers than ever before, mutating ever faster – increases the nightmare exponentially. 'In the early years of digital, we were a little out of control,' the lexicographer and *OED* historian Peter Gilliver told me. 'It's never-ending,' one *OED* lexicographer agreed. 'You can feel like you're falling into a wormhole.'

Adding to the challenge is a story that has become wearily familiar: while more people are consulting dictionary-like resources than ever, almost no one wants to shell out. Sales of hard-copy dictionaries have collapsed, far more calamitously than in other sectors. (OUP refused to give me figures, citing 'commercial sensitivities'. 'I don't think you'll get any publisher to fess up about this,' Michael Rundell told me.) While reference publishers amalgamate or go to the wall, information giants such as Google and Apple get fat by using our own search terms to sell us stuff. If you can get a definition by holding your thumb over a word on your smartphone, why bother picking up a book?

'Go to a dictionary conference these days and you see scared-looking people,' Rundell said. Although he trained as a lexicographer, he now mainly works as a consultant, advising publishers on how to use corpus-based resources. 'It used to be a career,' he went on. 'But there just aren't the jobs there were 30 years ago.' He pointed to his shelves, which were strikingly bare. 'But then I'm not sentimental about print; I gave most of my dictionaries away.'

Even if the infrastructure around lexicography has fallen away or been remade entirely, some things stay pleasingly consistent. Every lexicographer I spoke to made clear their distaste for 'word-lovers', who in the dictionary world are regarded as the type of person liable to scrawl 'fewer' on to supermarket signs reading '10 items or less', or recite 'antidisestablishmentarianism' to anyone who will listen. But love is, most grudgingly admit, what draws people to spend their lives sifting and analysing language. It takes a particular sort of human to be a 'word detective': something between a linguistics academic, an archival historian, a journalist and an old-fashioned gumshoe. Though hardly without its tensions – corpus linguists versus old-school dictionary-makers, stats nerds versus scholarly etymologists – lexicography seems to be one specialist profession with a lingering sense of common purpose: us against that ever-expanding, multi-headed hydra, the English language. 'It is pretty obsessive-compulsive,' Jane Solomon said.

The idea of making a perfect linguistic resource was one most lexicographers knew was folly, she continued. 'I've learned too much about past dictionaries to have that as a personal goal.' But then, part of the thrill of being a lexicographer is knowing that the work will never be done. English is always metamorphosing, mutating, evolving; its restless dynamism is what makes it so absorbing. 'It's always on the move,' said Solomon. 'You have to love that.'

There are other joys, too: the thrill of catching a new sense, or crafting a definition that feels, if not perfect, at least right. 'It sounds cheesy, but it can be like poetry,' Michael Rundell reflected. 'Making a dictionary is as much an art as a craft.'

Despite his pessimism about the industry, he talked with real excitement about a project he was about to join, working with experts from the Goldfield Aboriginal Language Centre on indigenous Australian languages, scantily covered by lexicographers. 'Dictionaries can make a genuine difference,' he said. 'They give power to languages that might have had very little power in the past; they can help preserve and share it. I really believe that.'

Throughout it all, *OED* churns on, attempting to be ever so slightly more complete today than it was yesterday or the day before. The dictionary team now prefer to refer to it as a 'moving document'. Words are only added; they are never deleted. When I suggested to Michael Proffitt that it resembled a proud but leaky Victorian warship whose crew were trying to keep out the leaks and simultaneously keep it on course, he looked phlegmatic. 'I used to say it was like painting the Forth Bridge, never-ending. But then they stopped – a new kind of paint, I think.' He paused. 'Now it's just us.'

These days *OED* issues online updates four times a year; though it has not officially abandoned the idea of another print edition, that idea is fading. Seven months after I first asked how far they had got into *OED3*, I enquired again; the needle had crept up to 48.7 per cent. 'We are going to get it done,' Proffitt insisted. If the update does indeed take until 2037, it will rival the 49 years it took the original *OED* to be created, whereupon it will presumably need overhauling all over again.

A few days ago, I emailed to see if 'mansplain' had finally reached the *OED*. It had, but there was a snag – further research had pushed the word back a crucial six months, from February 2009 to August 2008. Then, no sooner had Bernadette Paton's entry gone live in January than someone emailed to point out that even *this* was inaccurate: they had spotted 'mansplain' on a May 2008 blog post, just a month after the writer Rebecca Solnit had published her influential essay 'Men Explain Things to Me'. The updated entry, Proffitt assured me, will be available as soon as possible.

Nappies, takeaways and bubble wrap: could I remove plastic from my life?

STUART HERITAGE, IAN JACK AND COCO KHAN

STUART HERITAGE, 37

No man is an island. However, if I were an island, I'd probably be the best one ever. When the *Guardian* asked me to record all the single-use plastic I got through in a week, I scoffed. Piece of cake, I thought.

I work from home, so I never use coffee-shop cups. I have a reusable metal water bottle that I carry around in lieu of disposable plastic ones. I make my own soup for lunch each week and store it in reusable pouches. If it wasn't for my reliance on gelatinous stock pots when I'm cooking, I'd barely use any single-use plastic at all. What an island I'd be. The greatest.

But I'm not an island. I have a wife and two kids under the age of three. My wife has a fiendish sparkling water habit and gets through several two-litre bottles a week. My toddler is an unquenchable soft-fruit fanatic and ploughs through punnets of berries like they're going out of fashion. And the number of nappies we get through is astonishing. Conservatively, I'd say we use about 60 a week (the two-year-old is potty training), but the five-month-old has been poorly lately so, frankly, all bets are off.

'You know, if Henry VIII had worn disposable nappies, they'd still be in a landfill now,' says Rachelle Strauss of Zero Waste

Week, an organisation that encourages households and businesses to produce less waste. She has kindly agreed to be my guru for the week. And, while this did make me briefly entertain the idea of Jurassic Parking a new Henry VIII out of his ancient bum DNA, the permanence shocked me. Three billion nappies are sold in the UK every year, and they're all getting lobbed into holes.

Strauss is brilliantly unmilitant about waste reduction. Her journey began with the simple step of not using single-use carriers at the supermarket and, step by step, she's slowly reduced her household waste to the point where she hasn't needed to have her bin emptied for six months.

'This is all about compromise,' she told me. 'Pick your battles. What are the things that make you think, "OK, I can do without that"? But there will also be things where you think, "This is the 21st century and I'm not going to give that up." And that's OK. I'd rather everyone just gave up 50 per cent of their waste, because the collective impact of that is so much more than one family going to crazy lengths.'

Which was heartening, but there was still the nappies issue. Strauss had suggested not giving up disposable nappies entirely – they're useful in an emergency – but, in order to cut down, I ordered some washable alternatives online and texted my wife to tell her.

She texted back the emoji of a guy with crosses for eyes. To be fair, it's much nicer to be able to sling away a smelly nappy without much thought, but the new generation of reusables do make it easier. There are waterproof wraps with washable, absorbent bamboo inserts, so it's all much more civilised than it used to be. It's cheaper, too. A birth to potty reusable nappy kit is about £200, plus laundry costs of about £100. Disposables are much more expensive – even using the best bulk deals available, we spend £250 a year per kid on nappies, plus probably another

£75 on wipes. And the baby doesn't seem to notice the new setup, so everyone's happy.

When I told Strauss how much space was taken up with two-litre water bottles, she was surprisingly sympathetic. 'That's a prime example of where compromise comes in, because it's not fair on her to go without.' So what should I do? 'I would go back to the 1970s and think about getting a SodaStream. They're still around, and they still fart when you press the button. You'll save loads of money, and they just use tap water, so there'll be no waste.'

So, to make amends for the added strife of reusable nappies, I bought my wife a SodaStream Fizzi. Even though it was the cheapest model, it still cost £70, the equivalent of 700 litres of bottled water. There are cheaper brands, like Limo Bar, or Olympia, but even with SodaStream's gas exchange programme – you send them your empty CO_2 cylinder and they fill it for free – it's easy to see how the outlay would put people off. But then I imagined 350 empty bottles in a landfill, jostling next to all that theoretical medieval poo.

In all honesty, once you start paying attention to the waste you create, it's easy to trim it back. In just a week we've made a nappy dent, massively cut back on plastic bags and got rid of plastic water bottles altogether. We still create waste, but by the end of the experiment, for the first time since our kids were born, I didn't have to elbow-drop my bin bags to fit them into the dustbin. As Strauss suggested, once the simple steps we started with become habits, we'll begin to cut down elsewhere. But you can prise those fancy gravy pods from my cold dead hands.

IAN JACK, 73

I was born in the age of tin, glass, paper and jute. Beans, peaches and shoe polish came into our home encased in tin cans; jam, lemonade and Hydes Anvil Ales in glass jars and bottles; sausages, custard slices and haddock in paper wrappings and bags; coal in jute sacks. Some items – potatoes, for instance – went into mum's shopping bag without any protection at all and left behind the soil and dust of the fields. Some required cardboard – I am thinking of Barratt's Sherbet Fountains and St Bruno pipe tobacco.

And then plastic arrived.

Other than the Bakelite knobs on the radio set, my first memory of plastic is a plaything I was given as a birthday or Christmas present somewhere around 1950 and which, astonishingly, I still possess. A little plastic Mexican (you can tell by the hat) sits on a little plastic mule – white mule, pink rider – with his arms outstretched to hold reins that have gone missing or were never there in the first place. The pink Mexican and his steed were alone in their plasticness when I set out my lead soldiers for their battles on the carpet and had to be given separate roles – scouting forays on the settee, say – to make the difference less obvious.

From Greenland's icy mountains, from India's coral strand – to borrow from a hymn I associate with those faraway times – discarded plastic litters the world and threatens the future of its rivers, lakes and oceans, and all that lives in them.

Thanks mainly to my wife, a tireless campaigner on this front for more than 20 years, we try as a family to do our best by the environment. Our milk comes to the doorstep in returnable glass bottles, we refill old containers with washing-up liquid and laundry detergent at a nearby store, and, as far as we can, we buy fruit, veg, bread and cheese from local independent shops that use brown paper bags rather than packaging. We take our own bags with us wherever we go and rarely need to acquire plastic ones. We eat very little meat – which tends to use more plastic than veg to keep it safe and healthy – and some of us (not me, so far) take reusable hot drinks cups in our bags wherever we go. We never buy water in plastic bottles.

Oh, how noble we feel! And yet, as we discovered when we tracked our usage, we still generate a dismaying amount of plastic every week. We kept everything in a box in the basement. The pile would be much smaller if we hadn't succumbed to a frequent weakness for a takeaway Vietnamese supper from a local restaurant that has recently abandoned containers made of tinfoil and cardboard. And smaller still if we had given up salads for one from a minimarket in the high street – portion control rather than taste is the attraction here – and the occasional tub of hummus or box of falafels. But there surely comes a point when no further reductions can be made. Shampoo, toothpaste, bleach: all kinds of personal and household cleaners come in plastic bottles and we aren't about to stop buying them.

We're lucky. We live in a prosperous part of London that has independent shops, and we can afford to use them. Cutting down on plastic is harder when your only choice of shopping is between a supermarket and an online catalogue. The truth is that a little money can make virtuous living a lot easier.

COCO KHAN, 29

I knew when I started this challenge that it would be impossible to eliminate all the single-use plastic from my life. But I hoped I might get close. I'd found the eco tweaks I made a few years ago painless. I stopped using straws – metal, paper or plastic. (After all, what's wrong with the humble cup? It's a design classic.) I bought a reusable water bottle, which I've never lost despite being a chronic misplacer, and I often carry my own cutlery (there is nothing like the expression on a bouncer's face when they search your bag and pull out a fork). On the makeup front, I reduced my daily routine to coconut oil and eyeliner pencil (the harder plastic that makeup is packaged in is especially difficult to break down in landfill). And in the kitchen I've nearly blinded three housemates by stacking up takeaway boxes for potential reuse so precariously high that an innocent rummage for a salt shaker is a reckoning with gravity.

Those amends to my life were a doddle and made my existence easier, so I was optimistic about continuing the journey. I started by noting my single-use plastic consumption. Thanks to smug friends and colleagues gleefully piping up with 'Did you remember to include xyz?', I learned that my clothes were a bit plastic (polyester, microfibre and fleece all contain plastic fibres); that even the foil-looking bags for crisps and nuts are plastic; and, worst of all, teabags also count (they use it to seal the bags). My optimism quickly disappeared. I found myself frustrated by the sight of food packaged in perfectly good recycled paper, only to be ruined by a plastic window pane (presumably because you might think the label is lying?).

Payday arrived in the middle of my week logging plastic use, and I was surprised to realise that having less money made me consume less plastic. When I'm watching the pennies, I eat more home-cooked meals. When I'd been paid, I found myself much more likely to reach for the takeaway menu, to spend money on lunchtime meal deals and deli-counter pleasures all served in plastic bags.

But I still felt frustrated by the constant dodges I was having to make to avoid plastic in my daily life. Luckily I was given a pep talk by plastics campaigner Lizzie Carr. In 2016, Carr became the first person to paddleboard the length of England, on what she called a 'plastic patrol', a one-woman crusade to highlight the impact of plastic on the UK's waterways. Carr took up paddleboarding on the Isles of Scilly in 2013 when recuperating from a cancer diagnosis. When she moved back to London and attempted to paddleboard on the city's canals, she found them to be 'disgusting', filled with plastic waste.

'That was the start of everything for me,' she told me. 'The waterways and paddleboarding had been a way to restore my health, it was where I went to get better. And yet, I was among all of this trash, the waterways coated in rubbish.'

She decided to take photos of every piece of plastic she saw, logging it on a map. Last year, she launched an app so people could contribute. She advises me to look for easy wins, and to consider switching to a glass milk bottle. 'If you can organise a milkman you can get glass bottles with a foil top, but if not, many supermarkets sell milk in a glass bottle. These little changes all add up.'

Later that evening I decide to put some of Carr's other tips to the test. She recommends places that sell produce loose and in bulk so you can bring your own containers and fill up, but recognises these may not be an option for people outside major cities. I take a plastic box and foil to my local supermarket and head for the cheese counter. I'm surprised by how accommodating they are. The cheese is wrapped in the foil, the sticker showing the price stuck on top for checkout, bish bash bosh. My local independent butcher doesn't mind me popping a couple of chicken breasts in my own Tupperware, and in my local grocery store I even get a freebie out of it ('the scotch egg is on me,' says the friendly assistant).

At the time of writing, I still haven't finished things like my liquid handwash, which I will replace with regular soap, my washing machine detergent, which I will replace with powder that comes in a box, and fairy liquid which I will switch to Ecover (it's plastic, but is refillable and doesn't put harsh chemicals into the water system). The number of changes I could make are exhausting, but Carr's energy has rubbed off on me. Besides, there are few things more motivating than out-smugging your friend: 'I see your reusable bag, and I raise you a bamboo toothbrush.'

If it's a care home for me, bring on the pole dancers

MICHELE HANSON

Last week a bold care home in Dorset invited a troupe of pole dancers to perform for its elderly residents. What a thrilling breakthrough, in a number of ways. First, it makes a change from the usual fairly dreary entertainments, and second, the residents chose it themselves, from a list of options. Fancy that! For once they were given a choice, asked their opinion, listened to, and got what they wanted. They fancied 'more modern activities'.

They were perhaps sick and tired of bingo, singalongs, banging tambourines, crosswords, telly, chair-yoga, arts and crafts, mindfulness and reminiscences. Not that I want to criticise these pastimes – they're all lovely, if that's what you like – but pole dancing makes a refreshing change.

Only last week, while visiting my solicitor to organise power of attorney in case I am suddenly incapacitated or lose my marbles, I told him that I'd rather hurl myself from my perch and drop dead than live in a care home.

'We all feel like that,' said he, 'but I think you'll find, when the time comes, you won't care so much.' Could be, but in the meantime I have to cope with the dread. I imagine myself, corpse-like, stuck in a brown armchair, precooked slop food, telly burbling on, no dogs allowed. My fears are probably exaggerated, but this pole dancing story has made me feel a tiny bit less desperate. Perhaps this is the new zeitgeist – less bossing about of old people, more acceptance that we still have minds and can make them up for ourselves. Marvellous.

Of course the pole dancing afternoon had its po-faced critics. 'In my view it's inappropriate for a care home. It's not really the sort of entertainment I'd have thought that residents wanted,' said local councillor Peter Hall. Why inappropriate? It looked more like gymnastics than rudeness to me.

The costumes were not at all saucy, just your average gym clothes – leotards, shorts, crop-tops. What are they meant to wear? Crinolines? And the pole dancers were various shapes, sizes and ages. A realistic assortment, no Hugh Hefner-type mandatory bunny-shape. They looked perfectly respectable to me, like acrobats, twizzling themselves into remarkably clever positions. I couldn't hang straight out sideways or upside-down from a pole, or twirl myself into knots. It must be thrilling to watch people doing so.

But so what if they had looked sexy, or some of the mixed audience of men and women thought they did? May one not have any form of sex life, or even thoughts, after 65? Perhaps the care home's critics feel slightly sickened at the thought of any link between older people and sex. But on this occasion they needn't have worried. The residents may as well have been watching football, because pole dancing is now provisionally recognised as a sport. One day there may be pole dancing at the Olympics. That's what the International Pole Sports Federation is aiming at.

So the residents were watching a highly skilled sporting activity, to background music of mainly Abba, which they perhaps preferred to Vera Lynn, because, remember, many of the current elderly population were brought up in the time of rock'n'roll, not the second world war. We may prefer the opera. Whatever turns us on.

Sadly, this hasn't sunk in with many of the people that 'care' for us in old age. We're not all the same age, or the same class, we don't have the same tastes, and we're not all thick. We still have our own minds and like to make them up. So if some of us fancy watching pole dancing, then we don't need any condescending stuffed shirts telling us we shouldn't. So thank you, local Dorset pole dancers, and I'm so pleased that you've been invited back to perform again.

This was Guardian *columnist Michele Hanson's last comment piece before she died of a stroke on 2 March 2018.*

28 FEBRUARY

Queer Eye isn't just great fashion TV – it's the best show of the year

HADLEY FREEMAN

'We are living through the golden age of TV. Why isn't there any decent coverage of fashion on it?' Joanna, by email

I grew up as a devoted fan of CNN's *Style with Elsa Klensch*, but after Elsa hung up one of her 10 million Geoffrey Beene jackets in 2001 I pretty much gave up on fashion TV. After all, it so often reduces fashion to the two-dimensional visuals, when the real joy of fashion goes much deeper than that – and I'm not talking about Trinny and Susannah insisting that all Britain's housewives need to cheer themselves up is more colourful V-necks in their cupboards.

Well, colour me wrong, because – at last – a great fashion show has arrived. But this show is about so much more than fashion, as any great fashion show should be. In fact, it is definitely the best TV show to premiere so far this year and one of the most important TV shows for a long, long time. I speak, of course, of Netflix's *Queer Eye*.

'What? A gimmicky reboot of an already gimmicky reality TV show? Important? You've lost your mind, Freeman!' I hear the readers cry as one. I, too, scoffed when I heard about Netflix's revival of the show – yes, scoffed, I said. After all, I hate reality TV and my feelings about the original *Queer Eye for the Straight Guy*, which aired from 2003 to 2007 and was predicated on the stereotype that gay men are stylish and straight men are clueless schlubs, could largely be summed up as 'meh'. Whatever charm the show had came entirely from the personalities of the five gay male presenters.

But the new series is flat-out amazing. Only eight episodes long, I devoured it in two sittings. It takes on everything from Black Lives Matter to loneliness. What it is really about, though, is masculinity and the problems it causes – and it seems to me there is no more important subject on our planet right now.

But this is to make *Queer Eye* sound extremely po-faced, when in fact it is hilarious and fabulous. Like the original show, it features five gay men, AKA the Fab Five, each with his own speciality: interiors designer Bobby, who does the most impressive makeovers on the show; silver-fox fashion expert Tan, who, in his Doncaster accent, is convincing American men one at a time to throw out their combat shorts; the tongue-lollingly gorgeous Karamo, who is there for 'culture', but is essentially the therapist of the show and thus the source of some of its most amazing moments; scene-stealing grooming expert Jonathan, who has an endearing habit of giving exposition by asking a series of questions and answering them himself ('Did I realise this was my moment to shine? 100 per cent. Did I take it? Take a look!'); and 'food and wine' guy Antoni, who can't actually seem to cook. Sure, he will pronounce 'tamale' with a lyrical Spanish accent, but the fanciest meal he makes is hot dogs. Now, there is a fine line between making things easy for the cooking-phobic guests who appear on the show and not being able to cook yourself, but Antoni looks suspiciously like the latter. Put it this way: he is no Ted Allen.

But what is really amazing about this show is its heart. I can't remember the last time I cried at a TV show and I have cried at nearly every damn episode of *Queer Eye*. There was Tom in the first episode, the self-described ugly redneck who wanted to win back his ex-wife, and Cory the cop in episode three, who keeps his late father's old suits in his closet as a way to stay close to him.

But most of all there was AJ, gay and semi-closeted, who wanted to come out and stop dressing like the assistant manager of a sofa store. I have now watched this episode three times and each time I have cried absolute buckets: there is so much emotional truth going on here and not for a second does it feel manipulated. It sums up the excellence of this show: it has political nous, it has heart, it has style and it feels utterly relevant to now. Fashion finally has the TV show it deserves and 2018 has the TV it needs.

Spring

I have prostate cancer.
But I am happy

GEORGE MONBIOT

It came, as these things often do, like a gunshot on a quiet street: shocking and disorienting. In early December, my urine turned brown. The following day I felt feverish and found it hard to pee. I soon realised I had a urinary tract infection. It was unpleasant, but seemed to be no big deal. Now I know that it might have saved my life.

The doctor told me this infection was unusual in a man of my age, and hinted at an underlying condition. So I had a blood test, which revealed that my prostate-specific antigen (PSA) levels were off the scale. An MRI scan and a mortifying biopsy confirmed my suspicions. Prostate cancer: all the smart young men have it this season.

On Monday, I go into surgery. The prostate gland is buried deep in the body, so removing it is a major operation: there are six entry points and it takes four hours. The procedure will hack at the roots of my manhood. Because of the damage that will be caused to the surrounding nerves, there's a high risk of permanent erectile dysfunction. Because the urethra needs to be cut and reattached to the bladder, I will almost certainly suffer urinary incontinence for a few months, and possibly permanently. Because the removal of part of the urethra retracts the penis, it appears to shrink, at least until it can be stretched back into shape.

I was offered a choice: radical surgery or brachytherapy. This means implanting radioactive seeds in the parts of the prostate affected by cancer. Brachytherapy has fewer side effects, and recovery is much faster. But there's a catch. If it fails to eliminate the cancer, there's nothing more that can be done. This treatment sticks the prostate gland to the bowel and bladder, making surgery extremely difficult. Once you've had one dose of radiation, they won't give you another. I was told that the chances of brachytherapy working in my case were between 70 and 80 per cent. The odds were worse, in other words, than playing Russian roulette (which, with one bullet in a six-chambered revolver, gives you 83 per cent). Though I have a tendency to embrace risk, this was not an attractive option.

It would be easy to curse my luck and start to ask, 'Why me?' I have never smoked and hardly drink; I have a ridiculously healthy diet and follow a severe fitness regime. I'm 20 or 30 years younger than most of the men I see in the waiting rooms. In other words, I would have had a lower risk of prostate cancer only if I had been female. And yet ... I am happy. In fact, I'm happier than I was before my diagnosis. How can this be?

The reason is that I've sought to apply the three principles which, I believe, sit at the heart of a good life. The first is the most important: imagine how much worse it could be, rather than how much better.

When you are diagnosed with prostate cancer, your condition is ranked on the Gleason Score, which measures its level of aggression. Mine is graded at seven out of 10. But this doesn't tell me where I stand in general. I needed another index to assess the severity of my condition, so I invented one: the Shitstorm Scale. How does my situation compare to those of people I know, who contend with other medical problems or family tragedies? How does it compare to what might have been, had the cancer not been caught while it was still – apparently – confined to the prostate gland? How does it compare to innumerable other disasters that could have befallen me?

When I completed the exercise, I realised that this bad luck, far from being a cause of woe, is a reminder of how lucky I am. I have the love of my family and friends. I have the support of those with whom I work. I have the NHS. My Shitstorm Score is a mere two out of 10.

The tragedy of our times is that, rather than apply the most useful of English proverbs – 'cheer up, it could be worse' – we are constantly induced to imagine how much better things could be. The rich lists and power lists with which the newspapers are filled, our wall-to-wall celebrity culture, the invidious billions spent on marketing and advertising, create an infrastructure of comparison that ensures we see ourselves as deprived of what others possess. It is a formula for misery.

The second principle is this: change what you can change, accept what you can't. This is not a formula for passivity – I've spent my working life trying to alter outcomes that might have seemed immovable to other people. The theme of my latest book is that political failure is, at heart, a failure of imagination. But sometimes we simply have to accept an obstacle as insuperable. Fatalism in these circumstances is protective. I accept that my lap is in the lap of the gods.

So I will not rage against the morbidity this surgery might cause. I won't find myself following Groucho Marx who, at the age of 81, magnificently lamented: 'I'm going to Iowa to collect an award. Then I'm appearing at Carnegie Hall, it's sold out. Then I'm sailing to France to pick up an honour from the French govern-ment. I'd give it all up for one erection.' And today there's Viagra.

The third principle is this: do not let fear rule your life. Fear hems us in, stops us from thinking clearly, and prevents us from either challenging oppression or engaging calmly with the impersonal fates. When I was told that this operation had an 80 per cent chance of success, my first thought was 'that's roughly the same as one of my kayaking trips. And about twice as good as the chance of emerging from those investigations in West Papua and the Amazon.'

There are, I believe, three steps to overcoming fear: name it, normalise it, socialise it. For too long, cancer has been locked in the drawer labelled Things We Don't Talk About. When we call it the Big C, it becomes, as the term suggests, not smaller, but larger in our minds. He Who Must Not Be Named is diminished by being identified, and diminished further when he becomes a topic of daily conversation.

The super-volunteer Jeanne Chattoe, whom I interviewed recently for another column, reminded me that, just 25 years ago, breast cancer was a taboo subject. Thanks to the amazing advocacy of its victims, this is almost impossible to imagine today. Now we need to do the same for other cancers. Let there be no more terrible secrets.

So I have sought to discuss my prostate cancer as I would discuss any other issue. I make no apologies for subjecting you to the grisly details: the more familiar they become, the less horrifying. In doing so, I socialise my condition. Last month, I discussed the remarkable evidence suggesting that a caring community enhances recovery and reduces mortality. In talking about my cancer with family and friends, I feel the love that I know will get me through this. The old strategy of suffering in silence could not have been more misguided.

I had intended to use this column to urge men to get themselves tested. But since my diagnosis, we've discovered two things. The first is that prostate cancer has overtaken breast cancer to become the third biggest cancer killer in the UK. The second is that the standard assessment (the PSA blood test) is of limited use. As prostate cancer in its early stages is likely to produce no symptoms, it's hard to see what men can do to protect themselves. That urinary tract infection was a remarkably lucky break.

Instead, I urge you to support the efforts led by Prostate Cancer UK to develop a better test. Breast cancer has attracted twice as much money and research as prostate cancer, not because (as the *Daily Mail* suggests) men are the victims of injustice, but because women's advocacy has been so effective. Campaigns such as Men United and the Movember Foundation have sought to bridge this gap, but there's a long way to go. Prostate cancer is discriminatory: for reasons unknown, black men are twice as likely to suffer it as white men. Finding better tests and treatments is a matter of both urgency and equity.

I will ride this out. I will own this disease, but I won't be defined by it: I will not be prostrated by my prostate. I will be gone for a few weeks but when I return, I do solemnly swear I will still be the argumentative old git with whom you are familiar.

14 MARCH

A life in science:
Stephen Hawking

IAN SAMPLE

Stephen Hawking always had something to say. He shook up the world of cosmology with more than 150 papers, dozens of which became renowned. He was told he had only a brief time on Earth, but spent half a century captivating audiences in lecture halls, on TV and in the pages of his books. For newspaper editors, almost any utterance of his could make a headline, and he knew it. Hawking warned about the threats of nuclear war, genetically modified viruses, artificial intelligence and marauding aliens.

He pronounced on the human condition and once dismissed the role of God in creating the universe. The statement caused a fuss, as the denial of invisible superbeings still can in the 21st century.

It is an unwritten law of nature that when a personality steps into the foreground, their work must take a step back. In Hawking's case, being the most famous scientist of our time had a mysterious ability to eclipse his actual achievements. At his best Hawking was spectacular: he made intuitive leaps that will keep scientists busy for decades.

It began with Albert Einstein. Where Isaac Newton had thought gravity was an attraction borne by the fields of massive objects, Einstein said mass curved space itself. By his reckoning, the planets of the solar system circled the sun not because of some unseen force, but simply because they followed the curvature of space. The late US physicist John Wheeler once summarised the theory with characteristic simplicity: 'Matter tells space how to curve; space tells matter how to move.'

Einstein's formulation of gravity, set forth a century ago in the general theory of relativity, raised an exotic and somewhat unsettling possibility: that a truly massive object, such as an enormous star, could collapse under its own gravity, and would then become a speck of infinite density called a singularity. The gravitational pull of these weird cosmic dots would be so intense that not even light could escape them.

The idea that singularities were real and lurked in the darkness of space was not taken terribly seriously at first. But that changed in the 1950s and 60s, when a clutch of papers found that singularities – now known as black holes, a term coined by Wheeler – were not only plausible but inevitable in the universe.

This led to a surge in fascination with the objects that coincided with Hawking's arrival as a PhD student at Cambridge University.

Hawking was never one to think small. His goal was a complete understanding of the universe. So while others pondered the creation of black holes in space, Hawking applied the same thinking to the cosmos itself. He joined forces with Roger Penrose, the Oxford mathematician, and showed that if you played time backwards and rewound the story of the universe, the opening scene was a singularity. It meant that the universe, with all of its warming stars and turning planets, including Earth with all its lives, loves and heartbreaks, came from a dot far smaller than this full stop.

Even before they worked together, Penrose got a flavour of Hawking's sharp mind. Penrose had delivered a lecture on the big bang and Hawking, nearly a decade his junior, was in the audience. 'I remember him asking some very awkward questions at the end,' Penrose said. 'He obviously knew the weak points in what I was saying. It was clear he was someone to contend with.'

Hawking went back to black holes for his next act. Although the matter at the heart of a black hole is compacted into an infinitesimal point, black holes spin and have a 'size' that depends on the amount of mass that falls into them. The greater the mass, the larger they are, and the farther out the so-called event horizon, the point where light falling into the black hole cannot come out. A supermassive black hole such as the one at the centre of the Milky Way captures light from as far away as 12.5 million kilometres. If the Earth, at a mere six billion trillion tonnes, were compressed into a singularity, the resulting black hole would measure less than 2cm wide.

In the late 1970s, Hawking declared that a black hole could only ever get bigger. The maths behind the claim was strikingly similar to the equation that underpins one of the fundamental laws of nature – that entropy, a measure of disorder, can also only increase. When one physicist, Jacob Bekenstein, declared that the similarity was no coincidence, and that the area of a black hole was actually a measure of its entropy, Hawking and many other physicists balked. For a black hole to have entropy, it must be hot and radiate heat. But as everyone knows, nothing can escape a black hole, not even radiation. Or can it?

When Hawking set out to prove Bekenstein wrong, he made the most spectacular discovery of his career. Black holes did have a temperature, they did radiate heat – later known as Hawking radiation – and they could therefore shrink with time. As he remarked some time later: 'Black holes ain't so black.' It meant that, given enough time, a black hole would simply evaporate out of existence. For a typical black hole, that time is longer than the age of the universe. However, mini black holes, which are smaller than atoms, would be more dynamic, releasing heat with ferocious intensity until they finally explode with the energy of a million one megaton hydrogen bombs.

Hawking's revelation shocked cosmologists, and the claim threw up a fresh and thorny problem that became known as the black hole information paradox. As Hawking himself realised, if black holes simply evaporated, then all of the information they held from infalling stars, planets and clouds of cosmic dust could be lost for ever. It might not make for sleepless nights for most people, but most people are not theoretical physicists. The loss of information from the universe would contradict a basic rule of quantum mechanics. Hawking argued, nevertheless, that black holes destroyed information, while other physicists vehemently disagreed. In 1997, one of them, John Preskill at the California Institute of Technology, accepted a bet on the subject from Hawking. To the winner was promised an encyclopaedia of his choosing.

Marika Taylor, a former student of Hawking's and now professor of theoretical physics at Southampton University, says that while the information paradox remains a paradox today, most physicists now believe that information is not destroyed in black holes. The answer may lie in the principles of holography, the process of capturing a 3D image on a two-dimensional sheet. When applied to black holes, the holographic principle shows that the event horizon can keep an audit of whatever falls inside. How it does so is unclear, but according to the theory, it retains a kind of imprint of the information. 'Many people think that, effectively, the black hole event horizon itself behaves like a giant computer hard disk,' Taylor said. 'When the black hole evaporates into radiation, the information will be carefully encoded in the radiation that comes out.'

Hawking conceded his bet in 2004 and handed Preskill a copy of *Total Baseball: The Ultimate Baseball Encyclopedia*. But even as he admitted defeat, Hawking was convinced the information released by a black hole would be mangled and impossible to read. To make the point, Hawking quipped that he should have burned the encyclopaedia and given Preskill the ashes.

To settle the matter once and for all, scientists need to detect Hawking radiation as it streams from a black hole and read the information it carries. But that is a fanciful idea. 'We'd have to sit for millions or even billions of years to see this,' said Taylor. A more realistic hope is that subtle features of black holes may leave their mark on the gravitational waves that physicists can now detect with instruments such as Ligo, the US laser interferometer gravitational-wave observatory.

Hawking was, of course, far more than just a physicist. The stratospheric success of *A Brief History of Time* was driven by a blend of charisma, good writing, a profound theme and an excellent title. It put hard physics in the hands of millions, and even if millions did not finish the book, it changed the world. 'If you look at the popular science press in physics, it looks totally different from 30 years ago,' said Sabine Hossenfelder, a research fellow at the Frankfurt Institute for Advanced Studies. 'Everybody wants to know about black holes. People talk about the big bang over dinner. And Hawking has played a large role in this.' Hossenfelder read *A Brief History of Time* before she became a teenager. 'I hated it because I didn't understand anything,' she said. 'And it's the reason I'm a physicist today, because I thought I have to understand it.'

For Max Tegmark, a physics professor at MIT, Hawking was one of the most influential scientists of all time. The two worked together to raise publicity over the threat of nuclear war and the potential pitfalls of artificial intelligence. He was a person who wasn't afraid to think about the big questions, Tegmark said. Having been told he would die young, Hawking pushed for actions that would ensure humanity did not. He thought we should 'stop rolling the dice', Tegmark said, and 'plan ahead, to take advantage of this incredible cosmic opportunity we have'.

Hawking took opportunities whenever they arose, and his legacy will be richer for it. 'When you think of the impact that Albert Einstein, Isaac Newton and others have had, it's mainly in the past,' Tegmark said. 'But when you think of the impact of Stephen Hawking, it's clearly mostly in the future still. Stephen is going to be guiding our research for years to come.'

Stephen Hawking, 8 January 1942 – 14 March 2018.

23 MARCH

The people owned the web, tech giants stole it. This is how we take it back

JONATHAN FREEDLAND

I blame the T-shirts. The casual wear favoured by those founding wunderkinds of tech – Mark Zuckerberg, Steve Jobs, Sergey Brin, Larry Page and the rest – lulled us into a false sense of security. Even after they'd begun making serious money, too many of us took the aversion to a collar and tie to mean the likes of Facebook or Google were not really scary capitalist behemoths, but retained the spirit of the upstart startup: quirky, plucky and driven chiefly by a desire to do cool stuff with computers. They certainly saw themselves that way, Google charmingly distilling its mission statement into three words: 'Don't be evil.' It's amazing how long an initial image of laid-back informality can endure: for decades, Britons struggled to see Virgin as a corporate giant because Richard Branson had long hair and a goatee.

In truth, it wasn't just the look. The apparent idealism of the enterprise also encouraged consumers to give the tech goliaths the benefit of the doubt. In its infancy, the internet was hailed as a harbinger of equality and liberty. The new gospel held that 'information wants to be free' – free from censorship and free of charge. A new techno-utopia seemed at hand. Or, as Zuckerberg defined his company's purpose: 'Facebook gives people the power to share and make the world more open and connected.'

Those words leave a bitter taste now, after Carole Cadwalladr's ground-shaking revelation that Cambridge Analytica had helped itself to the Facebook data of 50 million users. But it was not so long ago that the internet, and specifically social media, were seen as forces that might transform the world for good, harming the powerful and strengthening the weak.

A crucial example is provided in *War in 140 Characters: How Social Media is Reshaping Conflict in the Twenty-first Century*, an insightful, richly reported book by David Patrikarakos. A correspondent who has covered several recent conflicts, he was struck by the emergence of what he calls *Homo digitalis*, the lone individual who, armed with nothing more than a smartphone, is able to shape global perceptions of the battle fought around them. He shows how a 16-year-old Gazan, Farah Baker, used a Twitter account to give real-time reports on the daily bombardments that came in the summer of 2014, steadily building up a vast international audience and leaving the mighty Israel Defence Forces playing catch-up. In the age of social media, he writes, even the most powerful 'states can win the physical battle on the ground but lose the political war'.

There are countless examples, from the Egyptian teenagers who used Facebook to rally protesters to Tahrir Square, eventually toppling the Mubarak regime, to the British blogger who methodically proved Russia had supplied the weapon that brought down Malaysian Airlines flight MH17 over Ukraine, leaving Moscow's denials in tatters. The asymmetry in each case was vast – and yet the weaker party won.

Thanks to social media, the internet had apparently decentralised power. In the old days, information was passed down from the mountain top – by a government, say, or a news organisation – to the crowd below. Now the crowd could speak to each other and to the world. At least one aspect of the techno-utopians' early hopes seemed to have materialised.

And it's that hope that Cambridge Analytica has shattered. For what we now understand is that those at the top, the political parties or governments that could afford it, have been engaged in a radical act of recentralising power. They saw the way social media was working, empowering individuals and networks of individuals, and they decided to grab those same weapons for themselves.

You can see why they were tempted, for our digital footprint is extraordinarily revealing. Witness the model built by researchers at Stanford and Cambridge that, simply by looking at your Facebook 'likes', can assess your personality with a startling degree of accuracy. It takes just 10 'likes' for the computer to know you better than your work colleagues. Give the machine 150 likes and it can predict you more accurately than your parents or siblings. Give it 300 and it knows you better than your spouse. No wonder the Trump campaign and so many others were ready to hand over big money to Cambridge Analytica. This week I met Hossein Derakhshan, a true *Homo digitalis* once known as Iran's 'blogfather', whose activities earned him six years in prison. 'Predictability is control,' he told me, recalling the hold his jailers had over him. Once you can predict someone's actions and reactions, you can control them.

Which is why the Cambridge Analytica/Facebook revelations are so significant. They represent an attempt to reverse the internet's previous upending of power, to restore the traditional imbalance between the ruled and their rulers. What Cambridge Analytica promised its clients was a return to the old form of media distribution, with those at the top sending their message to the crowd below. Except this time, that message would be disguised as if it were the organic word of the crowd itself, spread virally from one person to another, with no traces or fingerprints left by those at the top. As a Cambridge Analytica executive said, unwittingly caught on film: 'We just put information into the bloodstream of the internet and then watch it grow ... it's unat-tributable, untrackable.'

The hypocrisy is obvious. Here was the supposedly populist movement of Trump taking a tool that once empowered ordinary people and handing it back to the politicians, allowing them to manipulate voters and exploit their fears. Patrikarakos is not surprised. Digitally speaking, the 21st century 'belongs to the illiberals', he says. The technology is available to anyone, but it's Moscow that dares fund a troll factory, the Internet Research Agency in St Petersburg, pumping out lies and hate. London or Washington would not make so egregious a move, either because they'd regard it as a violation of their democratic norms or because they'd fear exposure, depending on your degree of cynicism. But the Kremlin bows to no such constraint.

Many shed their turn-of-the-century illusions about the internet years ago. And there will be more disenchantment to come. It can't be only political campaigners who used the likes of Cambridge Analytica to pickpocket our personal data; surely we'll learn soon of the major corporations that similarly played on our online hopes and fears to sell us stuff. But we don't have to have the full picture to know that we have to act. It could be regulation; it could be anti-trust legislation to break up those tech giants that act as virtual monopolies. I like Derakhshan's idea of obliging Facebook and others to open up a marketplace of algorithms: if you don't like the current social media preference for popularity (retweets) and novelty ('latest'), you should be free to choose a different algorithm that acts on different values.

This is not – yet – a lost cause. There are success stories, with the collectively curated Wikipedia perhaps the best example. But it will mean discarding our 00s-era naiveté. The tech companies are greedy corporations that need to be tamed – even if the boss came to work on a skateboard and is still wearing a damn T-shirt.

24 March

Time for change: Ireland's abortion referendum

ANNE ENRIGHT

Recently I spoke to a reasonable, sane Irish woman who said that she was against abortion and, because she was so reasonable and sane, I was curious what she meant by that. Was she against the morning-after pill? Certainly not. What about chemical abortifacients? They did not really worry her too much. So, what about terminations before 12 or 13 weeks, the time when women are often given the all clear to confirm their pregnancy to family and friends? This woman was not, all things considered, against terminations during this window, when pregnancy is not considered medically certain. She was also, just to make clear, in favour of abortion in cases of fatal foetal abnormality, rape and incest. In 1983 this woman might have voted 'against abortion', despite the fact that she is not against abortion, especially if it happens during those weeks when the natural loss of an embryo is called miscarriage. She just found abortion, in general, hard to vote 'for'. Had there been no referendum in 1983 – where people with a range of uncertainties were asked for a single 'yes' or 'no' – then limited abortion might well be available now in Ireland, in the way that the morning-after pill is legally available and widely used.

The 1983 referendum was a little like the Brexit referendum – a population voting about something that seemed, on one side, clear and, on the other, contingent and hard to describe. As it turned out, the language problem worked both ways. In order to bring the issue to a vote, a new legal term had to be minted,

one that did not appear in any previous laws. The eighth amendment to the Irish constitution acknowledges the right to life of
'the unborn' and this seemed to invent a new category of rights-
holder, possibly a new kind of person. By acknowledging the
'equal right to life of the mother' an impregnated woman was
changed from a human being into a relationship, that of mother-
hood, and a peculiar equivalence established. Pregnancy was a
binary state, in which two souls temporarily shared the same
blood supply. The question of who had it first was neither here
nor there and a fertilised egg was a grown adult, temporarily
inconvenienced by being a few hundred cells large.

In 2016, there were 63,897 live births in Ireland. The medical
estimate, according to the American College of Obstetricians
and Gynecologists, is that up to a quarter of pregnancies end in
miscarriage, which means that around 20,000 conceptions could
have failed in Ireland last year due to natural causes. If all life is
sacred, then all life did not get the memo.

The pro-life view is taken more from theology than biology.
Its supporters in Ireland did not foresee, or did not care about,
the medical consequences of their unnatural view – the decisions
gone wrong, the danger to the life of the impregnated woman,
such as the case of Savita Halappanavar who died of septic shock
in a Galway hospital, when a miscarriage could not be treated
until the foetal heartbeat stopped.

They did not care about the psychological consequences, and
the cruelty of that indifference was hard, as a society, to live with.
Arguments about suicide (how to believe her?), about rape (how
to believe her?) reinforced the fact that 'a mother' could not be in
charge of herself, because she had no self in the way we usually
understand the word – this was set aside, for the duration. Once
impregnated, a woman was reduced to a body, and that body was
no longer hers. On the one side we have miracle, on the other, meat.

In March 2014, a refugee Ms Y arrived in Ireland and discovered that she was pregnant as the result of multiple rapes in her country of origin. She had no passport or papers and was turned back at a British port, when she tried to travel there for a termination. Back in Ireland and suicidal, she was told she could be detained under mental health legislation, and she agreed to stay in a maternity hospital instead. There, she went on hunger strike, until delivered by caesarean at 30 weeks. In the years since 1983 we have learned that there is no answer to the question: 'How much suffering is too much suffering?' The question is irrelevant because the psychology of the mother is irrelevant, as are social or practical concerns.

Unlike Ms Y, most women are not confined to Ireland and many make the decision to travel to Britain to avail themselves of abortion services there. This is not so much an Irish solution (pretend it isn't happening) as a middle-class one. It depends on people having literacy skills, credit cards, supportive parents if needs be, an amount of spare cash. It is not a solution for people in denial about what has happened to them – the woman who doesn't want it to be true; the couple who took a chance; the woman who has other issues, who has enough going on, who is depressed, or poor, who has three children already and no time. The girl impregnated by her stepfather, or her uncle, or her father, or by any man who has power over her, or over the people who might help her. The woman unsure of her visa. The woman who is alone, or feels herself to be suddenly and overwhelmingly alone, just now.

Conservative figures from the charity Rape Crisis reveal that 3,265 Irish women went to Britain to procure abortions in 2016. This was down more than 50 per cent from a high of 6,673 in 2001. The biggest shift happened among women in their 20s (those born after the referendum of 1983), with numbers declining more than 60 per cent, from 4,089 to 1,563. Figures may be disputed in this fiercely debated topic, but there is no doubting a significant reduction over the same years in which the general population rose by nearly 25 per cent. A more open and secular society has not resulted in more abortion, but less.

Pro-life campaigners don't seem to trust people much, though in my experience people do the best they can. They talk as though floodgates were about to burst open, as though women are naturally opposed to the rights of 'the unborn'. But having children is a complicated business, it is not a war. Many children are conceived by accident, or in a state of doubt, and their mothers bring them – half in dread, half in hope – into the world. Other babies are born after long months of their mother's anguish and incomprehension that her body should be so used – and after her body, her life.

The referendum on abortion was held in 1983, when contraception was also illegal in Ireland. Can you imagine how freaked out that made everyone I grew up with about sex? Do it once, and everything changes. Perhaps this informs the way pro-lifers think about mothers in general, perhaps even their own – that she is always trapped; that we must be saved from her rage, her sense of life's unfairness, her murderous intent.

There is an overlap of nine months, when the smaller life depends on the bigger, and not the other way around. This is just true. If a foetus dies, the body surrounding it does not die, or not usually. The mother's life is the more powerful thing. This is very frightening, when you think about it. So, yes, women are very frightening, despite their almost universal willingness to please people, to smile and be nice.

The pro-life movement controlled the terms of the debate in Ireland, so it remained a religious discussion in which all conceptions are fully realised, as opposed to potential, human beings. This is something you either believe or you don't, but it is difficult to get outside their language, which has the weight of culture behind it. So I want to suggest two small shifts in the words we use. The first is to replace the word 'pregnant' with 'impregnated', to restore a sense of causality to a condition that is sometimes seen as self-enclosed. The other is to swap out the phrase 'unwanted pregnancy' with its echoes of unwanted gifts, or what used to be called 'unwanted advances' or 'attentions' (now called harassment), and to use the more radical 'pregnancy without consent'.

Sex without consent is a terrible thing, we are all agreed on that. We understand the horror of rape – to have someone inside you for 30 seconds, or 10 minutes, to enter your body without your joyful invitation, this is known to be a terrible violation, a trauma from which it is hard to heal. We see the power dynamic here. We imagine, or remember, the pain inflicted and the pleasure taken, and we condemn the act absolutely. But this sense of drama – of a battle of wills – is also a distraction from an ethical argument that might be made about your body: who gets to use it, and on what terms.

If a conceived embryo is already, and instantly, a full human being, this raises questions about what human beings can do to each other, and why. This is not the way I usually think – my thoughts about abortion are always uncertain and, I hope, slow to judge – but if you want an absolute argument about all this, then here it is. What right does another human being have to be inside your body for the best part of a year, to make their way out of your private parts in a bloody, difficult and painful way, and then turn to you for nourishment, not to mention love – perhaps for the rest of your life?

In the nine months' occupation that is a pregnancy, the embryo has no agency, it doesn't mean to be there, and no intention to cause harm. But an absence of intention does not confer any rights. Just because someone does not mean to use you does not give them the right to use you. The fact that an embryo cannot ask for consent does not mean that consent must be given. An embryo takes no pleasure from its presence in your body, but this does not give it ownership of your body any more than a grown man has ownership over your body's interior. The hidden fact in the eighth amendment is that the term 'unborn' does not mean 'human being' as the mother is a human being – if it did then the mother's rights might also be asserted. The 'unborn' here is code for 'biology', 'happenstance' or 'life itself'.

It may be argued that when a woman consents to unprotected sex she is also consenting to carry any resulting pregnancy to term, but I do not know if you can make an agreement with someone who does not yet exist. The hidden power, in this contract-with-no-one, lies not with the physically powerless embryo, or the legally powerless pregnant woman; it lies with the father, or with the father-as-state, who asserts control, from a sometimes indifferent distance, over both.

This argument may sound slightly absurd, not to mention harsh, but it is exactly as harsh and as absurd as the eighth amendment to the Irish constitution, which is widely understood without making any sense.

In 2016, people in Britain and the US voted for the tribal and the symbolic when they went for Brexit and for Trump. We know something about all this in Ireland because we had a tribal, symbolic vote in 1983. We saw the cruelty of that symbolic choice play out in our hospitals, and airports, and in our lives for more than 30 years. We know how debilitating it is to argue with the religious right and how wounding it is to face down their trolls.

If we, in Ireland, can repeal the eighth amendment, that shift will echo around the world. It will be heard in El Salvador, where women have been imprisoned for the natural loss of their babies, it will be heard in those Australian states where abortion is both available and illegal at the same time, it will be heard in Poland where 30,000 people marched against the further restriction of abortion laws, and won. It will be heard in the US, where state by state the rights conferred by Roe v Wade are being whittled away to the especial detriment of poor women; women who own little or nothing, not even the body in which they walk around.

The message it will send is not just about women's right to choose, it is about how countries work. Democracies must also be allowed to change.

4 April

Good times! How fashion got happy (and what it says about the world)

JESS CARTNER-MORLEY

Outselling all competition on River Island's website over a record-breakingly wet Easter bank holiday weekend was a £16.99 T-shirt that reads: 'It's All Good'. Meanwhile, over at J Crew, if you missed out on last season's 'UP BEAT' slogan tee, seen on several New York fashion-week showgoers, you can now buy one that reads 'ON THE BRIGHT SIDE'.

At Topshop, the top which reads 'You Make Me :)' is sold out in all sizes, and the long-sleeve tee with 'Be Happy' written above rainbow stripes is now only available in a size four, but you can cheer yourself up with an alternative that just reads 'Good Vibes'.

T-shirts with positive slogans are the new T-shirts with random French words on them. Except it is more than that. It is not just that happiness has overtaken feminism and French as the T-shirt aesthetic of the season; it's that the emotional tone of fashion has warmed up by several notches. Even Victoria Beckham, who more or less built a personality cult around her superhuman ability to refrain from the slightest mouth-twitch of a smile in public, modelled a T-shirt from her new collection that reads 'A Dark But Happy Place' to launch her latest Victoria, Victoria Beckham collection at Mark's Club in Mayfair a month ago. 'I wear sunglasses a lot so it's always dark in my world, but I'm happy really,' she said.

Smiles are replacing pouts in the images selling clothes, because the optics of online retail are ever more inspired by the aesthetic of social media influencers – who tend to go for a warm, approachable vibe – rather than trying to ape cover-girl chill. (Also, when the Asos T-shirt says 'Smile', the sell makes more sense if the woman wearing the garment is doing exactly that.) The visuals for the streetwear collaboration between Champion and Harley Viera-Newton, which will go on sale at Urban Outfitters this spring, show gaptoothed model-of-the-moment Slick Woods beaming in her cherry-print hoodie.

This is a seismic shift. Being borderline morose has been the only possible way to look hip for generations. On the front row, being cool, jaded, unimpressed and generally completely over it, expressing said attitude with an icy stare, a rigid no-smiling policy and layers of black, has gradually shifted towards expressing unguarded enthusiasm via selfie-taking and wearing colour. (Brights do tend to look better on the street-style blogs.) On the catwalk at London fashion week, rainbow stripes were the across-the-board standout motif, from Burberry's block-colour puffa to the sequin layer-cake dresses at JW Anderson and joyous diagonal stripes of Fyodor Golan.

The dopamine dressing that began last year with the yellow dress trend sparked by the film *La La Land* has stepped up a gear, with clothes that remind us in the most literal way possible that one day the rain will stop and the sun will come out. The real world doesn't show any signs of getting less problematic, but fashion is determined to look on the bright side. This is not how it is supposed to work. Fashion is supposed to reflect the world we live in. When the economy slumps and the geopolitical picture is dark, accepted wisdom is that hemlines will dip and the colour palette will contract. We will quit peacocking around and dress either to cocoon or armour ourselves. For fashion to take it upon itself to bring the positivity at such a moment is something of a turn-up for the books.

This can be seen as pure escapism, rainbows being as far beyond our grasp as those other pop cultural motifs of the moment, unicorns and mermaids. Perhaps these fashion choices represent us regressing into imaginative play – like children, or like the characters in Steven Spielberg's new film *Ready Player One*, who take refuge from the dystopian reality of 2045 in a virtual world called the Oasis.

But when fashion leans towards a cheeriness that challenges rather than reflects the zeitgeist, it flags up some interesting precedents. The exception to the rule that dark times mean dark clothes is that, when revolution is brewing, rebellious spirit sometimes shows up in what is worn on the streets before it bubbles over into actions.

For example: in the years immediately preceding the French revolution, the dire economic conditions in Paris were at odds with a trend for impractically high heels worn by both men and women. These became more and more vertiginous right up until Bastille Day, after which they disappeared from French fashion for several decades. Perhaps we will look back at this summer's rainbow T-shirts as a crucial staging post in the emergence of the resistance. OK, maybe not. But it is possible, surely, that fashion's refusal to have its vibe crushed by world events is part of a ground-level shift towards activism, or at the very least a rejection of defeatism as the only course of action. It's not just clothes. Rainbows are happening in food, as well as fashion. This spring's hot guilty-pleasure foodie pop-up, Grill My Cheese at Selfridges, is serving an eminently Insta-grammable rainbow toastie with stripes of beetroot, rocket and caramelised onion melted into goat's cheese.

Meanwhile, the rainbow layer cake has graduated from Insta-gram fantasy and is available off-the-shelf – complete with a unicorn horn fashioned from royal icing – in M&S. There is nothing more cheering than cake, and there is nothing more happy-making than a rainbow. Let them eat rainbow cake? Wait. What happened after that?

5 MAY

No Cinderella: the real Meghan Markle

MARGO JEFFERSON

In February I saw a photo of Meghan Markle and the Duchess of Cambridge sitting next to each other at the Royal Foundation Forum, wearing colour-coordinated dresses (lavender for Kate, deep purple-blue for Meghan). It wasn't their dresses I minded, it was how they sat – legs crossed neatly at the ankle, knees pressed firmly together. It was that *dulce et decorum* pose passed down to generations of girls and young women expected to demonstrate their good breeding on social occasions – expected to show they are 'ladies'. Both Kate and Meghan had folded their hands in their laps, the arms forming a gentle circle, the hands quietly clasped, as if ready to shelter a child or calm a kingdom's cares. But it was the legs that haunted me – in part because I'd been taught that same bit of etiquette when I was a young black midwestern girl in the 1950s and early 60s, a child of the manners- and achievement-conscious black bourgeoisie, which in those days we called the Negro elite.

In fact, things turned out better than I'd feared. In a subsequent photo Kate crossed her legs at the knee. And when both women were asked in the video about the causes they planned to take up, Meghan spoke out. The words 'MeToo' and 'Time's Up' flowed from her lips. So did the words 'I fundamentally disagree', as in: 'What's interesting is ... when speaking about girls' and women's empowerment you'll often hear people say: "Well, you're helping women find their voices," and I fundamentally disagree with that. Women don't need to find a voice, they have a voice, and they need to feel empowered to use it, and people need to be encouraged to listen.'

Rachel Meghan Markle, for those who have chosen or somehow managed to miss the ceaseless chronicling of her life thus far, is the only daughter of Thomas Markle (white), an Emmy award-winning cinematographer and lighting designer, and Doria Ragland (black), a social worker and yoga instructor who focuses on community mental health. This union of white Hollywood and black social-spiritual activism made her the offspring of a modern and ever more varied biracial bourgeoisie.

The family settled in Woodland Hills, a prosperous Los Angeles neighbourhood. Prosperous and largely white: Meghan's mother was regularly mistaken for her nanny there. This must have happened in the 1980s and early 90s when she was a young girl; it still happens in the US to every black woman I know who has a mixed-race child.

Meghan's parents divorced when she was six, and she lived with her mother after that, although she saw her father regularly. There are two half-siblings from his previous marriage, both quite a bit older. Relations with them, at least since the courtship and engagement, have been strained.

Markle majored in international relations and theatre at Northwestern University, Illinois. Besides becoming an actor, she became a feminist who worked for UN Women as an advocate for political participation and leadership. Yes, she has been praised and criticised as 'outspoken', but her style never risks being 'aggressive' or 'combative', or any of the other words thrown at women who are deemed insufficiently graceful when they disagree with men. Even when she makes staunch political statements, her manner astutely – sometimes cloyingly – balances the forthright and the pleasing. She's learned to use political maxims and assertions very effectively. As in: 'It's time to focus less on glass slippers and more on glass ceilings.' With the word 'fairytale' now a ubiquitous tag line for the royal romance, this should be a useful daily mantra.

The *Cinderella* story refuses to dwindle into a period piece; in the last 20 years alone there have been six film remakes with white, black and Latina leads. But Markle has not been plucked from poverty or – like the heroines of such romcom adaptations as *Pretty Woman* and *Maid in Manhattan* – from the low-status toil and trouble of working-class life. Her net worth as an actor has been estimated at around $5 million. An actor's fortunes can fluctuate, especially when that actor is a woman. But so can the fortunes of a wife. If the royal marriage were to end in divorce, Markle would not have to depend on the Windsor millions or, like many once-upon-a-time celebrities, design a skincare or jewellery line for QVC.

Love that results in the bride's near-magical social ascent is the key element in *Cinderella* tales. But is Markle automatically marrying up by marrying a prince? In the old-school way, yes: any 'commoner' who marries into any royal family is seen as marrying up. But Harry is marrying up too. He's marrying up by marrying out – out of long-entwined bloodlines, out of entrenched rituals and hierarchies, out of a lineage as constricted as it is privileged. We always ascribe social ambitions to commoners, but aristocrats have their own longings for a world elsewhere. Harry is marrying into all the possibilities of postmodernity. It's a world where – as Zora Neale Hurston said of black folk tales and music – hierarchies, styles, sites of social and cultural change are being made and forgotten every day.

In this world-elsewhere that is here and now, Markle's identities as a progressive biracial and black feminist are impeccable. When speaking of her role on TV series *Suits*, as the biracial lawyer with a black father, she said: 'Some households may never have had a black person in their house as a guest, or someone biracial. Well, now there are a lot of us on your TV and in your home with you.' And now there are even a few of us in the castles you see on TV.

Today the House of Windsor is like a venerable and all-too-predictable fashion house. Its cultural currency depends on history packaged as costume drama: *The Queen*, *The Crown*, *The King's Speech*, *Darkest Hour*. To flourish it must attract new designers, new ideas and new muses. Perhaps a better genre through which to read the complexities of the Meghan–Harry narrative is the romantic comedy. In the best romcoms, attraction is ignited by tension and difference. Thwarted too. The characters have to learn something from each other and something about themselves; negotiate across troublesome boundaries (gender and class privilege, temperament), and learn to take emotional risks.

For this union, Harry has had to renounce his protected status as a vivaciously shallow party boy whose transgressions took the form of booze-fuelled pranks, such as showing up at a friend's birthday party in a Nazi desert uniform with a swastika armband (the party's theme was 'colonial and native'), or hosting a game of strip poker in a Las Vegas hotel room. Reformation followed in three stages, each appealing to a different constituency. He served in Afghanistan. He recently confessed to emotional and mental health problems that began soon after his mother's death: a shutdown of feelings, bouts of rage and anxiety followed by psychological counselling.

Finally, there came his involvement with Markle. A professional woman, an educated woman, a 36-year-old divorced American woman, a woman of colour and a feminist whose presence in his life would soon require that he forcefully denounce racism and sexism in the British press (and, I trust, among his more un-woke friends and relations). 'I've never wanted to be a lady who lunches – I've always wanted to be a woman who works,' Markle once said. In show business she worked her way up. She didn't become a Hollywood superstar; she did become a skilled, well-paid lead in a highly rated TV series. She had a social conscience, which she acted on. And now, she is more famous and more influential than she was ever likely to be on her own. It remains the way of the world. Does Amal Clooney have more resources as a human rights lawyer and philanthropist now that she is married to George Clooney? No doubt.

Whatever we think of her new job requirements, Markle will remain a working woman with a lifetime of public performances ahead. Once a woman enters a royal family, every aspect and function of her body becomes a site of proprietary fantasy. The female body as a nation's procreative destiny: the only real change through the centuries is that fantasy has replaced realpolitik. For Diana Spencer, that meant her uncle certifying her virgin status in a tabloid newspaper interview shortly after her engagement to Charles. As if his niece's body parts were a bride price to be flaunted, eliciting leers and cheers.

For Markle, it means media warnings that she is 36 years old and shouldn't wait much longer. 'Meghan, Oh Baby! Meghan and Harry Planning a Honeymoon Knock-Up' went one headline. 'Meghan Markle Looks Gorgeous With Naturally Curly Hair in Childhood.' The published photo was charming, as is the video of her at 11, with a curly frizzy ponytail, chastising the ad industry for its sexism. Many of us used to ask if we'd ever see Michelle Obama in an updated version of the afro she wore in her pre-public figure days. Many of us used to answer that the furore it would cause – the afro as proof of the first lady's secret allegiance to white-hating black militants – probably wasn't worth the gesture. And since a small dust-up followed Meghan's recent appearance in a bun with wavy tendrils around her face, it's hard, alas, to imagine how anything, including the claim of biographer Andrew Morton that she is a direct descendant of Robert the Bruce, would atone for a full display of those racially marked curly/wavy/frizzy locks.

But if she never wears her version of a natural, she has already done race history a real service. She has helped scuttle false, foolish constructs of 'the mulatto' that were developed a few centuries ago to counter the very real threat that mixed-race people posed to the constructs of white supremacy. To serve popular culture, the female mulatto became a source of social and erotic intrigue, a figure who needed strict narrative policing. A key theme in these stories is the heroine's terror that, if she marries her white hero, she might bear a child whose skin colour would reveal the dreaded racial truth. I imagine there's plenty of spiteful, behind-the-scenes chatter about whether this 'touch of the tarbrush' will taint Meghan and Harry's offspring. Perhaps the 'blackamoor' brooch that Princess Michael of Kent was photographed wearing on her way to a royal event with Harry and Meghan was meant to signify such a dread: Meghan as the black ewe tupped by a white ram, who will produce a shamefully black offspring.

Still, to watch a divorced, interracial couple walk the royal red carpet has its own rewards when, once upon a time just 51 years ago, US law forbade their marriage.

In 2015 Markle wrote an essay for *Elle* in which she quite eloquently established that she is both biracial and black. She started with the blunt racial slurs of her childhood, which turned, as she grew, into the patronising queries and assumptions favoured by adults who think themselves liberal. A perfect example was the teacher who told her to fill in 'white' on a census because 'that's how you look, Meghan'. Intended as a compliment, no doubt. In the essay, she also discussed the institutional racism exposed by the police shootings in Ferguson and Baltimore. She recalled the flurry of racist tweets set off when Wendell Pierce was cast as her African American father on *Suits*: 'Ew, she's black? I used to think she was hot.' Then, having described both her struggles with, and her pride in, being biracial, she ended the essay with a tribute to her black ancestry.

'You create the identity you want for yourself, just as my ancestors did when they were given their freedom. Because in 1865 (which is so shatteringly recent), when slavery was abolished in the United States, former slaves had to choose a name. A surname, to be exact. Perhaps the closest thing to connecting me to my ever-complex family tree, my longing to know where I come from, and the commonality that links me to my bloodline, is the choice that my great-great-great-grandfather made to start anew. He chose the last name Wisdom. He drew his own box.' Excellently done, I thought. She's refusing to let white readers white out her black identity.

When it comes to issues of race, gender, sexuality and class, how much can Meghan Markle say and do? How much does she want to say and do? We simply don't know yet. Like any black and biracial woman, she has had a lifetime of learning to both confront and dextrously navigate codes that range from the puzzling to the vehemently punitive. Like every actress she's had to confront misogyny. But she has options that previous generations did not.

10 MAY

The Gender Recognition Act is controversial – can a path to common ground be found?

GABY HINSLIFF

They came in a steady stream, picking their way across a garden in central Oxford to the Quaker meeting room beyond. A crowd of largely middle-aged women, the sort you would find at any literary festival or school open evening; friends exchanging kisses, a baby squawking in a pushchair. Only the chanting protesters outside gave the game away. For this was a meeting called by the feminist organisation Woman's Place to discuss potential changes in the law on gender recognition, and that meant tension in the air.

At a recent meeting in Bristol, masked activists tried to stop speakers entering the building. In Cardiff, the venue cancelled the women's booking after threats were made. Last month, a trans activist called Tara Wolf was convicted of assaulting Maria Maclachlan, a 61-year-old feminist, during a protest at Speaker's Corner in Hyde Park where Maclachlan was filming trans activists.

Oxford's student-led protest went more peacefully, but some attendees were evidently shaken enough to leave by a back door afterwards; others were thrown at being on the sharp end of an equality demo. 'I'm usually the protester,' said one woman, emerging from the scrum. But this issue turns old certainties on their head.

Woman's Place formed last autumn out of a conversation 'literally around a kitchen table', according to teacher and co-founder Philipa Harvey, between a group of friends – trade unionists, academics, lawyers and others – worried that they had nowhere to debate freely. They wanted to discuss the potential implications for women and girls of sharing single-sex spaces – from domestic violence refuges and female prisons to swimming pool changing rooms and Brownie packs – with male-bodied people, and to explore what they see as the risk of predatory non-trans men finding a way to abuse such access to reach vulnerable women. They wanted to discuss bodies and biology without being told that mentioning vaginas excludes women who don't have them. And they suspected other women also had questions they weren't asking, for fear of being called transphobic. 'There are people who will say nothing about this in their workplaces, because their jobs are on the line; in social situations people won't talk about it,' says Harvey. 'But there is a change in the law being proposed and it will impact women. Women have a right to ask: "What will the impact look like for my daily life?"'

These are women who feel silenced, erased and intimidated – and yet it is clear that many trans women do, too.

'It is held against me that "you were raised with male privilege", but actually I was beaten up all the time for being effeminate,' says Clara Barker, a trans scientist at the University of Oxford, who also leads voluntary work with LGBT young people. 'Because I was trans I was severely depressed, I was bullied in my workplace, so it's like, "What privilege is that?"'

She considered going to the meeting after an invite from speaker Nicola Williams, an activist with the gender-critical pressure group Fair Play for Women (the pair met debating each other on TV). But she was afraid of encountering in real life the abuse she experiences online, where jeers about how trans women are really men jostle with threats to bash 'terfs' (trans exclusionary radical feminists, a derogatory term for women questioning trans rights). While the trans movement has its dark side, also hovering on the outer fringes of the gender-critical camp are a handful of men with far-right associations, attracted by a perceived fight against political correctness.

'I want to be able to engage, even if sometimes I'm going to hear things I don't like. I'm perfectly willing to listen to the other side,' says Barker. 'But it's got to be balanced, it's got to be reasoned. I tried to make a couple of comments [on Twitter] just to see if it was possible to find common ground and the truth is, it wasn't.'

Yet beyond the shouting, the beginning of a more nuanced debate is discernible; one involving trans women who crave equality but not at vulnerable women's expense, feminists with divided loyalties, and people wanting more than toxic Facebook slanging matches.

'There is a difference between social media debate and the conversations going on elsewhere,' says Sophie Walker, leader of the Women's Equality Party, who was torn apart over her party's trans-inclusive stance in one notable Mumsnet webchat, but is now more optimistic about the chances of reaching some consensus. 'I am encouraged by the number of women who have contacted me privately to say they want to find common ground.' Both Woman's Place and trans activists led by Stonewall have given well-received briefings to Labour MPs in recent months.

Six days after the Oxford meeting, meanwhile, 300 Labour party members reportedly quit in protest at trans women standing for parliament on all-women shortlists, exposing a split within the left that feels more generational than ideological; woke millennials versus older women who fear hard-won victories being eroded. This isn't just about politics. It's about what it means to be a woman, born or made, and feel dismissed. The story began in January 2016, when the new Commons equalities select committee – chaired by the Conservatives' former equalities secretary Maria Miller – made its Westminster debut with a report it didn't expect to be enormously controversial, on reforms to the law governing gender recognition.

The 2004 Gender Recognition Act (GRA) lets adults officially register a change to the gender assigned at birth. They don't necessarily have to undergo surgery, but must provide psychiatric assessments and proof of living for two years in the gender they wish to be officially recognised, a process activists see as intrusive and overly medicalised. Miller's committee broadly agreed, recommending instead a system of self-identification where changing gender was as simple as signing a form. Similar arrangements now exist in Portugal, Ireland, Malta, Belgium, Norway and Denmark, and activists insist there is no evidence of anyone abusing them for sinister purposes, although the numbers involved are relatively small so far (it is estimated up to 1 per cent of Britons may be trans, although there are no official statistics). An Irish government review of how the system is working there, due this autumn, is hotly awaited.

Shifting to self-identification doesn't, by itself, automatically mean trans women being treated in all circumstances as if they had been born female. Irish trans women may, for example, still be jailed in male prisons.

But crucially, the Miller committee's report also backed the curbing of exemptions in the 2010 Equalities Act, which currently allow trans people to be barred from certain jobs and services if necessary to protect other users – the loophole covering sensitive areas such as women's refuges. And that's where alarm bells started ringing. It was discrimination law, not the recognition process, that came under scrutiny in Canada after serial sex attacker Christopher Hambrook attacked two women in domestic violence shelters in Toronto, which he'd entered dressed as a woman. (The state of Ontario had previously passed a bill prohibiting discrimination against trans people.)

Significantly, when the then equalities secretary Justine Greening announced a consultation on simplifying the gender-recognition process last July, she did not take up the call to rewrite equality law. Women's shelters in the UK can still legally turn people away following risk assessments – including women who were born female if, for example, they have a history of offending that might endanger others. 'People always say, "Well, anyone could just say they're a victim of domestic violence", but to get into a refuge, we'll sit and talk to you for ages. There are all sorts of assessments to undergo,' says the Labour MP Jess Phillips, who sat on Miller's committee and has previously worked for Women's Aid.

What worries many gender-critical feminists is that organisations are having to make difficult choices in a climate where any deviation from the principle that 'trans women are women' causes a backlash. Advertisers have been lobbied to withdraw from the parenting site Mumsnet, after its anonymised message boards became a haven for gender-critical feminist debate. Topshop hurriedly introduced gender-neutral changing rooms after being publicly accused of transphobia by a customer barred from the women's cubicles. As trans activists pointed out, you may have been trying on clothes next to trans women for years without realising; it's just official now, meaning teenagers no longer risk public humiliation just to buy a T-shirt.

But what bothers opponents is the idea of changes such as these happening without women's consent. 'Small businesses can't afford to use the exemptions and big companies don't want to, because they don't want to be seen as anti-trans,' says Williams. 'We've got the law and there is good reason why it's there, but the law doesn't mean anything if nobody's using it. Everyone's too scared of getting it wrong.'

Trans men have flown largely beneath the radar of this debate, presumably because men don't feel threatened by sharing changing rooms with potentially female-bodied people. The exception, however, is trans boys. The Oxford meeting also heard from Stephanie Davies-Arai, of the pressure group Transgender Trend, who questions why most transitioning teenagers now referred to London's specialist Tavistock clinic were born girls when the reverse used to be true: could some have deeper reasons for questioning their gender? (Referrals to the Tavistock, the only NHS gender-identity clinic, rocketed from 97 cases in 2009 to almost 2,600 by the end of last year, and 70 per cent were born female.)

It's a furiously contested issue, but as a child, Williams says she might have been 'very attracted' to the idea of transitioning. 'It took me a long time to come to terms with the fact that I was a lesbian. I went through feeling uncomfortable with my gender as a woman because I didn't like being a woman. I didn't really fit, I didn't feel very good at being a woman. I think that's a path lots of lesbians have to tread, and now I'm proud to be a lesbian woman. But if someone said to me, "Actually you could be a boy if you wanted", I'd have found that amazing.'

However, any suggestion of children being rushed into transitioning, with its echo of 1990s arguments about homosexuality supposedly being 'promoted' in schools, is bitterly contested by those working with young people. 'It is 12 months before you see a gender doctor, probably 12 months of counselling after that,' says Barker. 'All the kids I see are saying: "It's been three years, when am I going to get hormones?"'

Her own hunch, meanwhile, is that the disparities in girls and boys transitioning themselves may even out in later life: 'Young boys still have the emphasis on toxic masculinity, which means they won't be able to admit they're trans until they're older. It's about being able to come to terms with yourself at an early age.' And that's a lifetime's work for some.

Sitting in the Oxford audience was physics teacher Debbie Hayton, one of the few trans women to have spoken from a Woman's Place's platform. While she agrees the GRA is too bureaucratic, she prefers the security of having a formal diagnosis and surgery to self-identification. 'As a trans person, I don't want my rights or protections to be based on feelings, because people don't believe it. They may tolerate it. But it takes away my credibility as a trans person.' As for all-women shortlists, Hayton says, 'hell would freeze over before I'd go on one, because I was socialised as a boy and I have those advantages still'.

Such views aren't necessarily popular among trans activists, and Hayton has been accused of being 'self-hating'. Yet in a movement focused on giving everyone the freedom to define themselves as they choose, it seems odd to deny her the same leeway.

For Hayton, sex is a biological fact; she describes herself as 'male, and I prefer people to relate to me as if I were female'. But in an ideal world, free of all stereotypes, what she would have liked is to present as a feminine man. 'This is really difficult to explain but by asking to be treated by society in the same way that they would treat a woman, I feel more comfortable,' she says. 'I transitioned because I couldn't cope with the way society was treating me as a man, the expectations it placed on me, and the restrictions. The problem is, as a teacher, if I express myself completely as non-gendered, I couldn't get on with the job. If somebody comes in saying: "I'm not a woman or a man", then every time I did a new class, you would have to go through that with them, when what you really want to be doing is teaching them.' Transition was, for her, a pragmatic if not ideal solution to a complex issue.

Channel 4 has been exploring the idea that gender identity is a spectrum – stretching from non-binary (identifying with neither gender), to trans, to gay, to a dizzying number of other possibilities, and that finding the right place on it can be complicated – in its reality miniseries *Genderquake* this week. The programme features 11 young people with different gender identities sharing a house for a month. While an ensuing studio debate between activists, including the trans model Munroe Bergdorf and feminist icon Germaine Greer, descended into chaotic scenes and aggressive audience heckling, the reality show struck a markedly different tone; by the end the housemates had clearly bonded, and in some cases, minds had been changed. Could it be that opinions in real life are less entrenched than public debate suggests?

The solutions to some points of conflict are likely, as Jess Phillips says, to be 'very, very practical'. While the Oxford meeting heard poignant stories about schoolgirls feeling unsafe sharing gender-neutral toilets with boys (ironically, the meeting's venue had unisex toilets), sealed cubicles, locks and other design features may go a long way to avoid any anticipated friction.

But finding common ground elsewhere may be trickier, unless both sides can overcome their fear of the other. After deciding not to go to the Woman's Place meeting, Barker ended up hovering a few yards down the street from the protest, ready to intervene if the chanting students from her university overstepped the mark. 'I felt for the people who obviously looked nervous going in, because I understand that,' she says. 'Those were the sort of people that I would love to sit down and have a chat with.' Perhaps it's not too late.

22 MAY

Patrick Melrose captures heroin addiction perfectly – it brought my memories flooding back

JOHN CRACE

I never flew on Concorde. I seldom dared leave London during my 20s. I was never sexually abused by my father. (I somehow managed to hate myself enough without being forced to endure that horror.) I never shot up heroin in the penthouse suite of a flash, New York hotel. I shot up heroin in grubby bedrooms and the back of cars.

But to concentrate on the differences between Patrick Melrose and me is to commit a major category error. Edward St Aubyn's five semi-autobiographical novels contain some of the most viscerally accurate depictions ever written of what it means – and how it feels – to be an addict. And watching them come to life in the virtuoso performance by Benedict Cumberbatch in the new TV drama has brought the memories flooding back. In just a few hours of television, superbly scripted by David Nicholls, the checklist has been near-enough complete.

It starts with the obsession. Nothing can be allowed to get between addicts and their drugs. I never set out to be an addict. Like many others, I thought I would be the exception that proved the rule – the person who beat the system. It would be me who controlled the drugs and not the other way round. As Patrick would say: 'Some hope.'

I often took drugs that I didn't even particularly like. Drugs such as coke and speed, which made me feel far too awake, and dope, which just made me feel stupid. I took them because they were there. Anything was preferable to being me. It sometimes felt as if I was a guinea pig in my own pharmacological experiment as I tried to calibrate the platonic ideal of absence.

The first time I took heroin was like coming home. For some people I knew, heroin was the final taboo. They would smoke dope and take coke, but draw the line at smack. Not me. I actively sought it out as if we were long-lost blood brothers. As if I had always known all the other drugs I had taken had been merely a build-up to the main event. My feelings of inadequacy and despair gave way to a warm embrace. No one and nothing could get to me.

I was invulnerable. I was me and not me. I was an outside observer delivering a running commentary on myself: Patrick's voiceover narration in the TV drama of a weekend he spends in New York collecting his father's ashes is no mere stylistic device holding the drama together. It's a powerful depiction of his dissociated state.

With heroin, the world had been refashioned in my own disconnected image. Every time I took it thereafter was a desperate attempt to recreate that first experience; a longing that met with ever-decreasing success. Before long, I was taking heroin just to feel normal. Or the closest approximation to normal that I could manage.

The drama captures the relentlessness. One of the striking features of Patrick Melrose is just how much everything revolves around drugs. Most of the first hour-long episode was taken up with Patrick buying drugs, coming off drugs or taking drugs. Patrick's ability to score in a foreign city in the early 1980s is impressive. I seldom left London in that era because I needed to maintain an umbilical link to my supply of drugs. And, even then, days could pass with me standing around outside phone boxes or sitting in a dealer's house. Just waiting. And waiting.

In many film and literary depictions of using, the drugs are often relegated to an incidental role because the nature of addiction is so profoundly boring. Here, they get pride of place, centre stage. For a heroin addict, it's the living that's incidental.

That's the way it is. Being a heroin addict is a full-time occupation. A deadly dull one at that. One without glamour. The first thing I did when I woke up in the morning was take some smack. The rest of the day would have a familiar rhythm: taking more drugs, trying to find some money to buy more drugs, waiting for the dealer to be in. The years I wasted hanging around, buying more drugs and taking more drugs. Only once that was all sorted could the rest of my life be fitted in. Friends came and went. Crap jobs came and went. It was a question of priorities.

Patrick Melrose captures the denial. The belief that no one else knows what a mess you are; that when they look at you, they see a person who knows what they are doing. This is one of the more perverse strands of arrogance. Patrick expects to be indulged. It doesn't occur to him that there is anything abnormal about being discovered by the concierge crawling along the hotel corridor on Quaaludes or opening his door naked to a valet. And if reality does briefly intrude, such as when Patrick is brushed off by a friend of his girlfriend, then it is instantly rebuffed with more heroin. Safety in powders.

Self-deception is an integral part of the addict's armoury. You intellectually understand that you are a junky and yet somehow convince yourself you're a different order of junky to those around you – a superior junky. Someone who could go straight if they really wanted to, but now just doesn't happen to be the right time. Tomorrow is always a better time to go cold turkey than today.

The chaos of the addict's life frequently descends into near-farce, something the addict chooses to wear as a badge of heroic pride – and Patrick Melrose has that comedy. I managed to miss almost all of my own wedding reception by holing up in a toilet with a dealer who, for the first time ever, was showering me with free smack. Patrick's weekend in New York is laced with humour as he picks up his father's ashes: he ends up being directed to the wrong body in the morgue, where he is greeted by enthusiastic mourners. But, beneath the comedy, there is pathos. Today, I just feel sad that I was absent on what should have been one of the most significant and happiest days of my life.

Patrick describes his life as one of 'ungovernable shame and violence'. And it's the shame that's the big one here: the violence is just collateral damage. Shame is the one that gets you every time, because deep down you know how worthless you are. You know that every day is another testament to your failure. And there is nothing you can do to stop it. Your anger turns in on yourself as the days turn into weeks turn into months turn into years. The self-destruction gets steadily worse. You end up doing all sorts of things you'd promised yourself you would never do and somehow you find a way to normalise them.

Until you can't. My own rock bottom came on my 30th birthday after nearly 10 years of addiction. I was holed up in a flat with a large bag of heroin, surrounded by the small handful of friends who had stood by me, and I'd never felt so miserable. I had obliterated a third of my life and had failed at almost everything. After that, I started overdosing regularly. Not because I desperately wanted to die, but because I wasn't that bothered if I stayed alive.

Edward/Patrick and I are the lucky ones; those who found recovery. A friend and my wife together persuaded me to get help, and I found, to my surprise, that I wanted to live more than I wanted to die. I went into rehab on 9 March 1987 and have been clean ever since. And, yes, I am still counting the days.

Many of the people I knew haven't been so fortunate. Some died while I was using. Some got clean and then relapsed and died. Some found the pain of living without drugs just too much and killed themselves. Others died of Aids and hepatitis C. The rate of deaths from cancer and heart disease has been far higher in those I knew who were addicts than those who weren't. At times it has felt attritional. The body count on my timeline is terrifyingly high.

The Patrick Melrose books get to the heart of the addict's condition. Even in recovery, St Aubyn never soft-soaps or descends to saccharine Hollywood endings. He tells it like it is. The blood, the dirty hits, the overdoses, the casual violence and the banality. No one gets off scot-free from heroin addiction. Yes, I'm unbelievably grateful for the second chance I have been given. I have a family I adore and of whom I am enormously proud. I have my dream job. Life in many ways could not be more sweet.

But there is a price. Edward/Patrick can speak for themselves, but here's my story. I have severe depression and anxiety. I have been in hospital with mental illness. I am still driven by the same feelings of inadequacy I had as a teenager. Futility and despair are still my default settings in life. I just choose not to use on them. It is not always easy. Most days, I still feel less than those around me. I still wake up feeling as if I have failed. I still find it hard to feel the love of those around me. I just know that taking drugs isn't the answer. So I plod on. One foot after another. One day at a time.

26 May

Philip Roth: 'the kind of satirical genius that comes along once in a generation'

MARTIN AMIS

Portnoy's Complaint (1969) was my introduction to Philip Roth. I read it in the first edition of the paperback, and I thought: here we have a really deafening new voice, and a whole new way of being funny – transgressive, corrosive, but with something ecstatic in its comedy.

Then I worked my way through the three predecessors: *Goodbye, Columbus*, *Letting Go*, and *When She Was Good*. They were engaging and diverting; they made you think, they made you smile, often, but they didn't make you laugh. Ah, I thought, he's what Saul Bellow calls 'an exuberance hoarder', restrained by High Seriousness and, in his case, restrained by an exaggerated reverence for Henry James. *Portnoy* was his real 'letting go'; now the comic energies will surely surge and swell.

It didn't work out that way. In fact, Roth's early career is one of the strangest in American letters. A writer's life is not as detached and monastic as some would like to think; and novelists, in particular, are unmistakably in the world. And what did the world make of *Portnoy*? It was critically acclaimed (it wasn't just a *succès de scandale*), and it outsold Mario Puzo's *The Godfather*. It also became a part of the national conversation – with talk-show one-liners zeroing in, of course, on chronic self-abuse (Barbra Streisand remarked that she would like to meet Roth 'but wouldn't want to shake his hand'). What would Henry James have said to that?

Roth reacted with reliable perversity: he wrote, or dashed off, three comic novels that were almost neurotically unfunny – *Our Gang* (featuring 'Trick E. Nixon'), *The Breast*, and *The Great American Novel* (400 highly facetious pages about baseball). Something other than the sensation caused by *Portnoy*, it seemed, was threatening his equilibrium.

All was explained in *My Life as a Man* (1974). Roth had spent the years 1959–63 writhing around in a nightmare marriage, the result of a weirdly reciprocal folly. She entrapped him (a low ruse with a pregnancy test), and he entrapped himself, magnetised by difficulty, complication, and the crew-necked earnestness of his (academic) milieu. 'Literature got me into this,' he wrote in *My Life*, 'and literature is gonna have to get me out.' The dud comic trio was his retaliation against literary values, and against High Seriousness.

But now he settled down. *My Life* inaugurated a long series of autobiographical novels (the Zuckerman books), culminating in what is called the American Trilogy (1997–2000): *American Pastoral*, *I Married a Communist*, and *The Human Stain* – a vast work of almost Victorian narrative richness. Along the way there were other triumphs: *The Counterlife* (the only postmodern masterpiece apart from DeLillo's *White Noise*), and *Sabbath's Theater* (which I found rebarbative, but it is loved by many, female as well as male). Around the turn of the century Roth retreated into sparer utterance (the late novellas), and eventually a dignified and equable silence.

Writers of genuine originality are always divisive. Roth alienated not just the occasional reader but entire communities, reviled, first, by world Jewry, and later by world feminism. This choric hostility was in both cases essentially socio-cultural, and not literary. You can understand the historical uneasiness, but world Jewry got it wrong about Roth, a proud Jew as well as a proud American. And the feminist objection is impetuously sweeping; it detects no distance between Roth and his (often deplorable) narrators. Besides, if you outlaw misogyny as a subject, then you outlaw *King Lear*, and much else.

My subjective impression is that *Portnoy's Complaint* is still the diamond in the crown. Here the Jewish-American novel is narrowed down to one idea: gentile girls, shiksas ('detested things'), where ancient laws of purity come up against American womanhood, and the inevitability of material America. In *Portnoy* all the great themes are there (all except mortality): fathers, mothers, children, the male libido, suffering, and Israel. Roth torches this bonfire with the kind of satirical genius that comes along, if we're lucky, perhaps once in every generation.

Philip Roth, 19 March 1933 – 22 May 2018.

29 MAY

The writer Katharine Whitehorn would rather die than live like this

POLLY TOYNBEE

This is a terrible thing to write – but I know that the old Katharine Whitehorn, the wittily honest *Observer* writer, would not have flinched. That's what her two loving sons say and they want it written the way she would have. Her friends and former colleagues have been told, yet it may appal some lifelong admirers to have it said out loud. But her ability to confront hard truths and break old ideas of decorum is the reason so many read her for decades. With her usual no-nonsense rationality, she wrote with fearless clarity on the end of life.

Katharine is now 90, living in a care home, suffering from Alzheimer's, with little understanding left, no knowledge of where she is or why. She often doesn't recognise people, can no longer read and curiously sometimes talks in French, not a language she knew particularly well: she will never read or understand this article. In other words, she is not herself. Her old self would not recognise herself in this other being who sits in the care home dayroom. What or who she has become is a difficult philosophical question, but she is no longer Katharine Whitehorn as was.

Pause here to celebrate the real Katharine, the breaker of conventions with pioneering humorous columns about everyday life. Now standard fare, her *Observer* column delivered an electric shock to women's pages of the 1960s, then filled with woollies, jellies and the etiquette of hats and gloves. Her 1963 praise of 'sluts' – slovenly women, nothing to do with sex – made her famous for asking, 'Have you ever taken anything out of the dirty-clothes basket because it had become, relatively, the cleaner thing?' Frankness about untidy lives was her hallmark. After joining the *Picture Post* in 1956, she wrote as a single woman in London; her *Cooking in a Bedsitter* remained in print for more than 40 years.

When I started out on the *Observer* in 1968 as a junior on its miscellaneous Pendennis column, she was a megastar columnist, 20 years older than me, culturally and politically of another generation in another firmament. Though unswervingly for women, she never quite belonged to the feminist waves that followed her. Her warm insight into women's actual lives – married to difficult men, coping, juggling – cast a caustic eye on mundane details and great questions alike.

Her sons say without doubt that if the real Katharine could see herself now she would be horrified, never having wanted to end up as she is. Indeed, most people find the prospect of this ending a negation of self, denial of a life's work and character, a mortifying indignity no one should suffer. Who wants to leave family and friends with a final memory of themselves as a vegetable, a distortion, an alien being?

But even those who think carefully about how they definitely don't want to end up find that rational plans, made in good health, usually slip away during a step-by-step medical decline, no longer in sound enough mind. Too late to say stop. St Joseph, the patron saint of the good death, deliver us from this evil – though it's the religious, with their 26 bishops and other believers in parliament, who have repeatedly prevented us from gaining the right to die in dignity, despite years of overwhelming public support for this final freedom.

Katharine wrote often of this, so we know what she thinks – or thought when she could still think. Ten years ago she reported for the *Guardian* on Oregon's right to die laws with strong approval – except she thought only allowing the terminally ill to choose death didn't go far enough. 'Oregon at least shows the way forward for dealing with a problem that is not brought about by too little health care, but almost by too much – by our ability to keep people alive long after they would once have served their term.' In a YouTube interview you can see her airing that view.

In 2013 she wrote a column headlined 'What the Death of My Cat Taught Me About Assisted Dying', asking why it's cruel to keep a sick and suffering pet alive, but not a human. She complained that the current endless debate on assisted suicide would 'limit it to people who are pretty certain to die in a short time anyway. If it were me, I would dread, far more than suffering just weeks before the end, the prospect of being incapacitated ... Nobody insists that a cat has to be within weeks of death before we let it go; surely we should not deny release to humans with nothing but wretchedness ahead.' She ends, 'How I wish one could wear a poison ring, as featured in Jacobean dramas, and refuse ever to be parted from it. No assistance would ever be necessary.'

But that mystic ring that, with one magic touch, one kiss, sends its victims to instant death is denied to us. The dying are forced to stay when they long for the end: my mother dying in pain asked the doctor acerbically, 'Where's Dr Shipman when you want him?' Not there, no easeful death. No doubt the law will change, by slow degrees, allowing a slight hastening of death to those with imminent terminal diagnoses. But the greatest horror of all is Katharine Whitehorn's fate, not dying, yet dead to all that makes life worth living.

If there is value in an existence living only in the minute, a mind with no yesterday, and no tomorrow beyond the next meal, that's not an existence she valued. And surely the real Katharine Whitehorn, the one in her right mind, is custodian of herself, arbiter of what or who is her real self and when to discard an empty husk? (And no, this personal custodianship has no bearing on the rights of disabled people.)

Yet that's denied to her, through no one's fault. She wrote a living will, which her sons say demand she not be officiously kept alive beyond her wits. Yet there she sits, in a state she strove to avoid. She is on no life-sustaining medication that could be withdrawn: a body can long outlast its mind. She has survived cancer. Her sons say if she ever suffered pneumonia – once called 'old man's friend' – they would obey her and tell doctors to withhold antibiotics. Until then, she sits in God's waiting room, surely a wicked God to wipe out all that makes a person who they are, without taking their life.

How many times have I sat with friends, promising one another that we won't let this happen to us. Yes, we'll find the pills to do the deed, find the willing purveyor on the dark web. (No, none of us knows how to access the dark web.) We will know the right day, just before losing our minds. But that's a comforting delusion. Chances are, we will not be in charge of our fate. Under current tyrannical law, a living will can't save us from dementia. Mostly, Katharine Whitehorn is placid, but in rare flashes of depressed lucidity, her sons say she asks for it to end, to stop now.

Summer

Does 'peak prosecco' spell the end of bubbly slogan tees and fizzy crisps?

LUCY MANGAN

Though I speak, as both my friends will attest, as an unparalleled fan of the stuff, I find myself crumpling with relief at the news that we appear to be hitting peak prosecco. Although nearly 36 million gallons were sold in the past 12 months of the cheaper, pretty-much-as-tasty and certainly-as-effective alternative to champagne that has come to dominate parties, supermarket aisles and the luxury wine market over the past decade, this represents a much smaller increase in sales than any year since 2011; just 5 per cent, when producers have been used to bubbly double-digit growth.

My relief stems from the hope that – while we will remain awash with the effervescent elixir itself – we may start to see the end of the surrounding merchandise. It has been getting ridiculous. You can't move – especially if you've had a few – for the things.

On Etsy, Notonthehighstreet and any other creatively unsupervised site, tote bags and T-shirts proclaiming your penchant abound. As golf is the spoiling of a good walk, so are slogans the ruination of innumerable perfectly fine tops. 'But first prosecco' is at least admirably succinct – and as good a philosophy as any to sport across your chest if sport across your chest a philosophy you must. But even if you squint at it through a third glass, 'Be there in a prosecco' barely makes the cut as legitimate wordplay.

Gym gear announcing 'Push ups + prosecco' is too cavalier an approach to health and safety for my taste, and alternatives reading 'No pain, no prosecco' are wrong on 17 levels.

I own a T-shirt that reads 'Espresso then prosecco'. I don't know how. I wear it, too. This is the way the world ends.

And yet, the clothes are not the worst of it. Oliver Bonas sells a 'Prosecco pong' game (it's like beer pong, but the glasses are posher and you play it with – you may be ahead of me here – prosecco) for £15 and a prosecco lip balm (£6, reduced – further fuel for my peak marching hopes to £4). I got one for Christmas. It tasted of despair.

You can buy customisable clocks and choose the hour whose numeral should be replaced with the rib-tickling legend 'Prosecco o'clock'. You can buy a doormat on whose unforgiving coir is writ 'Come in if you have prosecco', though within the reader-visitor's mind this is most likely to translate as 'Go home and drink to forget'.

And finally, you can buy prosecco crisps. Yes. Last Christmas Marks & Spencer sold prosecco-flavoured crisps scattered with edible gold stars. I ate them in my T-shirt, through my lip balm and tears. They were tangy, like a grownup Skip. I would buy them again, and this is why I drink.

1 JUNE

The refugees who gave up on Britain

KATE LYONS

On a drizzly afternoon in February, Philip Kelly made the short drive from his home near the centre of Derby to a street in

Normanton, one of the poorer areas of the city. He stopped at one of the terraced houses owned by G4S, which has a government contract to provide housing to asylum seekers in the region. The upstairs flat was occupied by Said Ghullam Norzai, an asylum seeker from Afghanistan, and his 11-year-old son, Wali Khan.

Kelly knocked on the door, but there was no answer. The police showed up; they had been contacted by Wali Khan's school and asked to check up on the boy after he had failed to attend. When they entered the house it was clear: Said and his son had vanished. Almost two years after smuggling themselves into the UK in the back of a lorry from Calais – and just seven weeks before an asylum appeal hearing that might have allowed him to stay and work legally in the UK, Said had smuggled himself and his son back out of Britain.

Said had arrived in the UK in May 2016, after a long, terrible journey from Kunduz province in Afghanistan. It took him almost a year, during which he was separated from his wife and their other children. More than a million people arrived in Europe by sea in 2015, of whom 50 per cent were estimated to be Syrians and 20 per cent Afghans.

A farmer and a family man, Said struggled with his new life in Derby. Here he was in an industrial city thousands of miles from home, confronting a world of bureaucracy in which his life was defined by Home Office letters, solicitors' meetings, healthcare forms and strict school pick-up times. 'I'm a simple man. I'm not educated,' he would often say, with a shrug.

Kelly first met Said and his son in the summer of 2016, when he knocked on their door to deliver a welcome box containing clothing, toiletries and toys – part of his work as a volunteer 'befriender' for a charity called Upbeat Communities. Since that first meeting, Kelly, a middle-aged engineer, had been their primary support in Derby.

Said came to rely heavily on Kelly, who took him to doctors' appointments and meetings with a solicitor to discuss his asylum claim. When Said, who is illiterate in English and his native Pashto, received post, Kelly would take Said into town to visit Aslam, an Afghan-British shop-owner, who would translate it.

It was thanks to Kelly that Wali Khan was enrolled in the local primary school. Said received a list of schools when he arrived in Derby, but did not understand the enrolment process. When Kelly visited one day and found the boy at home with his father, he scrambled, calling round local schools until he found one that had a free place.

Dates are not Said's strong suit. He has only a rough idea of his and his children's ages, but he believes he set off from Afghanistan in September 2015. He left home with his wife and their seven children – then aged somewhere between one and 15.

According to the account he later gave to the Home Office, Said fled his home in the Chardara district of Kunduz province because he was being harassed by the Taliban, whose power was growing in the area. They had been coming to his village in the middle of the night and shooting at people. One night they visited Said's home. They threatened him, smashing up his property and demanding that he spy on government forces for them. 'My children were frightened and said, take us away from here,' he said during his asylum interview. 'Our province has no security. There is no peace. My home was destroyed. Everything is destroyed.'

As for so many who have made that perilous voyage to Europe, Said's journey was unthinkably difficult. He and his family were among a group of about 100 people who had paid smugglers to take them across the mountainous border between Iran and Turkey when unseen attackers began firing on them. As the shooting started, Said was holding Wali Khan's hand, and they ran and hid together. But when they emerged, there was no sign of the rest of the family. The smugglers said they had gone on ahead, and they needed to keep moving.

Said and Wali Khan made it to Turkey, where Said thought he would be reunited with the rest of his family, but again he could not find them. He has had no word of his wife and six other children since.

Not long afterwards, Said and Wali Khan crossed the Mediterranean in an inflatable boat. (In October 2015, around the time of their journey, 221,000 people made that same perilous sea voyage, more than in any other month that year.) Eventually, after walking across Europe, through countries whose names Said does not remember, and then spending six months in the migrant camp at Calais, he and Wali Khan stowed away in the back of a lorry and arrived in the UK in May 2016.

When I first visited Said in Derby in February last year, to make a film about him and his son for a *Guardian* project called 'The new arrivals', he had not seen his family for more than a year. 'When my son comes home at night, he asks me: "Where is my mum, my brother and sisters?" If I had known I was going to lose them, I would never have left,' he said.

Said had been convinced that once he reached the UK, his problems would be over. Britain would give him papers, and help him find his family. He thought the battle had been to get here. He did not realise what kind of battle would be involved in trying to stay.

The process of becoming a refugee in the UK goes like this: after someone arrives in the UK (or someone already in the UK learns it would be dangerous for them to return home), they present themselves to the authorities and ask for asylum. At this point, they are classed as an 'asylum seeker': they are not officially a refugee until their asylum claim is successful. To obtain refugee status, you must lay out your claim in two separate interviews with the

Home Office. Said unwittingly created problems for himself from the outset. At the screening interview – a brief session designed to collect biographical data and the basic outline of someone's claim for asylum – Wali Khan told the Home Office he was nine years old. Since he and Said did not know their birthdays, they were assigned a birthdate of 1 January – like all asylum seekers who do not know their date of birth. (The producer and interpreter I worked with on this project, Shoaib Sharifi, who is British-Afghan, estimates that 80 per cent of Afghans in the UK, including himself, have that same birthday.)

This invented birthday meant Wali Khan was officially nine and a half when he arrived. Liz Clegg, a former firefighter who spent two years living in Calais and got to know Wali Khan and his father there, is convinced he was only seven or eight at the oldest when he arrived in the UK. This confusion would have led to Wali Khan being put in the wrong year at school – and moreover, Clegg said, such an apparently cavalier attitude to dates and years is likely to have been regarded by the Home Office as deliberate falsehood.

Said and Wali Khan were sent to live in a hostel in Birmingham, and then eventually to the flat in Derby. Asylum seekers who have no means of supporting themselves – roughly half of them – are provided with accommodation and a weekly allowance (at that time, £36.95 per person; it was increased by 80p to £37.75 in February this year) while they wait to hear about their asylum claim. During this time they are not allowed to work.

The next step in the asylum process is the 'substantive interview', which is conducted by a Home Office caseworker. This is an asylum seeker's main chance to lay out the reasons they should be granted asylum. Said's substantive interview took place in Birmingham on 10 November 2016, four and a half months after he arrived in the country. It took four hours. And it was a disaster.

It is hard to overstate the importance of the substantive interview. Because most asylum seekers are not able to bring documentary evidence proving the danger in their homeland, their claim is often decided based on how believable their story is. Just 32 per cent of initial asylum claims decided in the UK in 2017 resulted in someone being granted refugee status or another type of protection visa. Of all the initial refusals that went to appeal, 35 per cent were overturned by a judge. In cases involving people from Afghanistan, it was 52 per cent.

Though asylum seekers are entitled to a legal aid solicitor to help them with their case, Said went to his Home Office interview without ever having seen one. When I asked him why, he said he didn't know.

Said's interview transcript shows that he answered questions about the threats made to him by the Taliban – which might have helped him qualify for protection under the 1951 refugee convention – in an almost perfunctory way, though the Home Office interviewer repeatedly tried to get more information from him. Instead, Said dwelt on a feud he had with another individual in Kunduz. His responses were confused and hard to follow. Crucially, he did not fully explain discrepancies between his replies to that day's questions and what he had said in his screening interview five months earlier.

Liz Clegg told me that the 'erratic' state of Said's interview should have been a warning sign to the authorities that he was a vulnerable adult with mental health issues, rather than a liar. Leonie Hirst, a barrister who specialises in human rights and deportation cases, said that an asylum seeker who has been through traumatic events and may have PTSD 'is going to find it very difficult to give an account that is rational, coherent; what you get is a disjointed account. Trauma makes it difficult for people to tell their experience in a linear way, and that's often something relied on by the Home Office to determine credibility.'

Said's asylum claim was, unsurprisingly, rejected.

Said's case is not a Home Office horror story: his caseworker was not incompetent or insensitive during his interview, and his case was dealt with in a timely manner. But what his case does show is that the asylum system requires someone to be at the top of their game to navigate it. Said – illiterate, traumatised, grief-stricken – was thrown into a bewildering system and floundered. It was only because he had two dogged, passionate advocates in Liz Clegg and Philip Kelly that he got his appeal in, that he found a solicitor, and that he even made it to his substantive interview in the first place.

Last June, I visited Said and Wali Khan and shared an evening meal with them as Said broke his Ramadan fast. Every other time I had visited, Said had been dressed in western clothing, but today he wore a shalwar kameez of loose, khaki cotton and a red velvet cap.

Ramadan is traditionally a time when the community comes together: people visit one another, often dropping in unannounced. Iftar meals – eaten when the sun has set, which on that day, painfully for Said, was not until 9.35pm – are bountiful and social. But Said and Wali Khan had been marking the season alone. 'When a refugee or a poor person is upset, where can he go to celebrate?' said Said. It is too painful, he said, to be with others, because he was consumed with thoughts of his missing family. 'I'm alone, plus I'm living with the uncertainty of my family. Not just alone, but missing my loved ones.'

Said had been given an appeal date for August, but that would later be adjourned twice – rescheduled first for December, and then, just days before that hearing, adjourned again to 6 April this year. At this point it had been almost two years since he had been separated from his family. He couldn't understand why the process of securing refugee status – and with it the travel documentation that would allow him to go looking for his wife and other children – was moving so slowly.

'I have a sense of hopelessness. It started in the camp in Calais, but got worse when I came here,' he said. What made it worse? 'This feeling of statelessness.'

In Afghanistan, Said worked as a farmer. 'I used to grow melons on my farmland: they were called Qandak and Dilwayran and they were very sweet,' he said as we walked past a large display of melons at a fruit shop in Derby in August. 'In Afghanistan, melons are very sweet ... these are not that good.'

He described his life in Afghanistan as a simple one: he would farm during the day – onions, potatoes and chickens, as well as melons. 'I had a comfortable life there. I had a car, and in the evening I had a home to go to where I was welcomed by my children,' he said. 'The best memories were of us all going to the market together, or when I got home from work. I was surrounded by my kids; it was so special and comforting.'

In many ways, Wali Khan had been thriving in Derby. Everyone I spoke to who knew him remarked on how bright he was, how he had caught up at school, how well his English was coming along. He was cheeky, wanted to be a doctor, spoke English impressively, as well as some French and Urdu, and his native Pashto. He loved football and was – by his own telling – an excellent striker.

In August, Wali Khan said that although he thought about his mother every day, details about her were starting to slip from him. His feelings about being in the UK were complicated; he loved England, but when I asked him if he wanted to stay, he said: '[If] my mum is here, yeah, but [if] no, I want to go back. I want to live with my mum and dad, my sisters, I want to go with my family.' Asked how he would feel if his father was deported but he was allowed to stay in the UK, he said, 'I will cry after my dad if they send him back. Or I will run after him.'

During my visits, I often noted Wali Khan's tender inter-actions with his father. Because Wali Khan spoke reasonable English, he had been his father's interpreter throughout their time in the country. After Kelly left the deserted flat on that rainy February afternoon, he called Wali Khan's mobile repeat-edly. 'Eventually he picked up, and he was kind of subdued, he wasn't his normal self,' Kelly said. Wali Khan and Said had taken the train to London, where they had said farewell to a relative, and then caught a boat to France. Neither had passports, so they had to leave the country illegally. Kelly recalled the conversa-tion: '"My dad says we're going to go home and find our family and then we're all coming back," Wali Khan said. "It's really difficult to do that," I said, and he says yes, he knows. I asked: "Did you want to leave England?" And he goes: "no". It's super sad, really,' said Kelly.

Kelly was devastated – angry at himself, angry at Said, terrified for Wali Khan, whom he worried might try to make his own way back to England and end up at the mercy of traffickers.

The fact that they left just weeks before their appeal tribunal perplexed everyone who knew them. They were so close, why not wait a little longer? Mohammed (not his real name) is an Afghan asylum seeker who met Said and Wali Khan in Calais and stayed in touch with them in the UK. Mohammed knew Said was thinking of leaving the country – he had been threatening it since he was refused asylum in February last year. 'He told me: "I want to leave this country because they give me no chance, everything takes too long, they're never going to accept me and give me papers ... the government says I am lying. No future for me, no future for Wali Khan. I want to go and find my family,"' Mohammed told me.

Mohammed has spoken to Said and Wali Khan a few times since they returned to Kabul. 'Wali Khan said: "I'm not happy. No school, nothing,"' said Mohammed. 'I asked his father what's going on – will you put Wali Khan in school? He said: "No, I need to find my family, and if we find them I will send him to school."'

Said plans to search for his family in Iran, Turkey and Pakistan. If he finds them, he does not plan to return to Afghanistan, because of the danger there. In the first three months of 2018, there were 763 conflict-related civilian deaths across the country, and at least 57 people were killed in an explosion at a voter registration centre in Kabul in late April. But nor does Said want to return to Europe, for the simple reason, according to Mohammed, that, '[On the way to] Europe he lost his family.'

'Now I am here, I thought they would give me a passport,' he told me in February last year. 'I'm now waiting for a document so I can go to Turkey and look for them. If I can't find them, I'll go to Iran. Apart from this, what can I do? It is one year now since I lost my children. I don't know whether they are in Iran or Turkey, whether they are alive or dead.'

A year after we had that first conversation, Said decided that the British system had taken too long. Rather than wait any longer – even just seven weeks to make it to his appeal – he left, smuggling himself out of the country, just as he had smuggled himself in.

The last time Mohammed spoke to Said, he and Wali Khan were preparing to leave Kabul and travel to Iran and Turkey, retracing the steps of their fateful journey almost three years ago. This time, they go not in search of a better, safer life in Europe, but to find the family they lost on their way there.

2 JUNE

'The processed food debate is delicious, MSG-sprinkled class war'

GRACE DENT

In 1988, aged 15, I made my first expedition to a magical, other-worldly kingdom. It was cold, frosty and pale in places, like Narnia, while other parts were a Willy Wonka-esque explosion of colour and exquisite tastes. A land of limitless opportunity, it was just off junction 44 on the M6 near Gretna. The big Asda had come to Carlisle.

For the Dent family, this was akin to a religious awakening. My mother went first, while we were at school, after hearing about it on the local news. She arrived home breathless, the car loaded with dozens of fresh white rolls, boxes of Findus crispy pancakes and family-size microwave lasagnes. She had spotted her emancipation from the kitchen and she was grabbing it with both hands. Or at least she would once she had unloaded a family-size Sara Lee gateau and three bags of McCain oven chips from the boot of her Austin Princess.

Later that day, we drove back again as a family, marvelling at the traffic jams and the chaos in the car park, then stepping gingerly inside a world of pure imagination. Even as a sulky teen, steeped in existential angst from listening to the Smiths' *Hatful of Hollow* 86 times a week, I could not fail to be thoroughly seduced by the joy of processed food. Or just 'food', as we called it then. No one, certainly not me, was questioning where this tasty abundance of riches had come from. I just knew that, until then, we did the Friday-night big shop at a small supermarket called Presto that had only two types of choc ice, while Asda had 5,000 square feet of chiller cabinet, six flavours of squirty Ice Magic and sold Wall's Funny Feet by the box. Life would never be the same again. I have heard similar tales of joy regarding processed foods hitting 1980s Huyton, Llandudno and Scunthorpe, worlds that suddenly felt less grey, small and isolated once the big supermarkets arrived.

Nowadays, when the working classes are attacked, as they often are, for enjoying a dinner of Chicago Town pizza and Wall's Cornetto, I think how little is understood about why people make these choices. Or why it seems to be a constant surprise to well-meaning nutritionists that, when they advise against a KFC boneless bucket or Krispy Kreme doughnuts, the reaction is two fingers aloft, rather than forelock-tugging thanks.

I believe that at the heart of the processed-food debate is class war. Delicious, fructose-syrup-drenched, MSG-sprinkled class war. So, while I have no doubt Hugh Fearnley-Whittingstall and hapless Moby, who argues food stamps shouldn't pay for junk, are sincere, I wonder if they really know what they are up against, or how the noises they make really sound.

Perhaps because healthy-food campaigners always sound so posh, any debate can only ever descend into a bunfight over privilege. How dare you, multimillionaire Jamie Oliver, suggest a jacket potato is nutritionally better than a chicken and mushroom Pot Noodle? Do you not realise families on the fringes of society often share one microwave in a hostel? Why must you be so heartless? But, while it's satisfying to shout down the sharp-elbowed media classes for trying to tax doughnuts, the truth is much more complex. Yes, a relatively tiny percentage of British adults don't have cooking facilities; Ken Loach didn't pull *I, Daniel*

Blake out of thin air. And, yes, a jacket spud is probably better for your innards than a plastic carton of dehydrated noodles flavoured with monosodium glutamate, disodium inosinate and disodium guanylate. But the bigger, more disconcerting fact is that the majority of British working people have disposable income, access to a four-ring stove and a GCSE-or-above-level education and are fully conscious of the links between too many Greggs pasties and a profile like Homer Simpson's. And these people still love processed food.

As the *Guardian*'s restaurant critic, I have Britain's fanciest fine-dining restaurants at my disposal and a job that requires me – no, contractually compels me – to eat locally sourced, ethically harvested organic crops. Yet I love a dinner of Birds Eye potato waffle with spaghetti hoops, and a Heinz salad cream smile on the side of the plate. Processed food is easy, tasty and restorative. It hits the spot. It celebrates, it pacifies, it is a light of hope at the end of another tricky day. It is what you reach for when you need to get the job of eating done.

One of my happiest moments last year was going to a very long dance recital with my niece and 'rewarding' her afterwards with a late-night drive-thru McDonald's. I do not want her to grow up eating McDonald's. But, at the same time, I grew up being rewarded with McDonald's and remember those moments as pure happiness. I am an idiot and a hypocrite and someone trying to be a good auntie all at once. I didn't say any of this stuff was easy.

The fact is, my hackles rise whenever posh foodies talk of their childhood eureka moment. Forgive them, God, I often think, for they know not what they say. The cliche goes something like this: it was in Tuscany, or perhaps the Algarve, maybe Brittany, they say, while appearing on BBC One's *Saturday Kitchen* or Radio 4's *Desert Island Discs*. They were seven years old and until this point didn't understand the importance of real food. But as they ate al fresco by their *grandpère*'s orchard, they tasted a girolle and it shook their world. Suddenly they realised the importance of top-quality fresh food of exquisite provenance! And, from then on, they have firmly believed that everyone – yes, everyone – should eat as simply and freshly as this.

No one with a platform to discuss food in Britain admits the unfettered joy of their first trip to McDonald's magical golden arches. Mine was in 1983, on Edgware Road in London. Oh, the unwrapping of the cheeseburger, the slurping of the strawberry milkshake, the horror of the salty-sweet, snot-coloured gherkin slice, the crispness of the hot fries. We went back every day of our holiday in London, sampling the magma-hot apple pie and the Quarter Pounders. We also fed tame sparrows on our hands in Hyde Park and took pictures of 'real-life punks' in Camden. It is worth noting that, in the 1970s and 80s, most working-class mothers saw no correlation between sugar and a child's behaviour, so I will always feel conflicted when I hear modern middle-class parents obsessing about birthday party food or vending machines. When I was small, if you drank a blue Slush Puppie and started running about head-butting other kids, you were simply being 'a little shit' of your own accord. You would get your arse smacked and be sent to bed until you gave a full apology, after which you might well get another Slush Puppie.

At this stage, I should mention that the working classes are, and always have been, very diverse, so some readers will be screaming: 'Oh, how patronising – my family had no money throughout the 1980s, but my mother made lentil soup from scratch every day!' This I can only applaud. In fact, let me pause and pay tribute to those kids with a mother like Toni Collette in *About a Boy*, who never tasted mint Viennetta and were not allowed to eat Cadbury's chocolate rolls at birthday parties.

But let's turn back to more commonplace working-class Britain, where the comedian Peter Kay, with his reassuringly normal rounded frame, entered the *Guinness World Records* in 2013, selling 1,140,798 tickets over 113 arena dates, performing routines about the Friday-night big shop and the reassurance of finding Cadbury's fingers in a foreign supermarket ('Les Cadbury's Fingreses!'). Kay's routine about the sadness of your mam buying store-brand 'Rola Cola' when all you longed for was real Pepsi is so close to my life, it's as if he had CCTV footage of my teenage years.

I recognise Kay's descriptions of going to see your gran, who will tell you you have got fat, then bring out a plate piled high with Breakaways and Penguins. Or sedentary Sundays in the 80s, when true happiness was your family lazing around watching *Bullseye* with a big tray of cake. I believe that, for huge swaths of this country – and this very much includes Brits whose families arrived here from other parts of the world in the 1950s, 60s and 70s – the eating of processed food is our real shared British cultural heritage.

Still, when foodies mention this sort of eating, they sound disgusted. I can hear muffled middle-class loathing at the habits of normal, non-rich people like a dog whistle. 'This Domino's pizza is not real food,' rails the street-food entrepreneur, or the nutritional guru, or the saucer-eyed Instagram star. 'Um, OK,' think millions of people, 'but I ate that with my friends last Friday, and the Friday before that, and I'm still alive. Am I not a real person?' As I write today, now in my 40s and living the London life of a *Guardian* columnist – knee-deep in fancy quinoa, invites to juicing bars and nutritional yeast as a condiment – I confess that I have quit processed food almost entirely. I am at least two years clean since my last Greggs cheese pasty. My fridge is filled with the rainbow of fresh colours that nutritionist Amelia Freer advises us to eat. I am the perfect example of the working-class woman who took notice of all the health warnings. I spent time in California, where my colleagues lived on goji berries and activated sprouts and no one had more than 10 per cent body fat. Their skin gleamed, their bones stayed dense and no one was off work with gout. I cut refined carbs, factory foods and chemical flavourings from my life. What I am left with, alongside a Holland & Barrett loyalty card and a smaller waist, is a confused and jumbled identity.

Who am I without processed food? Am I even working class any more? I certainly still have to work. But I have spent years in the north railing against my family for adding Anchor squirty cream to already creamy items, for loving a Toby carvery. I have stood at Christmas gatherings reminding people that the only way not to gain weight in December is to eat no Quality Street or mint Matchmakers at all. The words 'preachy tosspot' surfaced from some of my closer family. I suppose I was trying to be helpful. Or trying to communicate my newer, fresher religious awakening. Sugar is the false god. The real saviour – gather round, people – is a Fitbit and fresh air.

To confound matters, it's a little-discussed truth that most working-class people who manage to stay at the bottom of the BMI chart are greeted with suspicion and vague slander anyway. Long before the fashion press began branding bouncy curves as the mark of the 'real woman', it was a given in my house growing up that thin people 'live on their nerves', 'could do with a feed' and have to 'run around in the shower' to get wet. At my gran's house, there was nothing worse than being 'a picky eater'. 'No wonder you're cold – there's nothing on you,' my mother will say. 'Have one of those Co-op flapjacks you like,' she will say, adding as a compromise, 'They're full of roughage – they're good for you.' I do like those Co-op flapjacks, she is correct, but I am currently smaller than I was when I was 20 and to stay here I must refuse all such rectangles of beige happiness. I must walk miles every day. I do squats. I drink three litres of water. In Costa Coffee, I have learned to say: 'No, thank you,' to the 'Anything else?' question and not: 'Yes, please – I will have a giant milk chocolate Tunnock's teacake as big as a child's head.' In the middle of all this, I have come to relish eating clean and training dirty.

But, as the great philosopher David Sylvian of Japan once said in their hit tune 'Ghosts': 'Just when I think I'm winning ... the ghosts of my life blow wilder than before.' I will never view eating Heinz macaroni cheese cold from the tin as anything less than heavenly. If I had a gun to my head and was asked to choose between 10 courses of Michelin-star fine dining at Claridge's or lying under a blanket on the sofa eating sour cream and onion Pringles, I would go for the latter. The thing that well-to-do food experts will never truly get is that, for millions of people, life is very hard and, via a million tiny ingrained cerebral signifiers, processed food is very cheering. You know these brands and they know you. They are our friends, even if they may be trying to kill us. Don't tell me a Sunday night hungover Domino's delivery, when you are dealing with the fear of another working week, doesn't feel just like a cuddle. I am from a land of garlic bread and circuses.

5 June

Summer Exhibition/
The Great Spectacle review
– a Grayson revolution

JONATHAN JONES

There's an orgy going on at the Royal Academy. People are tumbling over each other, cavorting in ecstasy, revealing all. Who knew the summer show could be so subversive?

This riotous assembly appears in a deliriously funny and rude satire on the Royal Academy's annual exhibition drawn by Thomas Rowlandson in about 1800. It's included in The Great Spectacle, a survey of the (nearly) 250-year history of what is now called the Summer Exhibition that runs parallel to this year's show. What a quarter-millennium it has been. Rowlandson's watercolour, called *The Exhibition Stare Case*, portrays fashionable society fighting its way up the spiral staircase in the Academy's old home in Somerset House. In their excitement, they've lost their footing. The dirty-minded Rowlandson imagines the crush turning into a mass ogle and grope.

This annual show was where Gainsborough and Reynolds, Constable and Stubbs competed for attention. From its first instalment at the year-old RA in 1769, through the Romantic age, it was the Turner prize of its day – with Turner in it. He exhibited his last new works here in 1850, the year before his death.

The Great Spectacle puts a brave spin on what happened next, celebrating the Victorian salon it became – there's a touching portrait by William Frith of Oscar Wilde at the 1881 private view

– but the reality was depressing. By 1900, the Royal Academy was a profoundly conservative institution, and its Summer Exhibition a parade of establishment taste. In his painting *Does the Subject Matter?*, the 1940s president of the Royal Academy, Alfred Munnings, viciously satirises modern art and its fans; the curators try to suggest he's ambivalent, but this is the same man who boasted that he and Winston Churchill wanted to kick Picasso in the balls.

The Great Spectacle can't hide the fact that the Royal Academy Exhibition stopped being a creative cultural force when Turner died in 1851.

Now along comes Grayson Perry.

In asking Perry to co-curate their summer show in their quarter-millennial year, the Royal Academy has let him turn it inside out and upside down. He's saved this open submission gathering of the famous and not-so-famous from the mediocrity that usually stultifies it by instituting a bold and ruthless measure. Usually, there are a lot of so-so works of art, the hard efforts of well-meaning plodders whose competence and sweat get them selected – a huge honour.

This year, getting selected is not such an honour. For Perry has filled the summer show with crap. I mean actual garbage: talentless, throwaway rubbish, a lot of it apparently made by jokers after getting home from the pub.

There are pictures made with eggs, monkey portraits, childlike banners, a marble relief called *Pig Man* (actually, that's by a 'proper' artist), and, most bizarrely, a whole collection of portraits of Perry, submitted either by fans or by people who hoped it was a sure way to get selected. They were right. Elsewhere, someone has embroidered over a photo of the Queen from the front page of the *Guardian*, while another hopeful has acquired a Ukip poster from the EU referendum and replaced the word 'Leave' with 'Love'. Only the cluster of TV cameras around it alerted me that it's by Banksy.

The biggest room in Burlington House is painted bright yellow and densely hung with weird and wonderful works. Olga Lomaka's elongated fibreglass sculpture of the Pink Panther, strung sideways through an abstract blue canvas, is perhaps the most bonkers of all – and she's a professional. Next to this hangs a deadly serious and adoring portrait of Nigel Farage by David Griffiths. Perry's show is politically as well as aesthetically promiscuous. Here, Banksy shares space with Farage. It results in a fascinating psychological delve into darkest Britain in 2018. By including so much art the selectors would normally put straight in the reject pile, this show charts the subconscious of our times. Haunted by Grenfell – I counted two works of art about it – and divided by Brexit, this is nothing like the garden party nation the summer show traditionally suggests.

Some established artists fit into the madness amazingly well. Rose Wylie shows a huge painting based on an African shop sign. Her sloppy splendour stands out for its design and colour. In an 'art world' context, she looks like an outsider: here you see how accomplished and clever she is.

Paula Rego, too, excels with a grotesque triptych of tortured bodies. David Hockney exhibits tremendous, vast photographic works that map his studio and expound his belief that western perspective limits how we see. Among all the amateurs he is amateur-in-chief, riding his hobby horse, glowing with intellectual enthusiasm.

There's something odd happening in art, and Perry has caught the moment. Boundaries of age and style, cool and uncool no longer seem to have anything to do with art's future. Perhaps its future lies in the past. Or vice versa. I don't know where I am after this crazy show. This is the most liberating exhibition of new art I've seen for ages, because it obliterates definitions of what's good or bad, archaic or modern, and invites us to sample all the ways people can use a thing called 'art' to express feelings and ideas. The more the merrier, the madder the better.

The barbarians have stormed the gates. And if ever a palace needed ransacking by the mob, it was Burlington House. I don't know what Constable and Turner would think. Rowlandson, however, would have a bloody good laugh.

7 JUNE

Word of the week: 'chaos'. Has British rail travel fallen into an abyss?

STEVEN POOLE

This week transport secretary Chris Grayling was accused of being 'asleep at the wheel', although trains don't have steering wheels, so perhaps he was asleep at the dead man's handle. There is still widespread 'train chaos' or 'rail chaos' or 'travel chaos' since train companies had to introduce new timetables and promptly failed to run trains according to them. This they weasellishly call 'disruption', though that word's original meaning, of a violent tearing-apart, is more apt.

In Greek mythology, chaos was the primordial void that existed before creation, and its first English sense was that of a boundless abyss. The meaning of utter disorder arises first in the 16th century with William Tyndale's translation of Matthew's Gospel. There an unnavigable maze is 'a confused Chaos, and a minglynge of all thynges together with out order, every thynge contrarye to another'. Rather like the privatised rail network.

The original cosmic chaos was at least a fruitful void. The first things to pop into existence were the Earth and the underworld. Then came Eros. So if all goes according to tradition, at least despairing commuters could find love on the overcrowded platforms.

12 JUNE

Solidarity of heirs on the Trump and Kim surreality show

JULIAN BORGER

The Singapore summit was destined for success. Donald Trump had predicted as much on waking at the Shangri-La hotel, and by his own account the president was not disappointed.

Trump had primed the world for a triumph. Like a dawn artillery barrage, softening up enemy lines and setting conditions for victory, Trump had fired off a string of tweets at 6am hitting out at his critics, the naysayers, and promising his followers: 'We will be fine!'

His hunch was proved right and his meeting with Kim Jong-un turned out to be as successful as he had foretold, something he was able to confirm within the first 10 minutes of meeting Kim.

'I feel really great. I think it's gonna be really successful and I think we will have a terrific relationship,' Trump said, sitting alongside Kim in the first session of a summit he had earlier described as 'getting-to-know-you plus'.

The hotel where the two men met, the Capella, is a former British barracks and a reminder of the pleasant life of colonial officers, spotless in white paint with wide verandas behind rows of grand arches. The colonnades, an echo of the White House, provided a photogenic backdrop for the two leaders to stroll up and down in conversation.

The personal warmth only got deeper as the day went on. By the end of five hours, after Kim had signed the joint statement and flown back to Pyongyang, Trump was talking about a special bond between them, and appeared ready to defend Kim to the bitter end.

Asked about the North Korean leader's penchant for killing his own relatives and starving his own people, Trump replied: 'Well he is very talented. Anybody that takes over a situation like he did at 26 years of age and is able to run it and run it tough.

'I don't say he was nice,' the president cautioned unless anyone had got the wrong idea. 'He ran it, few people at that age. You can take one out of 10,000 could not do it.'

The remarks added ballast to a hitherto speculative notion that Trump identified with Kim's backstory. They both took over the family business at a young age from unscrupulous but idolised fathers. It was solidarity among heirs.

At his side Kim said little, apparently content to allow Trump to act as a master of ceremonies and cheerleader. With his perpetual flow of honeyed adjectives and careful stage-management, the US president, a former reality show host, conducted the summit as if it were a TV dating show – one in which Trump was both compère and suitor.

As the two delegations sat down for a working lunch, Trump called out to the waiting Singaporean photographers: 'Getting a good picture everybody? So we look nice and handsome and thin? Perfect.'

Kim, who probably does not hear too many fat-guy jokes back in Pyongyang, looked astonished.

There are no pictures to record the look on the North Korean leader's face when Trump produced an iPad and showed Kim and his aides a specially commissioned advertorial video on the benefits of complete, verifiable and irreversible dismantlement. Produced in the style of the trailer for a straight-to-video 1980s action movie, it cast Kim and Trump as a pair of heroes struggling to save the world and its 7 billion people.

'There comes a time when only a few are called upon to make a difference, but the question is what difference will the few make?' the portentous narrator asked. 'One moment. One choice. What if? The future remains to be written.'

Trump was so delighted with the video that he had it shown to the press while they waited for his arrival. 'We had it made up,' he declared. 'I showed it to [Kim] today. Actually during the meeting. Toward the end of the meeting. I think he loved it.'

It has been a long time since Trump has been this ebullient. He claimed to have tried to persuade Kim to look at his country from a 'real estate perspective', speculating on what the beaches currently used for war games might fetch on the open market.

'I said look at that view. That would make a great condo,' Trump said.

He joshed with almost every reporter he called on to ask a question, and even pleaded with his spokeswoman, Sarah Sanders, to allow the session to run overtime. 'I don't care,' Trump said. 'Hey, you know, it just means we get home later in the evening, right?'

No amount of scepticism or snarkiness from the press was going to dent Trump's mood. He seemed genuinely unaware that the promises he had received about North Korean denuclearisation had been made, in somewhat firmer language, by Kim's father and grandfather in earlier decades.

This time it would be different, Trump promised, because this time there was 'a different administration and different president and a different secretary of state'. It was, in a way, a statement of the Trump doctrine.

The ethereal, somewhat quirky nature of the venue helped the atmospherics. From early in the morning, the streets of central Singapore were blocked off and lined by police as the two leaders set off in their motorcades from their separate hotels for the island of Sentosa, a name apparently derived from the Sanskrit for peace and contentment.

It was an improvement on the old Malay name, Pulau Blakang Mati, which meant 'the island where danger lurks behind your back', reflecting a dark past as a pirates' lair.

The Singapore tourist industry had gone one step further in the island's rebranding, dubbing it the State of Fun, a place to escape the realities of everyday life.

Along the way to their meeting, the two leaders drove past a turreted Disney-inspired castle and a rollercoaster, both set in lush foliage. The whimsical backdrop was not lost on Kim, whose father was a film fanatic and whose family has stayed in power in part because of their ability to create an alternate reality for their population.

At one point within the first few minutes, as they were strolling down the white-arched colonnade, Kim turned to Trump and said: 'Many people in the world will think of this as a ... form of fantasy ... from a science fiction movie.'

He could have had no way of knowing that Trump had actually had a science fiction movie made, starring the two of them as messianic saviours of the planet. But judging from the outcome of the summit, it is just possible that his instinct for handling Trump was far better than the American's much-vaunted intuition about dealing with Kim.

13 JUNE

'People scoffed at it!'
The unstoppable all-female
Shakespeare uprising

CHARLOTTE HIGGINS

'Quite a senior male director, who will remain nameless, went around calling it *Julius Beaver*,' remembers Josie Rourke, artistic director of London's Donmar Warehouse, where Phyllida Lloyd's all-female version of the Roman tragedy was staged in 2012. 'People would just scoff at it. And scoffing did two things: it trivialised it, and it made it look experimental.' But for Rourke and her partner at the Donmar, executive producer Kate Pakenham, *Julius Caesar* was a serious statement of intent about addressing the lack of representation of women in theatre. It came to define their Donmar tenure which is about to end: Pakenham steps down this month and Rourke next year, when she will be succeeded by Michael Longhurst.

By 2016 the Donmar, a tiny but high-profile theatre in Covent Garden, had put on not one but three all-female Shakespeares, each with the great actor Harriet Walter, directed by Lloyd and with an ethnically diverse cast drawn partly from ex-offenders. The trilogy – which includes *Henry IV* and *The Tempest* – has already been staged back to back in a large tent in King's Cross and travelled to New York. Now it is to be aired on the BBC.

Scepticism about what many considered to be a quixotic idea continued even after *Caesar*'s first triumphant run in London. According to Pakenham: 'There were people close to us, who

said to us, "Well, you've done that all-female thing now."' As in –
now's the time to go back to the proper business of the theatre.
Those people were, I infer, the Donmar's board, though they
are too discreet to be drawn. I sense that Rourke and Pakenham
encountered opposition in their desire to shake up the Donmar
which, under Rourke's predecessor Michael Grandage, had
become famous for a particularly gilded, beautifully made and
radiantly cast classic play – a model that became important
to the theatre because of the way it operates financially. As
Pakenham explains, very little of the Donmar's income comes
from Arts Council England, and only 35 per cent, owing to its
tiny size, from box-office receipts. The rest – 55 per cent – comes
from philanthropy. 'The theatre got very good at fundraising in
Michael's tenure around star-driven, classic titles. The fear on
us was that risk, or social mission, or inclusivity, could mean
a disintegration of the value of exclusivity that was driving the
business model.'

Rourke's chosen direction was not to take the path of
burnishing the 'jewel' that is the Donmar but of 'disrupting' the
life of the theatre – both in terms of commissioning new writing
and insisting on trying to open up its work beyond its traditional
tiny well-heeled audience. Rourke has been committed to big,
looming current affairs issues: there was James Graham's play
Privacy, which bounced off the Snowden leaks, Graham's *The Vote*,
looking at democracy to coincide with the 2015 election, and
Steve Waters's drama *Limehouse*, taking the long view of Labour by
way of the birth of the Social Democratic party.

Pakenham thinks their stubbornness paid off. 'The Shakespeare trilogy has a feminist mission, a social mission, an
inclusivity mission, an education mission. And that actually
drove philanthropy and partnerships and funding that made the
theatre richer in every way.' Rourke adds: 'The board has been on

a phenomenal journey to embrace the things we have wanted to do. It has had its undulations but I think we got there.'

Rourke says her only regret about the Shakespeare productions is that 'the dazzling conceptual brilliance' of Lloyd's direction got somewhat lost amid the focus on gender. 'If it had been directed by Ivo van Hove or another one of those big auteur directors I do think her work would have been understood more deeply and seriously,' she says. There is also the matter of Harriet Walter – undoubtedly one of the great actors of her generation, whose deep interpretations of Brutus, Henry IV and Prospero were theatrical events in themselves.

Looking back on the world as they found it when they were young guns in their mid-30s, some things have changed. Issues of gender in theatre have become more visible, not least since, in 2012, director Elizabeth Freestone and a team of researchers at the *Guardian* drew attention to a serious gender gap in all roles in England's largest subsidised theatres. The bastion of the theatre establishment, the Royal Shakespeare Company, will this year mount a summer season directed entirely by women, while its artistic director Gregory Doran will then direct a *Troilus and Cressida* cast 50-50 between men and women. It is hard not to feel that Lloyd's trilogy has played its part in a small but perceptible shift of attitude.

Rourke is preparing her Donmar production of *Measure for Measure*, which she predicts may 'get me into tepid-to-hot water'. The idea is to play it in two versions in a single evening – first in a 17th-century setting and then in a modern one, but with the two central roles of Isabella (Hayley Atwell) and Angelo (Jack Lowden) flipped. She is also in the process of debating edits to her first feature film, *Mary Queen of Scots*.

But they do not, the pair say, have a clandestine strategy for world domination, so much as an urgent need for time to breathe. One senses that Pakenham, in particular, has become radicalised by her time at the Donmar. 'I want to hear women's voices and voices we don't usually hear,' she grins. 'I definitely have become braver ... The good girl has been squashed. And the rebel has been born.'

Diversity in publishing is under attack. I hear the sound of knuckles dragging

HANIF KUREISHI

The furore over Penguin's wise and brave decision to 'reflect the diversity of British society' in its publishing and hiring output seems to have awoken the usual knuckle-dragging, semi-blind suspects with their endlessly repeated terrors and fears. They appear to believe that what is called 'diversity' or 'positive action' will lead to a dilution of their culture. Their stupidity and the sound of their pathetic whining would be funny if it weren't so tragic for Britain. You might even want to call it a form of self-loathing; it is certainly unpatriotic and lacking in generosity.

The industries I've worked in for most of my life – film, TV, theatre, publishing – have all been more or less entirely dominated by white Oxbridge men, and they still mostly are. These men and their lackeys have been the beneficiaries of positive discrimination, to say the least, for centuries. The world has always been theirs, and they now believe they own it.

Some of us have been fortunate enough to force a way through the maze and make a living as artists. It was a difficult and often humiliating trip, I can tell you. There was much patronising and many insults on the way, and they are still going on.

We are still expected to be grateful, though those in charge – never having had to fight for anything – have always been the lucky ones. And these lucky ones, with their implicit privilege, wealth and power – indeed, so much of it they don't even see it – are beginning to intuit that their day is done. Before, with their sense of superiority and lofty arrogance, they could intimidate everyone around them. No more.

It was never not a struggle to become an artist, with racism, prejudice and assumption all around, visible and invisible. I remember standing in a room with Salman Rushdie in the early 1990s, just after *The Buddha of Suburbia* had been published, discussing how it could be that we were the only people of colour there – indeed, the only people of colour in most of the rooms when it came to books. And that was the case with all of the culture industries. The first TV producer I ever met asked me why my characters had to be Asian. 'If they were white, we'd make this,' he said to me.

It is not coincidental that at this Brexit moment, with its xeno-phobic, oafish and narrow perspective, the ruling class and its gatekeepers fear a multitude of democratic voices from elsewhere and wish to keep us silent. They can't wait to tell us how unde-serving of being heard we really are. But they should remember this: they might have tried to shut the door on Europe, refugees and people of colour, but it will be impossible for them to shut the door on British innovation. We are very insistent, noisy and talented.

When I was invited to join Faber, in 1984, the fiction editor was Robert McCrum. He was excitable then, and so was I. I couldn't wait to be on his list of writers, since he was publishing Kazuo

Ishiguro, Milan Kundera, Josef Škvorecký, Peter Carey, Mario Vargas Llosa, Caryl Phillips, Paul Auster, Lorrie Moore, Danilo Kiš, Marilynne Robinson and Vikram Seth. Not long before, Rushdie had won the Booker prize for *Midnight's Children* and that masterpiece, with its echoes of Günter Grass and Gabriel García Márquez, suddenly seemed like a great opportunity. The world was coming in. What had been a narrow and sterile place was opening up. These books were successful; readers discovered that they wanted them. Today something similar can happen to Penguin.

This is not a gesture that can be made only once. It has to be repeated over and over again. British culture – the single reason for wanting to live in this country – has always thrived on rebellion, cussedness and nonconformity. From pop to punk, from Vivienne Westwood, Zadie Smith and Damien Hirst to Kate Tempest, from Alexander McQueen to Oscar-winning Steve McQueen, the voices of the young and excluded have made British culture alive and admired. There is no other country in Europe with the cultural capital of Britain, and no more exciting place for artists to live. This is where art and commerce meet. These artists' work sells all over the world.

The British creativity I grew up with – in pop, fashion, poetry, the visual arts and the novel – has almost always come from outside the mainstream: from clubs, gay subcultures, the working class and from the street. Many of the instigators may have been white, but they were not from the middle class – a class that lacks, in my experience, the imagination, fearlessness and talent to be truly subversive.

The truth is, the conservative fear of other voices is not because of an anxiety that artists from outside the mainstream will be untalented, filling up galleries and bookshops with sludge: it's that they will be outstanding and brilliant. Those conservatives will have to swallow the fact that, despite the success of British artists, real talent has been neglected and discouraged by those who dominate the culture, deliberately keeping schools, the media, universities and the cultural world closed to interesting people.

It is good news that the master race is becoming anxious about whom they might have to hear from. At this terrible Brexit moment, with its retreat into panic and nationalism, and with the same thing happening across Europe, it is time for all artists to speak up, particularly those whose voices have been neglected.

No one knows what a more democratic and inclusive culture would be like. It is fatuously omniscient to assume it would be worse than what we already have. The attempt of reactionaries to shut people down shows both fear and stupidity. But it's too late: they will be hearing from us.

19 JUNE

How Gareth Southgate became an unstoppable style icon

ALEXANDRA TOPPING

There are pressing questions to be answered in the wake of England's victory over Tunisia in their opening game of the World Cup. Should Dele Alli have been subbed earlier? Is Marcus Rashford a cert for starting against Panama? But for an – admittedly niche – section of the football-loving English populace, one question overshadows all others: just when exactly did Gareth Southgate become a style icon?

The Southgate look – the three-piece suit tailored to within an inch of its life, neat beard, expensive shoes – is not an overnight phenomenon. Last night's impressive dark blue number, teamed with a red, white and blue tie, is merely the apogee of a style journey at least a decade in the making.

And what a journey it has been. Cast your mind back, if you will, to 1990s Southgate. A classic image shows him staring wistfully across a training pitch in a ballooning plaid shirt, dark T-shirt visible underneath, vast collar splaying inelegantly across his chest. He looks like an apologetic bloke who pretended to be into the Stone Roses, but really loved Ocean Colour Scene.

But Southgate is making apologies no longer. Here is a man who knows that quality tailoring can act as a suit of armour. He is now one of those rarest of creatures – a well-dressed man in football. Pep Guardiola achieved this for a time, as did Jose Mourinho (although these days he has got the look of a sleep-deprived hoarder, rumpled clothes thrown on with abandon). Antonio Conte – who teams slim black shirt, skinny black tie and luscious hair transplant like no other – is perhaps also an inspiration.

The most elegant man to have played the beautiful game – and I will quite literally take down anyone who claims otherwise – is obviously Juventus legend Andrea Pirlo. Southgate is not yet in the same league as the Maestro; perhaps he never can be. And yet we have not given up hope of a vintage pair of sunglasses, designer holdall thrown over his shoulder, as he arrives in Nizhny Novgorod before Sunday's game.

And while it is hard to be a stylish man in football – the travails of Cesc Fàbregas and his epaulettes on the BBC show just how wrong well-intentioned attempts can go – it is harder still if you're English, when a well-cut suit or even a stylish scarf inspire derision and distrust. A lone England fan mourned on Twitter that Southgate was not 'a tracksuit manager'. But, seeing the 47-year-old – a man recast in the smouldering embers of Euro 96 – sufficiently confident to display the glory of his snug waistcoat last night, suit jacket abandoned in the heat of Volgograd, the message was clear: I have nothing to fear.

21 JUNE

Rattle bows out at Berlin with Mahler, Merkel and standing ovations

MARTIN KETTLE

After 16 years not just at the heart of Europe but also at the head of the continent's most prestigious symphony orchestra, Sir Simon Rattle bowed out as the chief conductor of the Berlin Philharmonic this week, in an emotional farewell concert in the German capital.

The Liverpool-born conductor, who in 2002 became the first Briton ever chosen for the Berlin job, was never the traditionalists' choice to take charge of the jewel in Germany's musical crown. But, in his last performance in Berlin's Philharmonie Hall before returning to the UK to take over at the helm of the London Symphony Orchestra, all that was history. Rattle received the kind of loud cheering, standing ovation and bouquets of flowers from admirers that used to be reserved for opera divas.

The conductor's final concert with the Berlin orchestra consisted of a single work, Gustav Mahler's searing and fateful Sixth Symphony. Rattle had conducted this 80-minute work in his first engagement with the orchestra in 1987, at a time when, in his 30s, he was dragging British concert life into the modern age as chief conductor of the City of Birmingham Symphony Orchestra.

There was no disputing the rapport between conductor and orchestra in this final performance together in their home hall. As the applause continued long into the hot Berlin night, a clearly moved Rattle made a short speech in German, addressed to 'my wonderful orchestra' and 'my dear Berlin public', thanking them for their support. '*Danke für alles*,' he concluded.

Even Germany's politically beleaguered chancellor, Angela Merkel, a keen concert-goer, took time out from trying to keep her coalition government afloat, to attend one of the many farewell events for Rattle. During the conductor's long stay in Berlin, Rattle seems to have won over doubters with his enthusiasm, his emphasis on modern repertoire, his involvement in educational work and his encouragement of new programming.

After Rattle's first concert in charge in 2002, the *Guardian*'s reviewer proudly concluded: 'Our boy has well and truly arrived.' Sixteen years on, the Rattle era has not been without its ups and downs, but the 63-year-old conductor, now white-haired and balding, departs from Berlin garlanded with honours, affection and respect – not to mention regret. The political echoes are hard to miss. The Berlin Philharmonic's house magazine contains a cartoon of a curly-haired man conducting from the stern of a ship named *Britannia* as it puts to sea with his orchestra on the quayside still following his baton. 'Bye bye Sir Simon' says the caption.

Now another ship docks. From the autumn, the Berlin Philharmonic will be led by its first Russian-born chief conductor, Kirill Petrenko, currently the music director of the Bavarian State Opera in Munich. An outstanding musician, Petrenko's opening concert as chief conductor in September is a striking contrast to Rattle's Berlin opener 16 years ago. Back then, Rattle began with *Asyla* by British composer Thomas Adès, followed by Mahler's Fifth. In

September, Petrenko opens with a more familiar programme of Beethoven and Richard Strauss. Our boy will be missed.

22 JUNE

The NHS, Windrush and the debt we owe to immigration

GARY YOUNGE

A few weeks ago, while looking for the family railcard, I found my mother's first passport. It's blue and hardbacked, with a lion and a unicorn perched on Latin and embossed in gold. The kind the Brexit types bang on about. The kind we will have when we get our country back. The ones that will be made in France.

Only mum's was a bit different. For above the crest it says British Passport and below, in the same gold lettering, it reads Barbados. It was issued by the governor of Barbados 'in the name of Her Majesty', and cites her nationality as 'British Subject: Citizen of the United Kingdom and Colonies'. Barbados did not gain independence until 1966. My mother didn't cross the border to come to Britain – the border crossed her.

The black and white picture inside is of a teenager, just 19. High hopes, high cheeks and high hair, with dark skin against a crisp, white cotton blouse. On the penultimate page are the only two stamps. One, an entry certificate listing her as a student; the other from the immigration officer at Gatwick marked 20 August 1962 (a year later than I had previously thought).

She arrived four months after the passing of the Commonwealth Immigrants Act – the first piece of legislation that sought to weaken ties and obligations with those whose colour was no longer deemed a good fit for the crest. The Labour leader at the time, Hugh Gaitskell (no radical he), branded it 'cruel and brutal anti-colour legislation'.

Even as Britain started trying to keep black people out, it sent for my mother, her passage paid upfront with an agreement that she would pay it back later, because the country desperately needed nurses. And so, as was the case for all my aunts who settled here, that would be her job for more than a decade.

This summer will see the celebration of two 70th anniversaries – the creation of the National Health Service and the docking of the *Empire Windrush*, bringing with it the symbolic arrival of postwar migrants from the Caribbean.

The first will honour Britain's most cherished institution. The NHS makes us more proud to be British than the monarchy, even as we are more dissatisfied than ever with the way it is run. If there must be patriotism – and for now it appears there must – then let it be for a collective institution set up to care for everyone, regardless of their ability to pay, and paid for by everyone who is able to contribute their taxes. For the second, the nation will throw its arms awkwardly around a group of people it has relatively recently decided to revere – older Caribbean migrants – even as it seeks to avoid any substantive discussion of another, albeit related group that we continue to revile – immigrants in general. Our bigotry is both selective and fickle, but no less passionately felt for that. We pride ourselves, simultaneously, on being both tolerant and hostile: those we deport today we may dedicate a commemorative day to tomorrow.

For the most part, these anniversaries will be marked separately – as though their age were the only thing they had in common. But we would grasp the historical importance and contemporary challenges of both much more clearly if we sought to understand them together, since their histories are intimately entwined.

The NHS, like so much of postwar Britain, was built by immigrants and could not have survived in its current form without them. There were recruitment campaigns for nurses in Malaysia, Mauritius and elsewhere in the empire as well as the Caribbean. By 1971, 12 per cent of British nurses were Irish nationals. By the turn of the century, 73 per cent of the GPs in Wales's Rhondda valley and 71 per cent in nearby Cynon valley were south Asian. Today, roughly a third of the tier-2 visas for skilled migrants go to NHS employees.

There is a certain civilising logic to this. For all the talk of national culture, ethnic diversity and racial difference, we are all human. As obvious as that may sound (and when babies are being snatched from parents on America's southern border, or boats of refugees are being turned away from Italy, the question of immigrants' humanity has yet to be politically settled), it explains why health would be a sector that favours migration. The human body is the same the world over. Whatever sense of racial or national superiority one may harbour, it is likely to be tempered when the black foreigner in the white coat is the one charged with keeping you alive.

Nonetheless, there is a contradiction that must be confronted. The institution that we value the most has been sustained by people whom we value the least. Even as Margaret Thatcher's rhetoric about being 'swamped' by people of a different culture gained traction, British lives were, literally, being saved by professionals from the swamp. If Enoch Powell's 'rivers of blood' prophecy had ever become true, the victims would have been patched up by doctors from India and Pakistan whom he invited to the country several years earlier, when he was minister of health. No claim about the strain that immigrants place on the

NHS can be taken seriously without a concomitant appreciation of the strain it would be under were it not for the immigrants working in it.

This is not a problem of the past. That fundamental inability to understand immigrants as people who stay and contribute, rather than as people who come and take, remains a central obstacle to any meaningful debate about immigration. Not only are we failing to have the discussion in terms of our human obligations; we are not even having it in the national interest.

In few places is this clearer than the NHS. According to an NHS Improvement report, in February this year 35,000 nurse vacancies and almost 10,000 doctor posts were unfilled. There has been a growing exodus of European nursing staff since the Brexit referendum. Yet earlier this month the *Financial Times* reported that 2,360 visa applications by doctors from outside the European Economic Area had been refused in a five-month period. Last week the shortage forced the Home Office to exempt medical professionals from the cap on skilled workers that was set by Theresa May several years earlier.

The outcry over the treatment of the Windrush generation shows that we are capable of both appreciating the contributions that immigrants make and protesting against the capricious and cruel state harassment that can be meted out to them. It has yet to fully sink in that what was wrong for the Windrush generation is wrong for all immigrants, and that when we argue for a more humane and less hostile environment for immigrants we do so not just for the sake of foreigners. We do it for ourselves. Our health depends on it. Seventy years after *Windrush* docked and the NHS was created, we should have learned by now. If we don't watch out, our xenophobia will literally be the death of us.

23 JUNE

Brick by brick, Glasgow must recreate its lost masterpiece

IAN JACK

It has been said that a certain class of person can spend their entire life inside the same kind of institutional architecture, never leaving the mellow English stone of the 17th century in their inevitable progress from boarding school to Oxbridge college to an inn of court. But most of us make a less splendid and more various journey. My primary school dated from 1912, my secondary school from 1934, and my tertiary place of education from 1931.

The first of these was the most attractive: 'blocky red sandstone art nouveau', says the Fife volume of the *Buildings of Scotland* series. Nothing much can be said for the other two, though it was from a classroom on the top floor of the third, the Scottish College of Commerce, that I first noticed the structure that has since become one of the most famous buildings in Scotland – perhaps, since its destruction, the most famous of all.

Only a few streets away, its roofline stretched across the near horizon provided by one of Glasgow's urban hills. From where I sat, it had a military look: small windows set in plain grey walls, odd little protuberances that suggested a fort or a beached destroyer. It was, of course, the Glasgow School of Art (GSA).

I didn't know much about architecture and I wasn't aware of the art school's significance. Cities such as Glasgow seemed to have much more in them, then. More shops, more cinemas and theatres, more factories and offices, more pubs, more secondhand bookstores, more newspapers, more streets, more big, black

Victorian buildings with unknown histories and purposes – and many more people, because Glasgow's population has almost halved in the 50-odd years since.

To the newcomer, the GSA was no more than one small part of this rewarding density. Not much was made of it. In 1960, a guide to the city, even quite a respectable history of the place, might ignore the name Charles Rennie Mackintosh, even though his designs had given Glasgow the most extraordinary building it will probably ever see.

Mackintosh was a 28-year-old assistant in the Glasgow architects' firm Honeyman & Keppie when in 1896 it won the competition to build a new art school for the city, which outside London was then Britain's foremost centre of artistic enterprise. He did all the drawings, but at first got none of the public credit. The first part opened in 1899: a three-storey studio block that ran east to west along the Garnethill ridge, it had wide, Italianate eaves and big windows to let in the northern light – each window with the square footage of a small flat – as well as ornamental wrought iron in front and unexpected touches of Scots baronial to the rear.

Then work stopped and didn't resume until 1907, an interval during which Mackintosh grew interested in the aesthetic of the Vienna Secession; so that when he came to design the building's second stage, the western elevation, it looked dramatically different to the rest of the building and unlike anything else in the country. Its trio of square bay windows, each about 20 metres (65ft) high, soared above a steep little side street that had a terrace of shabby pre-tenement dwellings on the other side. I stood below it one day and wondered what age this glazed cliff came from: it had an old/new look that suggested a cathedral on the one hand and the Odeon cinema on the other.

How 'beautiful' this was is a difficult question to answer. 'Striking', 'handsome' and 'functional' may be better words.

Beauty was a more obvious quality of the inside, where Mackintosh combined un-Victorian amounts of light with plain stone, ironwork and wood. He was, after all, a gifted interior designer as much as an architect: country houses and a chain of tearooms also bore his mark. Nothing, however, surpassed the art school's library, which was said to be the loveliest room in Glasgow and, according to the late Gavin Stamp, his 'finest, most personal and most mysterious creation, a complex space, at once dark and well-lit, in which every detail was personal and deliberate'.

Stamp, who taught at the art school from 1990, wrote those words in the *London Review of Books* after the first fire destroyed the library in 2014, and then added a sentence that was sadly prescient in its scepticism: 'The management of the GSA, which, despite warnings about fire, allowed a student to combine expanding foam with a hot projector in the basement, now cheerfully assures us that most of the building is safe.'

After the night of 15 June, only the walls remain, and even they may be too heat-damaged to support much more than themselves. What's to be done? 'Restoration' is too mild a term for the damage that would have to be rectified. The National Trust spent five years restoring Uppark, a West Sussex country house, after a disastrous fire in 1989 left its ground floor more than a metre deep in wet ash and rubble: it was a remarkable feat of conservation, but the house was much less ruinous than the GSA and many of its contents survived.

The choices facing the Glasgow building seem to be: demolition and replacement; 'facade-ism', in which a new interior sits behind the old walls, or some other elements of the old are incorporated with the new; or a faithful replica.

The last possibility has prompted a small outbreak of: 'What would Mackintosh have wanted?' Glasgow architect Alan Dunlop argues: 'He was an innovator, working at the cutting edge. He would want to see a new school of art fit for the 21st century.' But ghosts are bad witnesses, and the chances are slim that a new building will stand in relation to the 21st century as Mackintosh's did to the 20th – as a delightful, singular work that prefigures the future and reflects the past. The better answer, for me and I suspect many others, is a replica.

This week, watching the aerial footage of the GSA's burnt-out shell, I remembered those terrible pictures of German cities in 1945 – many square miles of buildings in the same state, destroyed by carpet-bombing and firestorms. By some calculations these cities – Berlin, Cologne, Hamburg, Dresden, Leipzig and the rest – lost four-fifths of their historic buildings. Many vanished for ever. Others, such as Dresden's Frauenkirche, have been wonderfully recreated.

The latest and possibly largest of these recreations, built at a cost of £500 million, is the City Palace in Berlin, which is scheduled to open next year as the home of the Humboldt Forum museum with the former head of the British Museum, Neil MacGregor, as its founding director. MacGregor, a Glaswegian, firmly believes the art school should be rebuilt as it was before. 'Just to let it go would be such a loss,' he said this week. 'A replica shouldn't be seen as a fake. It's a way of a city reasserting its history.'

It would be absurd to compare Glasgow to Germany. Nonetheless, at the hands of planners, developers and the all-too-visible hand of economic decline, the city has had a real mauling. To make Mackintosh's great building anew would be a long and expensive project, but skills would be preserved and passed on, and there would be something to marvel at finally. Every stone, window, beam, stair, shelf should be faithfully copied – and every ceiling fitted with sprinklers.

29 JUNE

Speak for England, Danny Dyer. You've blown the lid on Brexit

MARINA HYDE

'It's getting tickly now,' Alex Ferguson famously observed during a title run-in. 'Squeaky bum time, I call it.' This was in 2003, seven years after arguably the definitive Premier League bum-squeak. More of a follow-through, in fact, as the then Newcastle manager, Kevin Keegan, succumbed to his now legendary Ferguson-induced rant. 'I will love it if we beat them – love it!' he frothed, of Manchester United. The rest, of course, is history.

To watch Theresa May come out of this week's EU summit with just six weeks of negotiating time left on the Brexit clock, and declare the EU was risking the lives of its citizens by not striking a security deal with her, was to experience a similar look-away moment. The prime minister is this close to jabbing her finger at the camera and declaring the EU27 have got to go to Middlesbrough and get something. Of the many roles in which May has cruelly miscast herself, that of crap blackmailer is the most excruciating.

Still, what happened at the business end of things – the by now traditional bit of an EU summit where May has to leave while the other countries talk about the important stuff? *Pas devant les enfants*, as my grandmother used to say. In summary, they seem to have come to a tentative arrangement on migration. And the EU's Michel Barnier appears to be broadly in agreement with the Queen Vic's Danny Dyer.

Look, without wishing to involve you in what might sarcastically be described as 'my process', I no longer remark that things are 'sentences I never expected to type'. We passed the Typed Lands in 2016. Wherever this place is, this is normal. Nor does my keyboard raise so much as a ??? to report that the prime minister's official spokesman was today formally asked if the prime minister concurred with *EastEnders* actor Dyer that her predecessor, David Cameron, was 'a twat'. This is where we live now. Try not to choke on it.

If you haven't seen Dyer's outburst on ITV's *Good Evening Britain*, I urge you to take 36 seconds to do so. As fellow studio guests including Pamela Anderson and Jeremy Corbyn cock their heads thoughtfully, Danny begins by observing that Brexit is a riddle. 'So what's happened to that twat David Cameron, who called it on?' he wonders. The inquiry turns out to be rhetorical, as the *Real Football Factories* legend expands: 'He's in Europe, in Nice with his trotters up, yeah? Where is the geezer?! I think he should be held account for it. He should be held account for it.'

As the producers pan out to get reaction shots from studio guests such as Harry Redknapp and the Conservative party deputy chairman, James Cleverly – like I said, this is where we live now – Dyer can be heard lobbing in a final 'Twat'. Speak for England, Danny! Or rather, speak for south-east metropolitan centres, Scotland and Northern Ireland! The rest think you're the twat, but that's showbiz.

Wherever you stand on Brexit, though, we can at least thank Dyer for his hilarious addition to Westminster's annals of quotable quotes. God knows, they can always use the material. I was reminded this week that Neil Hamilton once won the *Spectator*'s Parliamentary Wit of the Year – an award that certainly puts Nigel Mansell winning Sports Personality of the Year twice into perspective.

Danny's latest pensée is easily as amusing as his rumination on the 11th anniversary of the attack on the World Trade Center.

'Can't believe it's been nearly 11 years since them slags smashed into the twin towers,' this ran. 'Still freaks my nut out to this day.'

It is, however, not as amusing as the big-hitting Brexiters and four-star political commentators who have spent the hours since Dyer's Brexit communique mobilising to condemn the reaction to it. Why are people listening to an actor, wonder various sorts who take themselves rather too seriously. I don't know, guys – but let's face it, they'll probably have better luck down the bookies than if they listen to newspaper columnists.

Why is his ghastly swearing being lionised, runs another line of inquiry. That I do know the answer to – it's because it's funny. And at this stage in the Brexit U-bend, arguably the best we can hope for is a shit deal on services and a cheap giggle. Contrary to what half you lot told us, they can't do us a bespoke/haute-couture/red-white-and-blue/money-spraying Brexit. The pretend landlord of the Queen Victoria pub appears to have figured this out, and is trying to salvage a point from the tie. Why haven't you?

Chiefly amusing, however, is the erstwhile *Danny Dyer's Deadliest Men* presenter scooping David Cameron on his own memoirs. I don't know what the former prime minister has been tossing off in his £25,000 shepherd's hut over the past 23 months, but I can already tell you it will lack the sparse precision of Dyer's summary. In fact, if they want to sell the book to people other than nerdy completists like me, then the publishers should consider running Danny's precis as a cover quote. I've no idea what the book's title will be – let's hope it's one of Cameron's catchphrases, like It Was The Right Thing To Do – but I'd love to see the words 'Twat ... Danny Dyer' emblazoned above the title, to bring in the punters.

As for how Theresa May will characterise the coming summer of heatwaves and cabinet warfare in her own eventual memoirs, who can say? But with the UK's chief Brexit negotiator privately warning there are just six weeks to go before both sides are required to sign a final deal, the situation must – in the words of the Chips Channon *de nos jours* – be freaking her absolute nut out.

30 JUNE

'It's nothing like a broken leg': why I'm done with the mental health conversation

HANNAH JANE PARKINSON

I am bleeding from the wrists in a toilet cubicle of the building I have therapy in, with my junior doctor psychiatrist peering over the top of the door, her lanyards clanking against the lock. Her shift finished half an hour earlier.

An hour later she calls the police, because I have refused to go to A&E or to let her look at me. Four policemen arrive. They are all ridiculously handsome. One of them is called Austin. Austin doesn't have a Taser like all the others and when I question this, Austin says he hasn't done his Taser training and all the others laugh. I feel bad for Austin.

I want to go home but I am not allowed. I am crying. The police ask me to tip out the contents of my jacket. Tampons fall out, with four sad coffee loyalty cards, each with a single stamp. Then I make a break for it because, seriously now, I just want to go home. The four officers surround me at the building entrance. One officer who has done his Taser training threatens to section me if I do not stop struggling.

As if you can just section me, I say. You can't just say someone is sectioned and then they are sectioned. That is not how it works.

It turns out this is exactly how it works.

I am put in handcuffs. Three other police turn up in a van – seven now. A woman searches me, running gloved hands along my calves. It is cold. It is dark. I am scared. I ask to call someone. A police officer says, now is not a good time. I say: I feel like this is totally a good time. I am bundled into the van. As if in a TV drama, my psychiatrist reappears in the gap between the doors before they clang shut.

The hospital is 10 minutes away but I end up in the van for 40 minutes, backed up behind ambulances. I'm offered water when I arrive, but they don't want the cuffs taken off, so the lead officer holds a cup up to my lips. All of my possessions are taken away from me. I am kept in a small room in A&E for 22 hours, before being found a bed in an inpatient unit.

I have experienced mental illness since the age of 13, and have been in the psychiatric system for a decade. In year 8, I spent so much time absent from school that a social worker was called. At 16, I dropped out of A-levels with incapacitating depression and barely left the house for nine months – the empty days stretching out while friends clubbed and kissed. I was put on antidepressants and at 18 decided to move to Russia, alone, in a manic whirlwind, and had the time of my life. At 20, I moved to Oxford and was diagnosed with bipolar disorder. I was told I would have it for life. I moved again at 23, and there is now no hospital in north London I have not been treated in.

In the last few years I have observed a transformation in the way we talk about mental health, watched as depression and anxiety went from unspoken things to ubiquitous hashtags. It seems as though every week is now some kind of Mental Health Awareness

Week, in which we should wear a specific colour (although this year no one could agree on which: half wore green, half yellow).

In the last few years I have lost count of the times mental illness has been compared to a broken leg. Mental illness is nothing like a broken leg. In fairness, I have never broken my leg. Maybe having a broken leg does cause you to lash out at friends, undergo a sudden, terrifying shift in politics and personality, or lead to time slipping away like a Dalí clock. Maybe a broken leg makes you doubt what you see in the mirror, or makes you high enough to mistake car bonnets for stepping stones (difficult, with a broken leg) and a thousand other things.

Oh, I know how it's meant. The lack of stigma should be the same as telling people why your limb is in a cast. But you can't just put someone with a broken leg and an insane person side by side and expect people not to be able to tell the difference, like the Winklevoss twins or, can we be truly honest, Joanna Newsom songs.

In recent years the discussion around mental health has hit the mainstream. I call it the Conversation. The Conversation is dominated by positivity and the memeification of a battle won. It isn't a bad thing that we are all talking more about mental health; it would be silly to argue otherwise. But this does not mean it is not infuriating to come home from a secure hospital, suicidal, to a bunch of celebrity awareness-raising selfies and thousands of people saying that all you need to do is ask for help – when you've been asking for help and not getting it. There is a poster in my local pharmacy that exclaims, 'Mental health can be complex – getting help doesn't have to be!' Each time I see it, I want to scream.

The Conversation tends to focus on depression and anxiety, or post-traumatic stress disorder. It is less comfortable with the mental illnesses deemed more unpalatable – people who act erratically, hallucinate, have violent episodes or interpersonal instability. I don't want to pretend that this stigma is merely a hurdle to be overcome. Stigma exists from a place of real fear, and a lack of understanding of the behavioural changes that can accompany mental illness. Episodes of illness can be frightening, frustrating, tiring and annoying for both the unwell individual and those around them.

The key isn't to deny this, but to educate. Instagram slogans do not make it clear what depersonalisation is, for instance, and that it won't be solved by a picture of someone walking on a beach. It's good that Lynx deodorant teamed up with the male mental health Campaign Against Living Miserably, but is 'Find Your Magic' not the most patronising slogan of all time?

I am a newspaper journalist – for now. But I don't know how long for because the illness might grip itself around me so tightly that it cuts off everything I love and hold dear, and my ability to lead a normal life.

I will admit that I am not well. That writing this, right now, I am not well. This will colour the writing. But it is part of why I want to write, because another part of the problem is that we write about it when we are out the other side, better. And I understand: it's ugly up close; you can see right into the burst vessels of the thing. (Also, on a practical level, it is difficult to write when one is unwell.) But then what we end up with has the substance of secondary sources. When we do see it in its rawness – Sinéad O'Connor releasing a Facebook video in utter despair – who among us does not wince?

The primary danger used to be glamorising. It was cool to be a bit mad. It meant you were a genius or a creative. It wasn't just that certain mental illnesses were acceptable, but certain mental illnesses were acceptable in certain types of people: if you had a special skill or talent or architect-set cheekbones. All of this remains true. Sure, Robert Lowell, great poet. Madness excused. Amy Winehouse, voice of a goddamn goddess. We'll allow. Kathy, 54, works at Morrisons. Not so much. White woman who has recourse to a national newspaper (called Hannah). Perhaps. Black man who comes from a cultural background where mental illness isn't recognised and whose symptoms might be put down to the racist trope of aggression in people of colour. Nah, mate.

But now there is also a new danger. It is 'normalising'. This is meant to be a positive – as in, 'What is normal, anyway?!' Which is a fair question, but I don't think it's the woman who crept into my inpatient room, stole the newspapers I had, found me in the lounge and ripped them up slowly in front of my eyes. I don't think it's me, sitting in a tiny, airless hospital room, carving my name into the wall with a ballpoint pen, with three guards for company, one of whom later tries to add me on Facebook.

We should normalise the importance of good mental health and wellbeing, of course. Normalise how important it is to look after oneself – eat well, socialise, exercise – and how beneficial it can and should be to talk and ask for help. But don't conflate poor mental health with mental illness, even if one can lead to the other. One can have a mental illness and good mental health, and vice versa.

Don't pathologise normal processes such as grief, or the profound sadness of a relationship breakdown, or the stress of moving house. Conversely, don't tell me it is normal to blow thousands of pounds on sporadically moving house without terminating a current lease, or to send friends bizarre, pugilistic texts in the night.

The truth is: enough awareness has been raised. We – the public, the health professionals, the politicians – need to make our words and actions count for more. First, the Conversation needs to be more inclusive when it comes to rarer conditions, and to people whose voices are less loud. Second, we need to recognise that posting 'stars can't shine without darkness' on social media might piss someone off in the midst of desperation and that, actually, anxiety can be a normal reaction and is different from general anxiety disorder, a serious condition. That feeling down is not the same as depression.

When I am well, I am happy and popular. It is tough to type these words when I feel none of it. And sometimes when I am most well I am ... boring. Boring is how I want to be all of the time. This is what I have been working towards, for 12 years now.

I worry, and most of the literature tells me, that I will have this problem for life. That it will go on, after the hashtags and the documentaries and the book deals and Princes Harry and William – while the NHS circles closer to the drain.

Maybe it's cute now, in my 20s. But it won't be cute later, when I am older and wearing tracksuits from 20 years ago and not in an ironic hipster way but because I no longer wash or engage with the world, and it's like: my God, did you not get yourself together already?

When I left appointments and saw the long-term patients, walking around in hospital-issue pyjamas, dead-eyed (the kind of image of the mentally ill that has become anathema to refer to as part of the Conversation, but which in some cases is accurate), four emotions rushed in: empathy, sympathy, recognition, terror.

I've noticed a recent thing is for people to declare themselves 'proud' of their mental illness. It's not something that, when stable, I feel ashamed of, or that I hide. But I am not proud of it. I want it gone, so that I am not dealing with it all the time, or worrying about others having to deal with it all the time. So I don't have to read another article, or poster, about how I just need to ask for help. So that when a campaigner on Twitter says,

'To anyone feeling ashamed of being depressed: there is nothing to be ashamed of. It's illness. Like asthma or measles', I don't have to grit my teeth and say, actually, I am not OK, and mental illness couldn't be less like measles. So that when someone else moans about being bored with everyone talking about mental health, and a different campaigner replies, 'People with mental illness aren't bored with it!' I don't have to say, no, I am: I am bored with this Conversation. Because more than talking about it, I want to get better. I want to live.

4 JULY

Middle-aged in a heatwave? I wouldn't wish it on a dog

ZOE WILLIAMS

This is a complete and unabridged account of the experience of being middle-aged in a heatwave, which you wouldn't wish upon a dog. Some buildup of brain bacteria over time compels you to mention climate change whenever there is any weather anywhere, but you remember from the 90s that everybody hates that person, so it's better to just head off weather chat mildly, absent-mindedly – 'Hot? I suppose it is' – and this gives you a bumbling, professorial air, as if you don't notice the world because you're busy thinking about Frankfurt School Marxists, except what you're really thinking is: 'I am way too hot.'

You can't wear jeans because it's like being stitched alive into your own nuclear-resistant shroud, which is the same for everyone except the difference is you don't have anything but jeans. What happened to all your T-shirt dresses and chiffon? Surely you once owned shorts? For the love of God, even some clamdiggers would help. You must have had a ritualistic bonfire of the fripperies, not planning for this eventuality, even though some kind of summer, realistically, will happen every other year. How is it possible to live so long, and accrue so little basic weather wisdom?

You are compelled to reminisce about 1976, even though you don't remember it any better than a millennial so you have to go on the internet and Google your own nostalgia. Did you know, by the way, that after two historically dry months, they appointed Denis Howell minister for drought, then three days later, thunderstorms arrived and it didn't stop raining until Christmas? But before that, he tried to boost the national water-saving effort by inviting reporters to watch him taking a bath with his wife, and that's the kind of politics – desperate, histrionic, obscurely sleazy, yet endowed with magical powers – that you don't see twice in a lifetime, however hot it is.

Around about day four of any given heatwave, a certain seen-it-all-before ennui beds in, because wasn't the year before last exactly like this, only more so? No, that was 2003. That incredibly recent year, when you stood on a tube platform reading about the temperature at which the cells of the human body start to change composition and can never change back, like scrambled egg? It was 15 years ago. That's why you're wearing a skirt in this memory, and reading '43C' on paper, not a screen.

You're too young to be in anyone's heat health news story, and too old to take it as an invitation to drink all day. You have too many pets who are, themselves, too hot. You are just shy of the sun-cream native generation, so it's a huge mental effort to remember it and you don't like the smell. If you're a man, the sun has blazed through your cycle helmet and you have stripes of tan on your bald pate, like a badger. If you're a woman, you wake up every morning thinking, is this a hot flush? Then you remember, no, it's just hot, and then you wonder why your memory is so bad, realising that is the other harbinger, and you're locked in a cycle of 'menopause-or-not?' that lasts roughly the entire day. Young people probably don't know why their boss is in such a bad mood, but you do: it's because they're slightly dehydrated and their gout is flaring up. You worry about your garden, but never quite enough to take measures to make sure nothing dies. You do not want to paddle, and ice-cream does nothing for you. And then, when it's over, all you can remember is how much you loved it,

7 July

Peter Preston, a *Guardian* hero who could have edited the *Daily Mail*

PAUL DACRE

I have a confession to make: I cannot claim to have known Peter Preston well. Not one for chitchat myself, our few social encounters invariably left me drowning in the sea of those famous unnerving silences, while my not infrequent mentions in his column were a mix of good, bad and, I suspect, deliberately elliptical.

That said, Peter was a hero of mine. I always felt – and here you must forgive my presumption – that in his love of, his obsession with, his addiction to journalism, we were kindred spirits.

As a young reporter on the *Express* when its circulation was about 4 million, I would sometimes have a late dinner at the

Kolossi Grill, known as the Colostomy, in the hope of catching sight of him. He was, after all, the journalist's journalist. The editor's editor.

Peter has been described as a private, shy, socially gauche individual who eschewed the swanky parties and glitzy first nights at which too many of his trade loved to be seen hobnobbing with the powerful and the celebrated.

I see a different man. I see a slightly lonely figure – one who was all too acutely aware that an editor who operates without fear or favour can't really have friends. And then again, good editors need to be outsiders because, let's be honest, most people only befriend journalists to get something into a paper or – more pertinently – to keep it out.

I also see a man who, even after the first edition had gone, was glued to the backbench, a microwaved pizza and plastic bottle of plonk on his desk. This was not because he was against gossiping in the pub but because, frankly, even after a 12-hour day, it was a wretched distraction from a job that had to be done. Like sharpening a headline, writing a cleverer intro or cropping a more dramatic picture. Because, let me tell you, when you're fixated by journalism like Peter was, there's virtually nothing more important in life than trying to produce the perfect paper. And on the rare occasions that you do, there's no greater buzz on this Earth.

Now, I am not going to provoke my own lynching by suggesting that I'd have made a good fist of editing the *Guardian*. But I am going to risk a collective cardiac arrest in this congregation by offering you the view that – politics apart; and actually, with the exception of his passion for Europe, I don't think Peter was ideological – it's not fanciful to say the man would have made a great editor of the *Daily Mail*.

After all, he came from the lower middle class. He was instinctively anti-establishment. Politically, he was difficult to define, though on the unions he was almost Thatcherite. He believed, to the deprecation of too many of his colleagues to whom profit is a dirty word, that it was actually rather a good thing for a paper to be financially prudent and commercially successful. He was evangelical about the need for what he called 'zing'. His mantra was 'serious doesn't need to be dull'. He initiated great women's pages. In *G2* he created a brilliant tabloid that has been imitated but never equalled.

He was fascinated by popular culture, and determined *Guardian* readers should not be excluded from the national dialogue because some of his staff had an aversion to anything that interested ordinary people. And his philosophy, outlined in his last media column – that readers in a jam should be treated like human beings and that a paper, by identifying with distress, becomes a functioning part of society rather than a commentary on its edges – should be the credo of every editor.

Above all, he loved features and beautiful words and brilliant writers, several of whom the *Mail* poached. Others were rogues whom he tolerated because of the glory of their writing. And the making flesh of those wonderful words, and a manifestation of Peter's genius for lateral innovation, was *G2*. Why, he asked, if it effervesced with flair, wit and creativity, should a tabloid be downmarket? Inevitably, there were the quali-pop sneers. Jonathan Miller, in self-condemnatory words, called Pass Notes a pollutant infecting culture. But *G2* had it all: jaw-dropping covers, a dizzying range of views and voices, bold pictures, important investigations and profiles. *G2* was both serious and salacious, even if there were, for my taste, a tad too many articles intellectualising the female orgasm. And not a week went by when, at its height, the *Mail* didn't buy one of its articles.

Now, I don't want to overstate this 'zing' factor, because ultimately Peter's *Guardian* was a very serious newspaper that broke important stories and pulled off some historic investigations. His specialists, particularly in Westminster, Whitehall, the City and sport, broke an embarrassment of exclusives, as I knew to my cost when news editing the *Mail* in the 80s.

He also, in masterminding the paper's journey from narrow socialism to broad liberalism, created a unique tone in which writers with many different voices, left and right, coexisted. But then, Peter's paper had a compassion, a burning desire to confront social wrongs, a reasonableness and a tolerance that eschewed dogma.

Others have rightly said that by seeing off the malicious militancy of the unions, and launching those highly profitable classified supplements, Peter saved the *Guardian* from oblivion.

But ultimately, it was *G2* and his daring redesign of the main paper – with its emphasis on creative white – that were hugely significant in the transformation of a somewhat austere, high-brow regional paper that haemorrhaged losses into a radical, young, modern, profitable, respected global liberal media brand that saw off the ferocious, predatory price-cutting of the *Times*, routed the incursions of the *Independent* and achieved, at its height, a *Guardian* circulation of 500,000.

I am told that in later years Peter was, rightly, proud of the *Guardian*'s online achievements. Whether he was ever reconciled to the digital revolution, though, I doubt. The reason, of course, was that he was, quite simply, a print man; he loved that magical symbiosis of newsprint, pictures, headlines, fonts and beautiful words.

Inevitably, sadly, those Fleet Street skills needed for that magic symbiosis are dying in an internet age that seems to have a vora-cious need for free, somewhat crudely expressed, round-the-clock information and gratification. Yes, of course, journalism will survive and may one day flourish again. But it will be different. Whether it will in future have the creative beauty and sheer power of Peter's *Guardian*, I don't know. But I do know – and there's no presumption here – that, for the sake of our industry's collective memory, we should salute a very great man of print.

Extract from the address given by Daily Mail *editor Paul Dacre at the service of thanksgiving on Thursday 5 July for the life of the former* Guardian *editor, Peter Preston (23 May 1938 – 6 January 2018).*

12 JULY

May's Brexit plan is here, and it's a dead duck already

POLLY TOYNBEE

Today, the government publishes its Brexit plan, two long years too late. The Chequers plan in this white paper should be a *Magna Carta* to lay out the country's economic future and the destiny of Britain's place in the world. In practice this poor specimen is dead on arrival. Never has there been a white paper of such profound potential importance and simultaneous absolute insignificance.

No battle plan survives first contact with the enemy, said Helmuth von Moltke the Elder, Prussian chief of staff; this plan has so many enemies it should never have made it past the drawing board. Least threatening to it are the hard Brexiters putting down killer amendments to kill off its central idea, Theresa May's facilitated customs arrangement (FCA).

If their mistaken aim is a show of strength, their amendments' failure will diminish their power, revealing possibly only some 30 or so backers. A useful display of their weakness will help remind everyone – broadcasters take note – that the likes of Jacob Rees-Mogg, Boris Johnson, Owen Paterson and Priti Patel are extreme mavericks: telegenic for their eccentricities, vanities and foibles, but a sideshow to the existential crisis facing the nation. (As for Nigel Farage, there is no political excuse for giving a man of no standing twice the airtime of, say, Sir Vince Cable, who leads actual MPs.)

The EU is not the enemy, but our closest friend: the Nato summit with Trump should have shocked us into remembering who our real friends are. But not even May expects her plan to survive first encounter with the EU27, who will reject her FCA. In evidence yesterday to the international trade select committee, Liam Fox admitted another obstacle: even the World Trade Organization may reject the legality of the FCA plan. May will be pushed to further softening compromises, inching towards a Norway-lite solution.

But what then? She has eventually brought to parliament a final Brexit offering that still pleases no one: far too soft for the fanatics yet still too menacing to the country's good to command enough MPs' support. Whatever new damage limitation it attempts, the deal will still leave us as rule-takers, budget contributors, with no MEPs and no seat on EU councils, brutally exposing how much we lose compared with what we have now.

What then? Gridlock. The head-counters see no majority in the Commons for accepting the deal: Labour and other parties will vote against, along with the Moggites. That will be a painful decision for some remainers, fearing rejection of a Norway-type deal will lead to something even worse. But they will still vote against, because the deal is still so bad for Britain. Barring the madmen, there will also be absolutely no majority in the house for an economy-killing no-deal crash-out. Then what?

This will be an unprecedented constitutional crisis, a logjam, an impasse with the deadline timebomb ticking. Labour will clamour for a general election, but why would a government – even this fractious ragbag – vote for no confidence in itself? They can throw out their leader, but that solves nothing. Do they go for a moderate compromiser – in which case, why not hold on to the one they have – or a Brexit ideologue, when there would still be no majority for either the dead-in-the-water deal or for crashing out?

This is the point where the only majority might be for asking the people to break the deadlock in a new referendum, as William Hague advocates and Labour doesn't rule out.

The Brexiters will protest that the will of the people has already been fixed for all time, but the mood in the country suggests people are already sick of the whole shebang. However, polling shows a majority would back a vote on the final deal – 48 per cent compared with 25 per cent against the idea (asked if they want a vote, people tend to say yes on most issues). Polling numbers point increasingly towards a victory for remain, by some five percentage points: some people are changing their mind, but more of the pro-EU young are reaching voting age as old Brexit-voters drop off the perch. Though once another virulently mendacious 'take back control', '80 million Turks are coming' campaign gets going, backed by 80 per cent of our press, dubious funding and subterranean foreign intervention, the result is unknowable.

Don't imagine deciding on a people's vote is a simple matter either. Parliament will choose the crucial wording of the question – and what will a gridlocked Commons choose? Question one – should the UK accept the deal or remain in the EU? The Brexiters would scream betrayal and demand instead question two – accept the deal or crash out without one?

Others suggest a three-way question, with all three options, which sounds fair. Except that offers the lethal likelihood that the moderate vote splits between remainers and deal-accepters, letting a minority of crash-outers win. So not even the people's vote is a simple answer to this poisoned constitutional conundrum. No one knows what comes next – and the time is short.

12 JULY

No more tears or pain now – this young England team deserves our applause

BARNEY RONAY

Leave the flags out. Have another glass. Take another look, if you can, at those moments from Kaliningrad to Moscow when this capable England team played above itself and turned a drowsy, toxic summer back home into something else.

Let's not have any anguish this time. England's four and a half weeks at the World Cup deserves a little better, even after a 2–1 defeat by Croatia in Moscow that was decided deep into extra time.

And no tears even at the memory of that goalscoring start when for a few moments the planes flew backwards through the sky, the cats barked, the police horses meowed and England did seem to be heading towards their first World Cup final on foreign soil.

Gareth Southgate's team played to their limits at the Luzhniki Stadium, as they had against Colombia and against Tunisia all those millions of years ago in the midge-mists of Volgograd.

In the end England found a superior opponent here, a team with deeper gears and with a mania to run right to the end.

Croatia came out like warriors in the second half, the craft and winning habits of Luka Modrić and Ivan Rakitić starting to intrude like a firm hand on the elbow as the game ticked down.

By the start of extra time it was a case of counting who could still run. England looked done, cooked. Harry Kane limped gamely. Jordan Henderson kept on chugging about like a cavalry captain on a dying pony. Jesse Lingard and Dele Alli found weird depths of energy, running on fumes.

The Luzhniki had been full to capacity at kick-off, the light above the lip of the roof fading to powder blue. The crowd was swollen by 10,000 England fans who made it here by lay-overs and nights spent on airport benches, and who pegged out the bed-sheet bivouac at one end, the familiar pageantry of painted flags, a tour of Albion from Exeter to Hartlepool.

With five minutes gone the evening seemed to be heading their way. Alli was fouled on the edge of the box. Kieran Trippier had been getting closer all tournament. As the ball dipped and curled and bulged the net the air seemed to rush out through the roof, then rush right back in as England's fans basked and bumped and rolled over each other in puppyish joy.

For 20 minutes this felt like England's game. On the touchline Gareth Southgate looked calm, striding about in his waistcoat, stroking his whiskery chin and resembling once again a very clever cartoon badger who drives an old-fashioned car and plays the violin.

Raheem Sterling ran hard but lacked edge. Harry Kane missed a chance he would normally gorge himself on like a starving man. And at half-time and 1–0 up England really did seem to have one foot jammed in the door for a return to this stadium on Sunday.

Except they didn't start again after the break. Croatia were suddenly driving the game, pressing England back on the flanks, finding holes that had previously been concealed. The equaliser came from the right, Ivan Perišić sticking a leg up above Kyle Walker's dipped head to deflect the ball in.

On we went into a bruising, draining extra time. The goal felt like it was coming, even before Mario Mandžukić peeled off the back of John Stones and finished smartly.

And so: exit music. England's World Cup summer is done. How will we remember those four weeks spent watching Harry and Dele and Harry from the dust of Samara to the semi-detached oddity of Kaliningrad?

Above all, this has been a dreamy, all-consuming piece of escapism. In tough times back home football has felt like a warm embrace, like a rush of chemical pleasure, like the best night out you've had in ages.

There will, of course, be that urge to give all this some wider meaning. It has been an odd feature of England's progress at this tournament that so many have latched on to the idea of a moral dimension to victory, the notion that England have won matches because their methods are righteous, their hearts pure, and not, say, because Mateus Uribe didn't hit his penalty kick two inches lower at the Spartak Stadium.

Sport is a chimera, it drags stories along in its wake. Champions are often blackguards. Losers are often nice. Sport and its storylines are just a decoration, a picture on the wall.

But it can still provide something uplifting. It is hard not to feel that part of the enthusiasm for this team comes from a feeling of relief. A lot of young English people have been told for the last few years that times are hard, that their lives are set one way and that things were always, always better in the past.

Watching this England team – and yes, it is of course just a football team – has seemed to provide a different kind of script. A young, unheralded bunch of players have gone further than those before who were more obviously talented, more golden, more authentic, finding ways to succeed through teamwork and energy and a refusal to be cowed.

It is hopeful to see this, to look at Alli or Harry Maguire or Jordan Pickford and say, well, people told them that they probably couldn't do it either.

Football isn't real life. It is a separate world packed with hammy emotions and big fat wet notes of drama, always straining to mean a great deal more than it does. But it can provide a little inspiration along the way, another kind of story. England in a semi-final, with a likable team led by the great Gareth, has been exactly this. No tears this time. There is St Petersburg on Saturday to follow. But they are, finally, coming home.

13 JULY

Special relationship? Trump and May's is almost pathological

JOHN CRACE

Not so much a press conference as a 50-minute couples counselling session. One in which the therapist was regrettably absent, leaving no one to mediate between two rapidly fragmenting psyches which were almost beyond help. The abuser and the abused.

When Donald Trump described his relationship with Theresa May as 'the highest level of special' he was for once telling the truth. It's just not a level of special to which most normal people aspire. More like pathology unplugged. The rest of us could only sit back in wonder as two of the most powerful people in the world unravelled before our eyes. A collector's item we will never see the like of again.

If the prime minister had gone into the final leg of the president's UK tour determined to grab some self-respect from her near-48-hour beating, she blew it right at the off. On the walk down through the Chequers garden towards the two wooden lecterns, the Donald had made a grab for her hand. And she had submitted. Yet again a handmaiden. The power relationship had been instantly re-established.

In her opening remarks, May struggled to recall anything positive that had come out of the visit. They had talked a bit about security and being ambitious for deals and that had been about it. There had been a few tough words – all from one side – because that's what being in a relationship was all about. Being bullied and shouted at. At this point she looked across to Trump as if for reassurance. The president didn't appear to notice, as his puffy eyes were closed to a narrow squint by the sun. Where were the sunbed goggles when he needed them?

'Thank you,' said Trump. Everything had been truly magnificent, the truliest magnificent. Even when he's reading from a script, he manages to sound slightly unhinged. What he had got from the trip had been that it had all been about him. Anyone he'd met had just been satellites orbiting round his ego.

He'd loved his historic buildings tour and it had been a great honour for people to meet him; he'd come 'from a productive summit that was truly a productive summit' and whatever Brexit deal Britain did would be fine by him, just so long as it was the kind of deal of which he approved.

So far so not very good, but things really fell apart when some of the assembled hacks got to ask questions. In particular about the interview the president had given to the *Sun*. May did the only think she knew how. She went into hostage video mode, repeating a few bland remarks about Brexit meaning leaving the EU while looking like someone who was praying for her ordeal to come to an end. Having the Maybot function sometimes has its advantages.

Trump, though, had barely got warmed up. The *Sun* interview had been lies. 'Fake news,' he spat. The things he had said about Theresa being completely hopeless and Britain having no chance of a trade deal with the US were obviously made up because he hadn't said them after all even though there was tape of him saying them. There was nothing he said that he didn't reserve the right to later contradict. The US press corps didn't bat an eyelid on this. The president's instability has long since been factored in. The Brits couldn't believe what they were hearing. Or their luck.

It soon got worse. Britain was a terrific place. The terrificest place. Apart from all the immigrants who had come over here. Each and every one of them were potential terrorists and should be locked up. Just as he was doing in the US. It was a fact that America was superior to anything that had happened before.

Then he went into overdrive. Sure, Boris Johnson would make a great prime minister. Why not? He was a great guy who had said some nice things about him. May looked as if she might throw up at that point. It was a while since a prime minister had been publicly insulted in her own back garden. Even when Trump went out of his way to praise her – 'She's doing a great job. The greatest job' – he somehow managed to sound patronising and condescending.

No, he wouldn't take a question from CNN because they were more fake reporting. But, hell, he knew about nukes because his uncle had been a professor of nukes. He was now full-on delusional, repeating lies about events and meetings that had never happened. A masterclass in uncontrolled narcissism made orange flesh.

May tried to drag him away and get him on the first helicopter out of Chequers but Trump kept dragging his heels. He loved the TV cameras. He needed the attention. It was the only way he knew he was alive. More, more, more. A seemingly endless stream of unconsciousness. Too far gone to notice that he'd reduced the office of president to a third-rate cabaret turn.

'We don't know how it worked': the inside story of the Thai cave rescue

MICHAEL SAFI

In the end it was a textbook rescue operation. Divers managed to carry, pull and at times swim the 12 young Wild Boars footballers and their coach along more than two miles of flooded and cramped tunnels in the Tham Luang cave complex, as billions of people around the world watched.

But briefings by Thai officials and interviews with six Australian, American, Chinese and Thai divers involved in the operation have revealed extensive details of a plan some were unsure could work, even after it started on Sunday morning.

'At the end, after we managed to get everyone out, we were just sitting there shaking our heads,' said Claus Rasmussen, a Danish diver who helped to execute the rescue. 'We have no idea how this worked or why, but it did.'

The plan to ferry the boys out accompanied by two expert divers, and escorted by a daisy chain of support workers, started to firm up as the most likely option on the evening of Thursday

5 July, said Ruengrit Changkwanyuen, a diver from Thailand who helped coordinate the diving teams – and to carry the first two boys to a field hospital when they emerged on Sunday.

By then the boys and their coach had been trapped for more than 13 days, after a fun excursion into the cave turned into a nightmare when flash floods cut off their exit. They were not discovered until 2 July, when John Volanthen, a Briton, found them huddled on a muddy slope nearly two miles inside the cave.

By the time the rescue plan was formed, more than 1 million cubic metres of water had been drained from the cave using pumps, but the boys would still be underwater, tethered to a diver, for much of the first 1.7km of the journey. For the last 1.5km, they would be on stretchers attached to a pulley system, guided home by more than 100 rescuers fanned out along the path.

Changkwanyuen helped to arrange the delivery of equipment including small wetsuits, full-face scuba masks and underwater lights, ordering huge supplies in case some of it failed. Anyone trying to buy a scuba mask in Thailand this week would be disappointed, he said. 'Basically every full-face mask in the country is here.'

Authorities had been trying to avoid bringing the boys out through water, which Rasmussen had earlier said was 'definitely the scariest option'.

But what was the alternative? Even keeping the boys in the cave chamber until January was looking increasingly risky, after medics reported that oxygen levels had depleted to 15 per cent and that the boys could fall into a coma if it fell to 12 per cent.

'That made us worry a lot,' Apakorn Youkongkaew, a rear admiral in the Thai navy, said. 'It was hard to fight nature. What would we do if the oxygen kept decreasing?'

Preventing disease in the dank environment would also have become increasingly difficult. 'It is very likely that infections would have started setting in, and the boys would have deteriorated a lot faster than they already were,' said Rasmussen.

Another plan, to drill approximately 600 metres into the boys' chamber from the thicket of jungle above, was also foundering. Engineers could not figure out where to drill. 'It was like finding a needle in an ocean,' said Youkongkaew.

Monsoon rain predicted for the morning of Saturday 7 July might have flooded the cave, making an extraction impossible. When it didn't come, rescuers knew they had to go for it.

'We had enough people to run the teams, the environment was right, we had a window with the weather,' said Rasmussen. 'We thought, this is going to be the best option we're going to get.'

Inside the cave on Sunday morning, unaware of the dangers ahead, the boys were excited, says Changkwanyuen. 'They were like, "Oh wow, I'm going to go diving,"' he said.

However, the rescuers were racked with anxiety. 'There were way too many unknowns,' said Rasmussen.

Chanin Wiboonrungrueng, nicknamed Titan, 11, the youngest of the group, was the focus of most concern. Rescuers sourced the smallest scuba mask they could find – but had to make it even smaller.

When Wiboonrungrueng started his journey out of the cave on Tuesday, they were still unsure whether the mask's seal would hold. 'We feared that it wouldn't fit him properly. That was the biggest worry,' Rasmussen said.

Rescuers planned to start with the strongest boy, said Changkwanyuen. 'But the Australian doctor Richard Harris evaluated the boys and said everyone was equally strong – so they picked among themselves to see who would come out first,' he said.

Thai officials said this week that the ultimate decision was made by the boys' coach, Ekaphol Chantawong. 'The coach selected. He wrote the order down: one, two, three, four, five,' said

Narongsak Osatanakorn, the head of the joint command centre coordinating the operation.

The boys were given anti-anxiety medication. Rescuers would not comment on its strength, saying it was a matter for the Thai government. 'If they were anxious, they could squirm,' Youkongkaew said. 'Some were conscious and some slept. There was no problem.'

Rasmussen was stationed at an area known as Pattaya Beach, about 3km inside the cave and the longest dry patch between the boys' chamber and 'chamber three' – a forward operating base for the rescue operation.

On each of the three mornings of the rescue, he would make the arduous two-hour trip to his designated area with two other divers, train his eyes on the dark water beyond him, and wait.

At about 2.30pm on Sunday, a diver emerged holding the first of the boys.

'As a team we were working together to put them in a stretcher as soon as they arrived on Pattaya Beach and getting them back into the water as fast as we possibly could,' he said.

'I was crouching, crawling, walking through water and over rocks, keeping the kids in the stretcher so they could be protected through all of this,' he said.

Navigating the steep, wet and muddy path in his section took about 20 minutes. Rasmussen worried about every second, aware that the boys would be in cold water for two hours, risking their core body temperatures falling to dangerous lows.

'Time was of the essence for us,' he said. 'If we fell or were slow it would interrupt not just the flow of what's happening but the whole rescue.'

Every diver interviewed said it was only at the end of the first day that they started to believe they might succeed. 'It was only when we made it out on Sunday and heard the kids were all very good and on their way to Chiang Rai hospital, we thought, fuck, this might actually work,' said Rasmussen.

The operation became more efficient with each day, but he said the slightest hitch – such as heavy rain – might have condemned some of the boys to staying inside the cave. 'We were still ready to back out completely on Monday night,' Rasmussen said.

About three hours after the last boys and Chantawong made it out on Tuesday, with the last navy personnel leaving the cave, the entire rescue system suddenly collapsed.

'All of a sudden a water pipe burst and the main pump stopped working,' Changkwanyuen said. 'We really had to run from the third chamber to the entrance because the water level was rising very quickly – like 50cm every 10 minutes.'

Australian divers in chamber three described hearing screams further up the tunnel, then seeing a rush of head lamps coming towards them.

'It was like a movie scene, everything was collapsing,' Changk-wanyuen said. 'It was one of those acts of God. The cave spirit didn't want us in there any more. It was saying, "I've had enough of you guys, it's time to leave."'

Rasmussen does not have a spiritual explanation, but agrees the timing was eerie. 'That everything breaks down as soon as everybody's safe? It's just weird,' he said.

The cave is now empty again, flooded and inaccessible. Divers will need to return in five months to collect their equipment.

Rasmussen said he would seek out two particular boulders that had bothered him. 'I'm going to find them and spit on them,' he said. 'They spent the week banging my toes and head.'

29 JULY

From Wales to the Champs-Élysées: the selfless rise of Geraint Thomas

WILLIAM FOTHERINGHAM

It is 11 years and one month since a chubby-faced Welsh youth stood on London's Tower Bridge marvelling, along with a slightly less chubby-faced Manx youth, at the fact that they were both about to make their debuts in the Tour de France. Both Mark Cavendish and Geraint Thomas were products of the legendary British Cycling academy in Manchester, run by the plain-speaking coach Rod Ellingworth, who moved with Thomas to Team Sky in 2010, where the pair have remained ever since. Thomas's Tour victory on Sunday marks another high point for Ellingworth's protégés.

In the coach's 2013 autobiography *Chasing Rainbows* (declaration of interest: I co-wrote it), Cavendish takes the starring role, in much the same way that Sir Bradley Wiggins did in the 2008 Olympic team pursuit four, where Thomas was a tower of strength while flying largely under the radar. There was some debate over whether Wiggins should partner Cavendish in the Madison relay, as the Londoner's form was dubious; the effervescent Thomas was the man who should have taken his place.

Only one cyclist has taken longer than Thomas to win his first Tour de France, from debut to triumph: Joop Zoetemelk, the rangy Dutchman who took the 1980 race, the highlight of a career spent in the shadow of Eddy Merckx and Bernard Hinault. Thomas has always raced alongside more ambitious men such as Wiggins,

Cavendish and latterly Chris Froome, notching up sufficient wins to remind onlookers of his innate talent, while inspiring a degree of frustration that he never quite made the definitive breakthrough. The past four weeks may have changed that.

Within British cycling the pattern is now firmly established along the template set by Ellingworth, but originally foreseen by Peter Keen, founder of the Lottery-funded cycling structure: track racing is used as a way to develop skills necessary for road racing. So Thomas won junior one-day Classics such as Kuurne–Brussels–Kuurne and Paris–Roubaix as well as racing amateur six-day track events with Cavendish.

During those outings Ellingworth, inevitably, recalls Thomas being involved in 'massive falls', including one in which he skinned his palms in a stage race and turned up at breakfast the following morning assuming he would abandon only to be told that he pedalled with his legs not his hands. The Welshman's arrival at the academy, a year early, took the entire structure up a level because of his sheer innate talent, the coach wrote.

Ellingworth also recalls how, tongue-in-cheek, he told a team meeting that a certain rival was such a strong favourite in one event that the only solution was to find a volunteer to fall off in front of him. 'It was Geraint Thomas who raised his hand,' to be told: 'Only joking, mate.' The ultimate team man, then, as Froome discovered in the 2015 and 2016 Tours.

Between stints in the service of others Thomas has built a fine all-round *palmarés*: two Olympic gold medals, a Commonwealth road race title, a one-day Classic – the Grand Prix E3 – and a wealth of stage races, beginning with the Flèche du Sud in 2006 and gaining in significance over the years; the Bayern Rundfahrt in 2011 and 2014, the Volta Algarve in 2015 and 2016, Paris–Nice in 2016, the Tour of the Alps last year before this season's diptych of the Dauphiné Libéré and Tour. The picture is that of a cyclist who can do anything – along the lines of Hinault, Merckx and Zoetemelk – from winning a major stage race, a prologue time trial or challenging in a major one-day Classic such as the Tour of Flanders or Paris–Roubaix.

Whether Thomas repeats this year's feat is open to question, not least because of the team leadership issue at Sky. At 32, he has only a couple of years available to win a second Tour de France, and he has already stated that returning to the one-day Classics might become an ambition. Winning multiple Tours in the modern era seems to be a matter for a specialist such as Froome. The obsessive strain of altitude training camps and extreme diets is not to be underestimated and Thomas is celebrated as a man who loves normal human things such as a couple of beers, as he made clear in his autobiography.

In one sense that barely matters. Thomas's win has massive implications for cycling in Wales. The council in Cardiff got in on the act on Sunday with a hastily arranged series of events to mark the occasion, and in the longer term that Welsh yellow jersey should provide fresh impetus to a sport which was already on a roll in the south Wales heartland thanks to the success of Nicole Cooke, Becky James, Thomas and his fellow Sky Welshman Luke Rowe. Over recent years a constant flow of youngsters has come on to the velodromes in Cardiff and Newport, and there has also been the foundation this year of a national under-23 team to act as a feeder for the Commonwealth Games.

Zoetemelk never won the Tour again but he retired happily in 1987, having taken the world road race title at the age of 38 to crown a remarkable all-round career. The modern sporting world expects repeat feats but in fact the trend is for cyclists to win the Tour only once; Wiggins was exceptional not in winning a single Tour but in never returning to it after his win. Whatever direction Thomas chooses to take, his history suggests he will succeed at it, if not without losing a certain amount of skin along the way.

31 JULY

Don't scoff at *Love Island*. It's British society laid bare

LEAH GREEN

Two TV shows have been endlessly debated during the long, hot summer of 2018. One was a vacuous, pointless and time-consuming programme where cartoonishly attractive, stupid people shagged endlessly in a tacky villa; the other a fascinating social experiment where the complexities of the heart, so often hidden from view, were laid out for inspection.

That is to say, no programme has split opinion like ITV2's *Love Island*. But those who use the first description tend not to have seen it. Or, they dipped into one episode, caught a ridiculous challenge where the men performed a fireman striptease, and couldn't fathom why this was ITV2's most-watched show ever.

As someone who watched the second season by myself, when it was still very much a niche hit, I can tell you that the *Love Island* experience is not complete without people to talk about it with. It's now a national conversation, lending itself to heated debate with your mates, your mates' mums, your hairdresser, or perfect strangers.

Sure, most of us watch *Love Island* because it feeds an addiction to trash television and we're extremely nosy about other people's sex lives. I don't see anything wrong with that and, taken simply on those merits, it really is one of the best programmes ever made. It won a Bafta for season three, and it's fair to assume the people behind the programme are no less intelligent than those who think themselves too intelligent to watch it. But denying how much more there is to the programme's appeal denies the power of mainstream television.

Even if you don't 'do' identity politics in your normal life, watching *Love Island* makes the complexities of British society so tangible they can't be ignored. Whether or not you backed the #MeToo movement, you will have an opinion on whether Adam Collard was a misogynist. You don't need to have read bell hooks to notice black contestant Samira Mighty being romantically sidelined, both by the male islanders and the show's producers. And after eight weeks of watching Dr Alex being kept on a show that was about finding romance, despite failing miserably at all attempts, it was fair to assume that his fanbase contained a lot of young men who can't date women and are angry with them about it.

Considering how some people go blue in the face trying to convince people that race, gender and sexual politics matter, and are still a thing, what is there to gain from scoffing at *Love Island*? If a programme watched by 1.5 million 18- to 34-year-olds is prompting these difficult questions, I'm all for it.

Admittedly, I didn't start watching so I could assess where we are with representation on UK television. And the *Love Island* WhatsApp group I'm in is more 'is that a birthmark or makeup above Alexandra's eye?' than 'does this programme pass the Bechdel test?' But when you reflect on the 48 (yes) hours of the programme you've watched, a lot of uncomfortable truths are thrown into sharp focus.

The world the islanders inhabit seems unreal: everyone is thin and beautiful, no one seems to eat meals, and women are still considered 'wife material' if they withhold sex from men (see Camilla from season three). But there is something very real about what the show tells us: the adverts that bookend the show might portray a rainbow Britain, but the show's first black female contestant was immediately relegated to the 'fun black best friend' that we were fed endlessly in 90s and 00s romcoms. You can't move for mixed-race men in the villa, but that only seems to be because they are so many of the white women's 'type on paper'.

Body-positive activism is on the up, but we are still drawn to skinny women with big bums, and men with six packs. Fourth-wave feminism has told women they can be sexually liberated, but Megan Barton-Hanson, who was open about enjoying sex and worked as a stripper and glamour model, is still mortally offended when someone guesses her sexual-partner count at 37. Even winner and everyone's favourite Dani Dyer says she won't sleep with Jack so he can 'look [her] dad in the eye'. Yes, that dad is Danny Dyer, but no one questioned the idea that she wanted to avoid having sex in front of millions of viewers not for herself, but for him (her mum wasn't mentioned).

So yes, we should hold our TV creators to account, but we can't let ourselves off the hook as we do it. *Love Island*, in its problems, is a reflection of society as it is, not as it should be. The show is basically a vacuous David Attenborough documentary, so simultaneously relatable and unrelatable that we can't tear ourselves away. It will be interesting to see how much changes for season five next year. My guess is not a lot, but we'll all be watching anyway, won't we?

11 AUGUST

My search for Mr Woke:
a dating diary

KIMBERLY McINTOSH

I tend to come to things late: Twitter, *The Wire* and puberty were
all delayed arrivals into my life. And losing my virginity was no
different. I rocked up to the University of Manchester in 2010
tragically chaste and sexually frustrated. It was what you might
call a pre-'woke' epoch; we were still drunk on lad culture. My
flatmate Liam quickly fashioned himself as the top lad; he would
confess later that he'd made a secret bet that he could shag every
girl in the group.

By the middle of my first year, my turn had come. I was in
his room on the pretence of 'watching a film', but the foregone
conclusion – have sex, then pretend it never happened – was
punctured irreparably. As we kissed, Liam whispered: 'I've never
had sex with a black girl before' – the anti-aphrodisiac for women
of colour everywhere. That was the end of that. Luckily, university was full of other young, drunk people with plenty of leisure
time, so it wasn't too difficult to get laid. But an awareness of
my race, and a persistent bout of thrush, followed me through
university and beyond.

I had spent most of my teens avoiding thinking about my
ethnicity; blending in and miracle boob growth were my prin-
cipal wishes at that age. But at university my sense of 'difference'
was heightened. It wasn't just confined to the obvious: the lack of
BME students or academics, or the history lecturer who claimed
that British colonialists were well-intentioned. It began to crop

up in my love life – such as the time I was asked whether my vagina was pink inside (FYI, it is).

The more I learned about racism and feminism, the smaller the pool of potential suitors became. While being thoughtful, funny, smart and able to put up with my unbearable flaws is a must, I became aware that my match also has to be serious about social justice to be my type on (recycled, sustainably sourced) paper.

Today, my work involves researching the links between race and inequality for two thinktanks. If 'woke' means being alert to injustice in society, especially racism, then I am on constant high alert. A potential partner needs to be at least on medium alert for it to be workable. Eventually, I took a vow to date woke men only. But only after numerous bad experiences.

It was on exchange at the University of Toronto, aged 21, when the first racist domino fell. No longer shackled by my virginity, I woke up naked but for a coat on a stranger's bathroom floor. I was pleased to find it was the flat of the best-looking guy at the frat party. We dated for a few months, but unfortunately Sam turned out to be a Republican and a biological racist. At a party, he told a confused group of fellow students that 'black people are biologically predisposed to violence', before tagging 'Kim isn't like that', on to the end. Lucky me. An important lesson was learned: check if they're overtly racist before intercourse.

I've shared a bed and overpriced meal with some less obviously deplorable offenders back home in the UK. With a university boyfriend, the incompatibility started small. I collected newspaper clippings about institutional racism in the Metropolitan police, but he wasn't convinced. I asked him not to smoke weed with me in public, explaining that the rules were different for me. He didn't understand why I cared. After we broke up, he admitted that he never spoke up when people made racist or sexist comments at work. I knew our friendship was finally over when he sent me an ill-judged treatise on race from the white male's perspective while 'finding himself' in India.

James Baldwin said that to be black and relatively conscious is 'to be in a rage almost all the time'. It's not the sexiest Tinder tagline, but dating someone 'not woke' does leave you in a state of constant fury. I'm all for debate, but I don't want my relationship to be reminiscent of *Question Time*. I'm looking for someone to be angry with, not at. There are enough other reasons in any relationship to be enraged, so why add another one?

But even after my vow to find a woke guy, things didn't go smoothly. There was the man who, while nice, wanted to talk about 'whether Cecil Rhodes was that bad' before I'd even had a morning cuppa. While on a date at a smart restaurant, he asked whether I had a dad, because he knew this was 'a problem' in my community. Once it became clear that he only dated women of colour, my doubts grew. Sure, people have types, but nothing makes you feel more like a trinket than being chosen for your ethnicity. No one would say 'all white people' are their type, apart from white supremacists. People specify and give details: brown hair, blue eyes, tall or short. Perhaps they'll even talk about personality! Black and mixed-race people are not a type.

When my white friend told me how much of a confidence boost Tinder was, I didn't have the heart to say that for me it was anything but. Black women receive the fewest messages on OkCupid and the fewest 'swipes right' on Tinder, and my inbox was no different. So, for 2018, I swore I'd meet people in real life. On New Year's Eve, I was asked out by a guy at a party. He was intelligent, attractive and, according to my wokeness calculator, 65 per cent woke – the highest score yet. To reach this level, you must be at ease with a few basics. For example: you know reverse racism isn't real; you never play 'devil's advocate' without knowledge of a subject; and you understand that poverty is not the fault of poor people. The rating couldn't go above 65 per cent in this case, because he is a civil servant with centrist foreign policy views. And he hadn't read the Malcolm X autobiography.

But after months of dates, attending parties together and the purchase of a Scrabble set, I had no idea whether or not I was still single. The funny thing about the Foreign Office is that it tends to make staff leave the country for years at a time, with no consideration of my dating plight. Would I have to start the whole, wretched woke man search from scratch?

Kind of. Turns out our expiration date is coming up faster than expected: he's getting a new post abroad. So when *Weekend* asked me if I would take part in their Blind Date series, I said yes. Fingers crossed he's wide awake.

HOW TO BE WOKE: THE DOS AND DON'TS
Don't say
All Lives Matter
OMG, I'm nearly as dark as you in this heat!
But you guys have Beyoncé?
I don't know much about this, but ...
I'm just not that into politics
You can't say anything any more
The N word or P word (even during Gold Digger)

Do say
Black lives matter
What pronouns do you prefer?
Racism is about power *and* prejudice
It's true, Britain didn't build the railways in British India
Poverty is not the fault of poor people
I don't know about that subject, tell me more

Names have been changed.

13 August

Halfway to boiling:
the city at 50C

JONATHAN WATTS AND ELLE HUNT

Imagine a city at 50C (122F). The pavements are empty, the parks quiet, entire neighbourhoods appear uninhabited. Nobody with a choice ventures outside during daylight hours. Only at night do the denizens emerge, HG Wells-style, into the streets – though, in temperatures that high, even darkness no longer provides relief. Uncooled air is treated like effluent: to be flushed as quickly as possible.

School playgrounds are silent as pupils shelter inside. In the hottest hours of the day, working outdoors is banned. The only people in sight are those who do not have access to air conditioning, who have no escape from the blanket of heat: the poor, the homeless, undocumented labourers. Society is divided into the cool haves and the hot have-nots.

Those without the option of sheltering indoors can rely only on shade, or perhaps a water-soaked sheet hung in front of a fan. Construction workers, motor-rickshaw drivers and street hawkers cover up head to toe to stay cool. The wealthy, meanwhile, go from one climate-conditioned environment to another: homes, cars, offices, gymnasiums, malls.

Asphalt heats up 10–20C higher than the air. You really could fry an egg on the pavement. A dog's paws would blister on a short walk, so pets are kept behind closed doors. There are fewer animals overall; many species of mammals and birds have migrated to cooler environments, perhaps at a higher altitude –

or perished. Reptiles, unable to regulate their body temperatures or dramatically expand their range, are worst placed to adapt. Even insects suffer.

Maybe in the beginning, when it was just a hot spell, there was a boom in spending as delighted consumers snapped up sunglasses, bathing suits, barbecues, garden furniture and beer. But the novelty quickly faded when relentless sunshine became the norm. Consumers became more selective. Power grids are overloaded by cooling units. The heat is now a problem.

The temperature is recalibrating behaviour. Appetites tend to fade as the body avoids the thermal effect of food and tempers are quicker to flare – along, perhaps, with crime and social unrest. But eventually lethargy sets in as the body shuts down and any prolonged period spent outdoors becomes dangerous.

Hospitals see a surge in admissions for heat stress, respiratory problems and other illnesses exacerbated by high temperatures. Some set up specialist wards. The elderly, the obese and the sick are most at risk. Deaths rise.

At 50C – halfway to water's boiling point and more than 10C above a healthy body temperature – heat becomes toxic. Human cells start to cook, blood thickens, muscles lock around the lungs and the brain is choked of oxygen. In dry conditions, sweat – the body's in-built cooling system – can lessen the impact. But this protection weakens if there is already moisture in the air.

A so-called 'wet-bulb temperature' (which factors in humidity) of just 35C can be fatal after a few hours to even the fittest person, and scientists warn climate change will make such conditions increasingly common in India, Pakistan, south-east Asia and parts of China. Even under the most optimistic predictions for emissions reductions, experts say almost half the world's population will be exposed to potentially deadly heat for 20 days a year by 2100.

Not long ago, 50C was considered an anomaly, but it is increasingly widespread. Earlier this year, the 1.1 million residents of Nawabshah, Pakistan, endured the hottest April ever recorded on Earth. In neighbouring India two years earlier, the town of Phalodi – the country's hottest ever day.

Dev Niyogi, professor at Purdue University, Indiana, and chair of the Urban Environment department at the American Meteorological Society, witnessed how cities were affected by extreme heat on a research trip to New Delhi and Pune during that 2015 heatwave in India, which killed more than 2,000 people. 'You could see the physical change. Road surfaces started to melt, neighbourhoods went quiet because people didn't go out and water vapour rose off the ground like a desert mirage,' he recalls. 'We must hope that we don't see 50C. That would be uncharted territory. Infrastructure would be crippled and ecosystem services would start to break down, with long-term consequences.'

Several cities in the Gulf are getting increasingly accustomed to such heat. Basra – population 2.1 million – registered 53.9C two years ago. Kuwait City and Doha have experienced 50C or more in the past decade. At Quriyat, on the coast of Oman, overnight temperatures earlier this summer remained above 42.6C, which is believed to be the highest 'low' temperature ever recorded in the world.

At Mecca, the 2 million hajj pilgrims who visit each year need ever more sophisticated support to beat the heat. On current trends, it is only a matter of time before temperatures exceed the record 51.3C reached in 2012. Last year, traditionalists were irked by plans to install what are reportedly the world's biggest retractable umbrellas to provide shade on the courtyards and roof of the Great Mosque. Air conditioners weighing 25 tonnes have been brought in to ventilate four of the biggest tents. Thousands of fans already cool the marble floors and carpets, while police on horseback spray the crowds with water.

Football supporters probably cannot expect such treatment at the Qatar World Cup in 2022, and many may add to the risks of hyperthermia and dehydration by taking off their shirts and drinking alcohol. Fifa is so concerned about conditions that it has moved the tournament from summer to a week before Christmas. Heat is also why Japanese politicians are now debating whether to introduce daylight saving time for the 2020 Tokyo Olympics, so that marathon and racewalk athletes can start at what is currently 5am and avoid mid-afternoon temperatures that recently started to pass 40C with humidity of more than 80 per cent.

At the Australian open in Melbourne this year – when ambient temperatures reached 40C – players were staggering around like 'punch-drunk boxers' due to heatstroke. Even walking outside can feel oppressive at higher temperatures. 'The blast of furnace-like heat ... literally feels life-threatening and apocalyptic,' says Nigel Tapper, professor of environmental science at Melbourne's Monash University, of the 48C recorded in parts of the city. 'You cannot move outside for more than a few minutes.'

The feeling of foreboding is amplified by the increased threat of bush and forest fires, he adds. 'You cannot help but ask, "How can this city operate under these conditions? What can we do to ensure that the city continues to provide important services for these conditions? What can we do to reduce temperatures in the city?"'

Those places already struggling with extreme heat are doing what they can. In Ahmedabad, in Gujarat, hospitals have opened specialist heat wards. Australian cities have made swimming pools accessible to the homeless when the heat creeps above 40C, and instructed schools to cancel playground time. In Kuwait, outside work is forbidden between noon and 4pm when temperatures soar.

But many regulations are ignored, and companies and individuals underestimate the risks. In almost all countries, hospital admissions and death rates tend to rise when temperatures pass 35C – which is happening more often, in more places. Currently, 354 major cities experience average summer temperatures in excess of 35C; by 2050, climate change will push this to 970, according to the recent 'Future We Don't Want' study by the C40 alliance of the world's biggest metropolises. In the same period, it predicts the number of urban dwellers exposed to this level of extreme heat will increase eightfold, to 1.6 billion.

As baselines shift across the globe, 50C is also uncomfortably near for tens of millions more people. This year, Chino, 50km (30 miles) from Los Angeles, hit a record of 48.9C, Sydney saw 47C, and Madrid and Lisbon also experienced temperatures in the mid-40s. New studies suggest France 'could easily exceed' 50C by the end of the century, while Australian cities are forecast to reach this point even earlier. Kuwait, meanwhile, could sizzle towards an uninhabitable 60C.

How to cool dense populations is now high on the political and academic agenda, says Niyogi, who last week co-chaired an urban climate symposium in New York. Cities can be modified to deplete heat through measures to conserve water, create shade and deflect heat. In many places around the world, these steps are already under way.

The city at 50C could be more tolerable with lush green spaces on and around buildings; towers with smart shades that follow the movement of the sun; roofs and pavements painted with high-albedo surfaces; fog capture and renewable energy fields to provide cooling power without adding to the greenhouse effect.

But with extremes creeping up faster than baselines, Niyogi says this adapting will require changes not just to the design of cities, but to how they are organised and how we live in them. First, though, we have to see what is coming – which might not hit with the fury of a flood or typhoon but can be even more destructive.

'Heat is different,' says Niyogi. 'You don't see the temperature creep up to 50C. It can take people unawares.'

16 AUGUST

A voice that gave America its heart and soul: Aretha Franklin

DORIAN LYNSKEY

'The Queen of Soul' was an honorific thrust upon Aretha Franklin by the Chicago radio DJ Pervis Spann during her first flush of fame, but it ended up being a job for life. When, decades later, *Mojo* and *Rolling Stone* ran polls to find the greatest singer of all time, she topped both and nobody was either surprised or disappointed. You could have tallied the votes anytime since 1967 and got the same result, because Aretha is the singer all others are measured against. 'When it comes to expressing yourself through song, there is no one who can touch her,' Mary J Blige testified in her *Rolling Stone* tribute. 'She is the reason why women want to sing.'

In 1967, *Jet* magazine equated her impact with that of Black Panther H Rap Brown and the Detroit riots by calling it the summer of ''Retha Rap and Revolt'. Comedian and activist Dick Gregory explained her importance as a civil rights figurehead by saying, 'You'd hear Aretha three or four times an hour. You'd only hear [Martin Luther] King on the news.' Franklin's publicist Bob Rolontz told biographer Mark Bego: '"Soul" was Aretha. Aretha came, and Aretha conquered and made the soul trend happen because it sort of united all the rest of the artists behind her. She hauled them along in a mighty wake.'

None of these claims felt like exaggerations yet none of them came from the woman herself, who saw her role in humbler terms. 'I sing to the realist,' she once said. 'People who accept it like it is.'

In Detroit in the middle of the 1950s, Aretha was already a big deal. As the daughter of Reverend CL Franklin, a powerful local figure who befriended Martin Luther King, Dinah Washington, Sam Cooke and gospel great Mahalia Jackson, she had a stage every Sunday at the New Bethel Baptist Church and she commanded it while still in her early teens. Her sisters Erma and Carolyn sang too but everyone knew Aretha was the star-in-waiting. Aretha recorded her first gospel album, *Songs of Faith*, in 1956, aged 14, but she also appreciated blues, jazz, Broadway and doo-wop and picked up tips from Cooke, another singer who ended up migrating from church to secular music. CL Franklin gave the transition his blessing but Aretha took a long time to get it right. John Hammond of Columbia Records, who signed the teenage Aretha in 1960 after hearing her on a songwriter's demo cassette, later admitted that he 'misunderstood her genius'. The nine albums of jazz, pop, R&B and show tunes that she recorded for Columbia weren't as bad as they're often made out to be but suggested an ongoing identity crisis – a light being hidden under a series of bushels.

By the time she joined Atlantic at the end of 1966 she was ready to find her real voice. She was 24, with a husband, three children and a decade of performing and recording under her belt. In short, she had lived. Atlantic's Jerry Wexler turned her career around with a simple idea: 'I took her to church, sat her down at the piano, and let her be herself.' After their first session together at Alabama's Muscle Shoals in January 1967, recording the throat-grabbing 'I Never Loved a Man (the Way I Love You)', the musicians were so astonished that they danced and sang and hugged each other with joy.

It was the first of five consecutive Top 10 singles in one spectacular year. Aretha's career, becalmed for so long, was suddenly
rocket-powered, as if America had been waiting for someone just
like her. The mayor of Detroit declared 16 February 1968 to be
Aretha Franklin Day and Martin Luther King himself presented her
with an award; that August she sang 'The Star-Spangled Banner' at
the Democratic National Convention. Her albums went gold, her
shows sold out and every talk show wanted her as a guest.

Between 1967 and 1972, Aretha released eight classic studio
albums and three live ones, showcasing a voice that sent listeners
scrambling for the keys to its uncanny power. Fans and critics
spent a lot of time pondering the definition of soul but they all
agreed that this is what it sounded like. In fact, her voice's perfect
alloy of pleasure and pain, suffering and endurance, sex and spir-
ituality, virtually constituted a scientific formula. 'This is a voice
that has not only sound but a smell and a depth,' said poet Nikki
Giovanni. 'A taste. You hear Aretha, but you also lick your lips.'

Wexler thought that Aretha had the full package of 'head,
heart and throat ... The head is the intelligence, the phrasing.
The heart is the emotionality that feeds the flames. The throat
is the chops, the voice.' It made her a spectacular interpreter of
other people's songs. She only took hold of a song if she could
feel it in her bones and, once she did, it was changed for ever. 'I
just lost my song,' said Otis Redding after hearing her blazing
feminist revamp of 'Respect'. 'That girl took it away from me.'
On *Aretha Arrives* (1967) alone, she tackled songs associated with
Frank Sinatra, Willie Nelson and the Rolling Stones and she later
unearthed the gospel classics hidden inside 'Let It Be' and 'Bridge
Over Troubled Water'.

Although she was a lifelong Democrat with a civil-rights
activist father, Aretha did not embrace politics as fully as some
of her peers. She was surprised that 'Respect' captured 'the need

of a nation' the way it did, and that 'Chain of Fools' became a hit with black troops in Vietnam. But she did release powerful versions of Curtis Mayfield's 'People Get Ready' and Sam Cooke's 'A Change Is Gonna Come' and recorded the blazing 'Think', with its battle cry of 'Freedom!' just days after King's funeral. By the early 1970s, she was wearing an afro and a dashiki and naming an album after Nina Simone's 'To Be Young, Gifted and Black'. An interviewer visiting her Manhattan apartment in 1971 noticed political texts by Frantz Fanon and Herbert Marcuse on the shelf. She was perhaps more radical in private than she was in public.

Even when her words resisted any kind of political reading, though, her voice spoke volumes. These were hard times and she was strong enough to take the weight. 'Soul music is music coming out of the black spirit,' she said. 'A lot of it is based on suffering and sorrow, and I don't know anyone in this country who has had more of those two devils than the Negro.' She might have added that black women were particularly attuned to these two conditions. On black feminist anthems such as 'Respect', 'Think' and 'Young, Gifted and Black', she sounded indomitable, drawing strength from the social movements of the time and repaying it twice over. 'I suppose the revolution influenced me a great deal, but I must say that mine was a very personal evolution,' she reflected. Ray Charles said that Aretha sang 'the way black folk sing when they leave themselves alone'.

So much praise and expectation could turn anyone's head, and Aretha certainly developed diva tendencies, but she liked to downplay her own exceptionalism and say that she felt the same pain that everybody did – it's just that she could sing that pain better than anyone else. And while the press fixated on her personal struggles to an intrusive degree (she divorced her abusive first husband Ted White in 1969), she didn't fetishise suffering in the vein of Billie Holiday. This daughter of the church was always moving on up, always overcoming. She might bend but she would never break.

Between 1968 and 1975, Aretha won the Grammy for best R&B female vocal performance every single year, until people started to nickname the award 'the Aretha'. With compositions such as 'Rock Steady', 'Day Dreaming', 'Call Me' and the title track of *Spirit in the Dark* (1970), she made a case for herself as a formidable singer-songwriter, not just an interpreter of other people's material.

After this creative high, however, she wobbled badly, with the Curtis Mayfield-produced *Sparkle* (1976) the sole highlight of a pretty wretched run. And in private, she wrestled with the worst depression of her life. The 1980s were a tough decade on a personal level. She lost her father and, just four years later, one of her sisters, Carolyn (her mother had died in 1952). The singer also developed a fear of flying that confined her to Detroit. But her career rebounded. When she sang 'Think' in the film *The Blues Brothers*, the *New Yorker*'s Pauline Kael marvelled: 'She smashes the movie to smithereens. Her presence is so strong she seems to be looking at us while we're looking at her.' She moved from Atlantic to Arista, where *Jump to It* (1982), produced by superfan Luther Vandross, took her back to No 1 and *Who's Zoomin' Who?* (1985) went platinum. That album's hit duet with the Eurythmics, 'Sisters Are Doin' It for Themselves', was followed by an even bigger one with George Michael, 'I Knew You Were Waiting (for Me)' – her first US No 1 since 'Respect'. In 1987, she became the first woman inducted into the Rock and Roll Hall of Fame.

After some less successful attempts to modernise her sound, she achieved another, more modest comeback with 1998's *A Rose Is Still a Rose*, working with Lauryn Hill and Puff Daddy. Demonstrating her rejuvenated range since she'd stopped smoking six years earlier, it came out just months after she filled in for a sick Pavarotti on 'Nessun Dorma' at the Grammys: hip-hop and opera in the same year. In 2014, after another batch of disappointments, *Aretha Franklin Sings the Great Diva Classics* found her tackling songs by women from Etta James to Alicia Keys. Her version of Adele's 'Rolling in the Deep' made her the first woman to earn 100 hits on the Billboard R&B chart, 54 years after her first.

She didn't really need to chase modernity, though. When she performed at Barack Obama's inauguration (as she had done for Bill Clinton and Jimmy Carter), she was as much a symbol as a voice, an essential part of the American story. She was the living defini-tion of soul and, once she set aside her youthful modesty, she didn't mind acknowledging it. 'My voice is better than ever, because of experience,' she told Mark Bego in the late 1980s. 'At the risk of sounding egotistical, it just gets better. I am my favourite vocalist.'

Aretha Franklin, 25 March 1942 – 16 August 2018.

16 AUGUST

The *Guardian* view on the press and Trump: speaking truth to power

GUARDIAN EDITORIAL

Press freedom was not invented in the United States, but there are few nations in which the importance of an independent press has been so closely woven into its long history. This great American tradition of civic respect for truth and truth-telling is now under threat. Donald Trump is not the first US president to attack the press or to feel unfairly treated by it. But he is the first who appears to have a calculated and consistent policy of undermining, delegitimising and even endangering the press's work.

Today, following an initiative by the *Boston Globe*, it is expected that some 350 editorial boards in news organisations across the United States will publish their own editorial comments on this issue. There is, of course, a risk in this initiative, and there will be differing press views about it. For some, including Mr Trump, it will feed the narrative that there is a partisan war between the press and the president. But the breadth of the response to the *Boston Globe*'s suggestion – and the fact that each editorial will be separately and independently written – suggests something different: that those who report and comment, day in and day out, in as professional and objective a manner as we can, are concerned that public respect for journalistic truth, reason and civility is under a new and present threat against which we must stand as best we can. As one editor has put it: we're not at war with the Trump administration, we're at work.

Mr Trump's sweeping abuse of the press is grimly familiar now. He calls the US press 'enemies of the people'. He accuses it – the instances now run into hundreds – of producing 'fake news' and being 'frankly disgusting'. He recently called the press 'dangerous and sick', and charged that they can 'cause war'. He has called journalists 'the lowest form of humanity'. The former FBI chief James Comey, later fired by Mr Trump, said the president asked him to consider jailing journalists for publishing leaks. His administration has removed reminders to respect press freedom from its internal manuals. He singles out four news organisations in particular – CNN, MSNBC, the *New York Times* and the *Washington Post* – insulting them in public (as he did at his Chequers press conference) and recently barring a CNN reporter from White House media events.

Inescapably, this campaign has consequences. Public opinion, especially among Mr Trump's most committed supporters, has become harsher in its views. Almost half of Republican voters (44 per cent) believe the president should be able to close news organisations for 'bad behaviour', according to a recent poll. In another poll this week a majority of Republican voters (51 per cent) say that the news media are 'the enemy of the people'. The anti-media mood at some Trump rallies has been intimidating. Social media trolling, violent abuse and threats to journalists (especially sexual threats to women journalists) have reached unprecedented levels. The United Nations human rights commissioner warned this week that Mr Trump's attacks on the press are 'very close to incitement to violence'. In June, five staff members at the *Capital Gazette* in Maryland were shot dead by a local man with a local grievance. They may not be the last.

It is not the press's job to save the United States from Mr Trump. It is the press's job to report, delve, analyse and scrutinise as best it can and without fear. The press has many faults. It can be self-regarding. Far worse, in Mr Trump's America, some parts of the media are partisan outlets which show a cavalier disregard for truth: the president has embraced these. But a free press must call out intimidation and incitement when it exists. And it must do what it can to preserve respect for the facts and for balanced judgment. In short, it must do its job. Mr Trump's insults and incitements are a calculated danger to that, and to the respect, civility and dialogue that should exist between the press and its readers. The *Guardian* stands with the US press in its efforts to maintain the objectivity and the moral boundaries that this president – like so many others in much more dangerous parts of the world – is doing so much to destroy.

28 August

Theresa May's take on no-deal Brexit

STEVE BELL

Index